Drive Right

2071 NW 86th St
Clive, W. Des Moines
-50322

Drive Right

Richard Kaywood

Richard A. Meyerhoff

Melvin M. Esarey

Margaret L. Johnson

Owen Crabb

Scott, Foresman and Company
Glenview, Illinois

Dallas, Texas   Palo Alto, California
Oakland, New Jersey   Tucker, Georgia

Authors

Richard Kaywood
Professor and Coordinator of Safety and
Driver Education
California State University, Long Beach
Long Beach, California

Richard A. Meyerhoff
Director of Driver Education
Waterloo Public Schools
Waterloo, Iowa

Melvin M. Esarey
Former Director of Driver Education
New Trier High School West
Northfield, Illinois

Margaret L. Johnson
Director of Driver Education
Glenbrook North High School
Northbrook, Illinois

Owen Crabb
Driver Education Specialist
Maryland State Department of Education
Baltimore, Maryland

Reader Consultants

Herbert Choy
Driver Education Instructor
San Francisco Unified School District
San Francisco, California

Amador Ramirez
Driver Education Teacher
David Crockett High School
Austin, Texas

Harry J. Sharper
Chairman of the Driver Education and
Highway Traffic Safety Department
Henrico High School
Richmond, Virginia

Grateful acknowledgment is made to the following
specialists for their critical reading of the
manuscript: Dr. William Fleischman, Optometrist,
Anaheim, California (Chapter 15, Qualifying
Physically); Benjamin E. Wheatley, Clinical Social
Worker, New Trier High School West, Northfield,
Illinois (Chapter 16, Emotions Affect Driving); Dr.
Richard Zylman, Associate Research Professor,
Center of Alcohol Studies, Rutgers University,
New Brunswick, New Jersey (Chapter 17, Alcohol,
Drugs, and Driving); Kenneth G. Perreault,
Automotive Instructor, New Trier High School
East, Winnetka, Illinois, and Warren G. Housinger,
Automotive Teacher, Thornton Fractional High
School, Calumet City, Illinois (Chapter 18, Owning
and Maintaining a Car).

ISBN: 0-673-10077-4 (Hardcover)
ISBN: 0-673-10078-2 (Softcover)

Contents

Unit 1 Preparing to Drive   1

Contents

Contents

Chapter 1

Driving in the Highway Transportation System

Objectives

1. List the three major elements of the highway transportation system (HTS).
2. Describe the job of the HTS.
3. List the various kinds of highway users. Explain why the HTS is so important in their lives.
4. Describe briefly the driving task.
5. Explain why driving is a "mental task."
6. Explain why driving is a "social task."
7. List the four steps of the driving task. Tell what the driver does in each one.
8. Explain what is meant by "multiple causes" of traffic collisions.
9. Name four official state government agencies or departments that regulate the HTS and briefly explain their responsibilities.
10. Explain why young drivers have the highest accident rate of all age groups and how this record can be improved.

Introduction

If you were to fly in a helicopter with a traffic reporter, you would see below you many drivers performing the *driving task*. This means the job of driving that each driver has to do. As you look at the variety and number of vehicles on the roads, it seems amazing that so many drivers can cooperate so smoothly. The drivers down there are doing a complex task. They must observe the whole traffic scene and identify possible problems around them. They must predict from previous experience what other drivers, motorcyclists, pedestrians, and bicyclists may do. Then they must choose actions that will not endanger other road users around them. Drivers must constantly make decisions while their cars are moving, and must control their cars with skill so they will not become a problem or a menace to other road users.

Knowledge and skill are essential in the safe operation of motor vehicles. Equally important is the willingness of each driver to share the highways with others in the system.

The Highway Transportation System

The highway transportation system (HTS) is made up of people, vehicles, and highways. Moving people and goods from one place to another safely and efficiently is the job of this system. Because so much depends on individual driver performance, each driver is an important part of this system.

Each part of the HTS is a people-machine-highway combination. The condition of each of these parts will vary from time to time. Of all the forms of transportation, the HTS is the most complex and changeable. Its operators—the drivers, motorcyclists, pedestrians, and bicyclists—have received less training than operators in other parts of the whole transportation system. Airline pilots and railroad engineers, for example, undergo long years of training and strict testing. They operate under a carefully controlled system.

DRIVERS AND OTHER ROAD USERS

Almost all people use the HTS in some manner throughout their lives. In the first few years of life, they ride in the family car on numerous occasions, and then as pedestrians and bicyclists, they use the streets around their homes and schools. These passenger, pedestrian, and bicyclist activities will continue for the rest of their lives.

People will also drive many hundreds of thousands of miles in a variety of four-wheeled (and possibly two-wheeled) motor vehicles. They may drive trucks or buses or taxis, pull trailers or drive campers. They will face problems developing from all these road users, including pedestrians, bicyclists, and animals. These problems will develop on a vast network of roads and highways under all types of weather and climatic conditions.

MACHINES

Consider the number of vehicles using the HTS. Over 130 million registered motor vehicles are driven more than 1.5 trillion miles each year on the streets and highways of this country. This includes 107 million automobiles, 27 million trucks, and over 6 million motorcycles. Add to those motor vehicles, at least 100 million bicycle riders of all ages who use many of the same streets and highways. At times the problems facing the users of the HTS reach a critical level.

Consider the different kinds of vehicles in the HTS. The smallest, and least protected, is the bicycle. At the other extreme is the huge semi-trailer rig weighing many tons when loaded with cargo. In between are the motorcycles, passenger cars (sub-compact, compact, intermediate, and standard size), vans, buses, pickup trucks, campers, and all sizes of trucks and trailers.

These kinds of vehicles range from the old "clunker" to the shiny new model just off the assembly line. They represent an equally wide range of performance in steering, accelerating, and braking, as well as a wide range of safety equipment. The running condition of each one varies as a result of the maintenance each has received over the years.

The machine part of the HTS clearly adds to the problems of moving people and goods from one place to another safely and efficiently.

Interstate Highway System

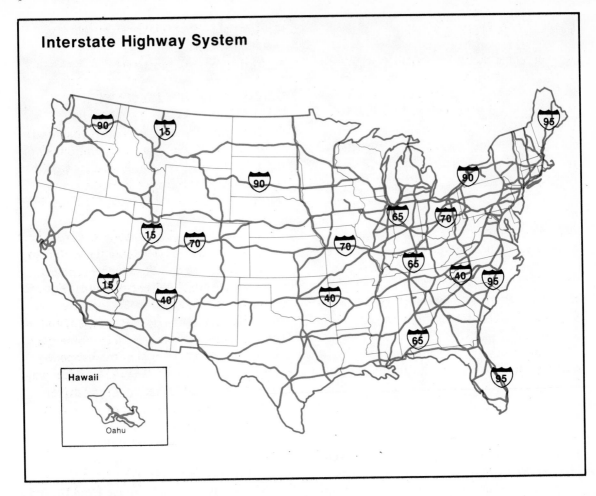

Hawaii

Oahu

ROADWAYS

The continued expansion of road building has brought paved streets and highways to almost every city and town in the country. Thousands of communities depend entirely on motor vehicles for all their supplies.

The Federal Aid Highway Act of 1956 provided vast sums of money for building the Interstate Highway System, a 42,500-mile network of multilane expressways that touch almost every city with a population over 50,000. Additional funds have been made available for improvement of state and local streets and highways. Funds are used for the elimination of hazards and for the upgrading of traffic-control devices, such as signs, signals, and pavement markings.

Since the energy crisis in 1973 and the increased attention given to mass transit, some state and federal funds raised by taxes have been diverted from road building to other forms of transportation. As more and more road users compete for space on our crowded roads, driving skill and cooperation will become increasingly important.

The Driving Task

Each driver in the HTS performs the driving task. This task includes all the skilled and properly timed actions a driver must make. These actions must be based on sound judgments and correct decisions and must be made for varying road and traffic conditions. To make decisions, drivers use their stored knowledge and the facts gathered from the present traffic situation.

To perform the driving task well, the driver must be able to:

- understand a motor vehicle well enough to know its limitations and to keep it in top operating condition.
- coordinate hands, feet, eyes, and other senses in controlling the vehicle.
- apply seeing skills and stored knowledge to read and interpret traffic scenes correctly.
- foresee situations and respond quickly and correctly.
- understand traffic laws, signs, and signals to use the roadway correctly.

- judge time-space relationships that constantly change.
- properly time all responses.

DRIVING IS A SOCIAL TASK

In order to move safely and efficiently, drivers must cooperate with other road users around them. Without this cooperation, safe and efficient movement on our roads would be impossible. It is a wonder that so many drivers, so varied in ability and life-style, can cooperate so well.

The driving task is a social task. Like other social tasks, this means interacting with many other people. They all have their problems, their own capabilities and limitations. For the most part, these people on the road are strangers. Some of them may be tired, and their reactions slower than usual. Some may be upset over something that has happened on the road or at home. Too many, especially at night, have been drinking. Every driver must adjust for any mistakes these drivers, pedestrians, or cyclists make.

Machines and built-in highway devices do some things automatically. But they cannot think. They cannot make decisions. Only people can be the decision-makers. Although decision-makers have a freedom of choice, they also have the responsibility for making the best choice.

YOUR BRAIN DOES THE DRIVING

Obviously safe driving is a thinking task. Driving is controlled by the brain. Feet and hands do only what the mind tells them. Skill in turning the steering wheel is of little use if a driver does it at the wrong time. Being able to brake in a fraction of a second may still be too late to avoid danger. The mind must tell the foot when to brake.

Some young drivers place too much emphasis on the physical part of the driving task. They think skillful car-handling is good driving. These basic skills must be learned well enough to become almost automatic. But it is the mental part of the driving task that gets most drivers into trouble.

A good driver must be alert and aware, and must be able to concentrate, reason, evaluate, plan, judge, and think well ahead. Using the eyes is essential in driving, but the eyes depend on the brain to interpret what they see.

IPDE PROCESS

Each driving event that is at all complex calls for a specific decision and action. For each event, the driver must go through the four major steps in the process:

- **Identify** information from the driving scene.
- **Predict** possible problems.
- **Decide** on necessary speed, position change, or other action.
- **Execute** the correct control responses.

Identifying Before a driver can identify anything in the driving scene, he or she must first sense it, generally with eyes or ears. The eyes or ears send messages to the brain

Identify

Predict

where they are checked against stored information.

A driver must be identifying objects in the driving scene all the time. The eyes can look at only one thing at a time, but they keep moving rapidly from one part of the scene to another to gather necessary information.

Predicting   A driver must try to foresee what might happen before it happens. To do this, the driver collects information from each part of the driving scene. The prediction is based on this information and also on the driver's stored knowledge.

The driving process would be impossible if every time we drove were the first time. What saves us is our ability to store information. We develop a "memory bank" of driving facts which help us predict correctly.

Deciding   A driver can learn to make good decisions by learning the reasons for various actions.

In any critical traffic situation there is a slim balance between snap judgments and delayed decisions. Each driver must find that balance. Otherwise, weighing facts and deciding may be done too quickly to produce the best decision. Or, with traffic moving, a decision delayed too long may be too late.

Deciding *when* to act is also part of the decision-making process. Delay brings about traffic changes. Then the driver must start the whole thinking process over again.

Executing   This step turns thinking into physical action. First, the driver must convert the decision into a set of instructions to arms and legs, which then operate the car controls: accelerator, brake, steering wheel, turn signal, gear selector lever, and horn.

Some of these coordinated responses become habitual with constant use, such as stopping at an intersection on a red signal. But many must be performed on a "first time" basis because of the unique set of traffic conditions.

Decide

Execute

Breakdowns in the HTS

When traffic congestion or a crash occurs, there is a breakdown in the HTS. More than 17 million crashes occur each year. Cars are involved in most of the crashes. The National Safety Council estimates that over 2 million people receive injuries each year that disable them beyond the day of the crash.

In 1973, over 55,000 people were killed in traffic. Since then, the number of fatalities has declined somewhat as a result of the 55 mph (88 km/h)* speed limit and reduced use of motor vehicles for non-essential purposes.

MULTIPLE CAUSES

Most crashes have several causes. For example, there may be a hole in the pavement. It does not cause a crash until a driver with worn-out shock absorbers fails to see it. When the car hits the hole, the worn-out shock absorbers fail to perform properly. If they had been in good condition, they would have absorbed the shock of the bump and the wheels would have gripped the pavement better. Instead, the car bounces so much when it hits the bump that the driver loses control. Another driver may not be fully alert and may hit the out-of-control car. Failure in the highway, the car, and the drivers all contributed to the crash. But one driver might have prevented it.

ACCIDENTS DON'T JUST HAPPEN

One helpful step toward clearer thinking about safe driving would be to stop saying "accident" when we mean collision or crash. The word *accident* suggests something that

*See tables of metric measures on p. 357.

just "happens" to a person—something a driver could not avoid. But most accidents don't just happen; they are caused. Those causes can be determined and steps taken to eliminate as many of them as possible.

REGULATING THE HTS

Driving is a privilege granted by the state through a license, which is earned by passing a state examination.

In accepting a license, a driver, in effect, promises to obey traffic laws. Failure to obey these laws or involvement in several collisions in one year can result in *suspension* of the license. In more serious cases, the license is *revoked*.

Many agencies and departments of state government play a part in regulating the HTS. The state legislature passes laws. These laws make up the *vehicle code.* State and local police enforce the laws, and the state department of motor vehicles sets up rules and regulations for the control of motor vehicles. The courts decide whether drivers or owners charged with violating the laws are guilty or innocent. In most collisions, one or more laws are broken. When laws are obeyed, the HTS has few breakdowns.

SOCIAL AND ECONOMIC LOSS

Collisions resulting from breakdowns in the HTS have serious social and economic consequences. It is estimated that traffic collisions cost this country over 20 billion dollars each year. Each tragedy brings with it costly damage to property, loss of wages or time away from school, lower wages after returning to work due to permanent impairment, medical

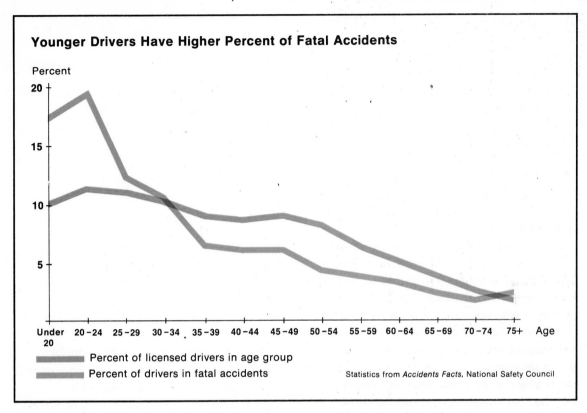

Younger Drivers Have Higher Percent of Fatal Accidents

Percent

Percent of licensed drivers in age group
Percent of drivers in fatal accidents

Statistics from *Accidents Facts*, National Safety Council

fees and hospital expenses, and insurance costs. What cannot be measured in dollars is the cost of broken homes, shattered plans, and human suffering caused by these collisions.

AGE GROUPS IN COLLISIONS

The youngest drivers have the highest accident rate. For the number of miles they drive, teen-agers are involved in twice as many fatal accidents as drivers over 25. A California study disclosed that since they drive only half as many miles per year as older drivers, on an average, their accident rate is *four times as great*. The study also disclosed that the difference between teen-age and adult drivers for traffic convictions are similar to those for accidents. Only 15

percent of male teen-agers have had neither accidents nor convictions during their first four years of driving. The reason for this poor record is a new driver's lack of experience, as well as certain characteristics of youth generally.

Many young drivers have proved that they can drive for years without collisions and without citations for violating traffic laws. They have established a firm foundation of knowledge and skill in the IPDE process as a result of their experience in driver education, and have practiced good driving habits.

Operating a motor vehicle safely in today's traffic requires far more skill, knowledge, and willingness to cooperate with other road users than ever before. Driver education can help establish the foundation for safe driving.

Vocabulary

collision, 10

deciding, 9

driving task, 7

executing, 9

highway transportation
  system (HTS), 4

identifying, 8

IPDE process, 8

multiple cause, 10

predicting, 9

revocation, 10

suspension, 10

vehicle code, 10

Summary

1. The highway transportation system (HTS) is made up of people, vehicles, and highways.
2. The job of the HTS is to move people and goods from one place to another safely and efficiently.
3. Most people use the HTS all their lives as pedestrians, passengers, drivers, and cyclists. They depend on the efficient operation of the HTS for transportation and movement of essential supplies.
4. The driving task includes all the skills and properly timed actions a driver must make in operating a vehicle safely and efficiently.
5. Driving is a mental task because the driver must make decisions that the arms and legs transform into actions to control the vehicle.
6. Driving is a social task because it requires interaction and cooperation with other road users.
7. The IPDE process has four steps: *identifying* information from the driving scene; *predicting* possible problems; *deciding* on necessary speed, position change, or other action; *executing* the correct control responses.
8. Most collisions have several causes. Some of the causes may be defects or failures in the highway or the vehicle, but mostly collisions result from poor decisions and actions of highway users.
9. State legislatures pass the laws which make up the vehicle code; traffic police enforce the laws; courts determine guilt or innocence of those charged with violating the law; departments of motor vehicles set up rules and regulations for the control of drivers and vehicles.
10. Young drivers have poor driving records because of inexperience as drivers, as well as certain characteristics of youth. Proper instruction in driver education can improve this record.

Driving Situations

You are driving and observe the traffic ahead as pictured in the four situations below. In each case, *identify* the possible problem, *predict* what may happen, and *decide* what action you should take to keep the problem from becoming worse.

1.

2.

3.

4.

Chapter Review Questions

The Highway Transportation System

1. What are the three elements of the highway transportation system? (4)
2. What is the purpose of the HTS? (4)
3. How are people's lives influenced by the HTS? (4-6)
4. How do people using the HTS add to the problems of the system? (4)
5. How do vehicles used in the HTS add to the problems of the system? (5)
6. How do the streets and highways of the HTS add to the problems of the system? (6)

The Driving Task

7. What five things must a driver do in performing the driving task? (7)
8. Why is the driving task a social task? (7)
9. Why is the driving task a thinking task? (8)
10. What are the four steps of the IPDE process that a driver goes through in each driving event? (8)

Breakdowns in the HTS

11. Why is collision a better word than accident? (10)
12. What state and local agencies play an important part in the regulation of the HTS? (10)
13. Why are breakdowns in the HTS of special significance for teen-agers? What can young drivers do about this problem? (11)
14. Is the poor driving record of young drivers caused by a small number of poor drivers? Cite evidence from this chapter to support your conclusion. (11)
15. What items are included in determining the costs of traffic collisions? (10)

Projects

1. Prepare a description of the HTS if it had to operate without traffic laws, law enforcement, traffic courts, or departments of motor vehicles.
2. Interview three professional drivers (for example, taxi drivers, truck drivers, salesmen). Ask them how their jobs would be different without regulation of the HTS by the vehicle code, police, courts, and the department of motor vehicles.
3. Ask these same professional drivers what they consider the most important part of the driving task.
4. Study a report of a traffic collision in your newspaper. Estimate the monetary cost of that collision.
5. Talk to an automobile insurance agent about the driving record of young drivers. What does the agent think about young drivers and about the value of driver education?

Chapter 1 ▪ Test

(Write the correct answers on a separate sheet of paper.)

True-False

1. The users of the HTS are responsible for more of the system's breakdowns than the machines or the highways. (4)
2. Because of their many safety features, motor vehicles do not contribute to many HTS breakdowns. (5)
3. The most important part of the driving task is the ability to react quickly to an emergency. (7)
4. Modern roads and automatic traffic-control devices have reduced the need for drivers to solve problems in traffic. (6)
5. Mental errors cause more problems for drivers than errors in driving skill. (8)
6. In order to drive safely, a driver must identify every object in the traffic scene ahead. (8)
7. In most traffic collisions, a single cause can usually be identified. (10)
8. Many state and local agencies of government participate in regulating the HTS. (10)
9. The accident rate of drivers under 25 years old is about 4 times as great as that of older drivers. (11)
10. Young drivers receive proportionally more traffic citations than do adult drivers, considering the number of miles they drive. (11)
11. Most breakdowns in the HTS can be prevented by obeying traffic laws. (10)

Answer the Question

12. What is the job of the HTS? (4)
13. What are the three parts of the HTS? (4)
14. Which part is responsible for most breakdowns in the HTS? (4)
15. In addition to driving skills, what important quality does a driver need for safe and efficient use of the HTS? (11)
16. Before drivers can decide what to do in performing the driving task, what must be done first? (8,9)
17. Which type of vehicle is involved in the greatest number of traffic collisions? (10)
18. What book contains state laws regulating the HTS? (10)
19. The ability to foresee what might happen in a traffic situation is related to which part of the IPDE process? (9)
20. Reduction in traffic fatalities have resulted primarily from what two changes? (10)

Chapter 2

Obeying Traffic Controls

Objectives

1. Describe the correct action to take or prepare to take for the red, green, and yellow phases of a traffic light.
2. Describe the correct action to take when approaching flashing red and yellow lights.
3. Explain two different kinds of traffic-light systems.
4. Give the meaning of the eight shapes and colors used on traffic signs.
5. Name some international signs the United States has adopted.
6. Name at least five different kinds of regulatory signs.
7. Describe the correct action to take at STOP and YIELD signs.
8. Name at least four different warning signs.
9. Describe the correct action to take when approaching school zones and school crossings.
10. Describe how to follow a route sign.
11. Describe the meaning of various pavement markings.

Introduction

Imagine driving in a city with no signals, signs, or pavement markings. Traffic jams would be common. The number of collisions would increase drastically. Traffic would move very slowly, if at all, and tempers would flare. Driving in the city would no longer be possible.

The highway transportation system, however, has signals, signs, and pavement markings. Together, they form the traffic control system.

How do traffic controls help the driver?

1. They *regulate* speed, direction, and movement of traffic.
2. They *warn* drivers of hazards ahead that may be dangerous or difficult to see.
3. They *inform* drivers of directions, distances, and services.
4. They *guide* drivers to their destinations by identifying the routes.

Knowledge of the exact meaning of each traffic control helps a driver identify a problem and make a decision. Correct knowledge leads to wise decisions that result in safe actions. Driving thus becomes the safe, pleasurable activity it is intended to be.

Traffic Control Signals Traffic control signals help move traffic smoothly in locations where congestion occurs often and where serious collisions have occurred. Traffic control signals include traffic lights, arrows, flashing signals, lane signals, and pedestrian signals.

TRAFFIC LIGHTS control busy and hazardous intersections.

STOP at stop line or behind crosswalk. Right turn is permitted when safe on red after stop and yield in some states.

WARNING. Light is about to change from green to red. Driver may not enter intersection if he or she can stop.

GO but first check for cars that might not stop. Yield to vehicles and pedestrians within the intersection.

ARROWS indicate direction.

GO straight ahead only after yielding to vehicles and pedestrians within the intersection.

GO left only. Be sure that oncoming traffic does not run the red light.

GO right only. Yield to pedestrians.

STOP. You may not go in this direction.

WARNING. The green arrow is about to end.

GO. Yield to **pedestrians** and vehicles already in the intersection.

FLASHING SIGNALS are placed at hazardous intersections.

STOP. A red flashing signal means exactly the same as a *STOP* sign. A *STOP* sign may also be posted at these intersections.

CAUTION. This flashing yellow light tells you to slow down, look carefully, and proceed with caution. Be ready to stop.

LANE SIGNALS are often used on streets and expressways to control the flow of traffic in lanes that change direction during different hours of the day.

STOP. You must never drive in a lane under a red X signal.

WARNING. Your lane signal is about to change to red. Look carefully and prepare to leave the lane safely before the red X appears.

GO. You may drive in lanes underneath this signal, but you must also obey all other signs and signals.

PEDESTRIAN SIGNALS are mounted on the same post as the traffic light but below it.

GO. Leave the curb to cross the street.

FLASHING. Do not leave curb, but if you have already started, complete crossing.

STOP. Do not leave the curb.

TRAFFIC-LIGHT TIMING SYSTEMS

The timing of traffic light changes may be arranged in several ways. Most lights change at regular timed intervals regardless of the traffic at the moment. Other lights are activated by pedestrians and traffic.

Progressive-Signal System Some cities set the lights on a street so that the drivers can travel at a constant speed of 25 or 30 mph. If they maintain speed, they will continue to go without stopping often at a red light.

Pedestrian-Actuated Signals At some intersections, a pedestrian can change the light by pushing a button mounted on a post. There are two kinds of pedestrian-activated signals: one stops traffic only on the street the pedestrian wants to cross and one stops traffic in all directions. School crossings often have pedestrian-actuated signals. When approaching a school crossing, look for children standing near the post. If they are present, there is a chance the light will change.

Traffic-Actuated Signals Traffic-actuated signals are usually placed on very busy main streets where cross-street traffic is light. Vehicles passing over a magnetic detector under the pavement change the light in their favor.

OFFICIAL'S SIGNALS

If a police officer, road construction worker, or fire official gives you directions contrary to those shown by signals, you must obey these officials. They may use both arms and a whistle to direct traffic. If an officer holds his or her hand with the palm up toward you, you should stop. A beckoning motion means go.

Traffic Signs

Signs inform drivers of traffic laws, warn them of possibly dangerous situations, and guide them in following the correct route.

Signs can be divided into three categories: regulatory, warning, and information and guidance. The shapes and colors of signs carry the same meaning everywhere. Learning the meanings is essential for safe driving.

SHAPES HAVE MEANING

Octagon:
Stop

Triangle:
Yield

Round:
Railroad Crossing

Vertical Rectangle:
Regulatory

Pentagon:
School

Pennant:
No Passing

Horizontal Rectangle:
Information and Guide

Diamond:
Warning

COLORS HAVE MEANING

Red:
Stop, yield, or
prohibited

White:
Regulatory

Black:
Regulatory

Yellow:
General warning

Orange:
Construction or detour

Green:
Expressway interchange
and information

Blue:
Expressway service
guidance

Brown:
Public recreation and
scenic guidance

INTERNATIONAL SIGNS

The United States has recently started to adopt some of the international signs used in other parts of the world. In the future, more of them may be used. Because these signs use only pictures and not words, people do not have to know the language of the country in which they are driving to understand a sign's meaning. Below are many of the international signs. In the rest of this chapter, see how many of these signs you can find that are now used in the United States.

Road narrows

Bumpy road

Falling rocks

Railroad crossing

Yield

No bicycles

Speed limit

No U-turn

Minimum speed

Expressway

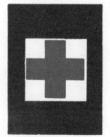

First-aid station

Gas station

REGULATORY SIGNS

Regulatory signs are posted to inform drivers of traffic laws. Therefore, a driver must obey these signs. They are generally white rectangles with black or red lettering, but some, such as STOP and YIELD, have unique shapes.

Stop Sign   STOP signs are generally placed on all streets or roads that cross main highways or through streets. The STOP sign always appears as a red octagonal (eight-sided) shape.

By law, drivers must come to a *full* stop at all STOP signs. After stopping behind a car that is waiting at a sign, you must stop again when you reach the sign.

The most important reason for stopping at a STOP sign is to yield the right-of-way to pedestrians and to cars that have already entered the intersection or may be close enough to risk a collision. Yielding the right-of-way means allowing other cars or pedestrians to use the intersection before you proceed. If you force a car or pedestrian to slow or stop when you are moving from a STOP sign, you have not yielded.

The locations of STOP signs and *stop lines* help a driver determine where to stop. First, when there is only a STOP sign, stop with the front bumper even with the sign. Second, if there is a crosswalk, ease up to, but not into, the crosswalk and stop. Third, when a stop line has been painted on the pavement, stop with the front bumper just behind that line regardless of the location of the STOP sign or crosswalk.

If you cannot get a clear view of traffic on the through street from where you have stopped, carefully move ahead. Stop again where you can see down the through street. Avoid edging out so far that the front of your car is in the way of traffic.

At some intersections, STOP signs are posted at all four corners. A small sign under the STOP sign may say, "4-way." At a 4-way stop, the driver must follow this procedure:
1. Every driver must make a full stop.
2. Other drivers should let the driver who stopped first, go first.
3. When cars at right angles stop at the same time, the driver on the left should yield the right-of-way to the driver on the right.
4. By releasing the brake pedal and moving slowly forward before proceeding through the intersection, a driver can signal an intent to go.
5. The driver should continue to glance left and right while moving into the intersection.

Yield Sign   A red triangular sign means yield the right-of-way to cross traffic. On seeing a YIELD sign, brake until you are sure you will not have to stop for traffic on the through street. If necessary, come to a complete stop. Proceed only when there is enough space for you to do so safely.

If you are driving on a street that has YIELD signs at cross streets, don't place too much trust in the protection of those signs. You could have a collision if you assume that all approaching cars will yield the right-of-way to you.

Speed Limit Sign   Most cities and all states set speed limits. White rectangular signs with black letters tell drivers what the speed limits are. Drivers must know and obey these limits even if signs are not present. Speed signs are posted on all major streets and highways to notify or remind drivers of the highest speed the law allows. In one-third of all fatal collisions, drivers were found to be driving over the speed limit or too fast for conditions.

Speed limits are established for ideal driving conditions. Because traffic, road, or weather conditions can make speeds unsafe, all state vehicle codes include a *basic speed law*. This law says that a driver may not drive faster than is safe for the present conditions, regardless of the speed limit.

Most states have also passed a *minimum speed limit law* that sets the lowest speed at which a car may travel on certain roads under good conditions. This law, which applies mostly to expressways, was passed to prevent a wide difference in speed among vehicles on busy roads. Many collisions occur when vehicles are moving at different speeds. A driver coming up behind a slow-moving car may not realize just how slowly the car is moving. If the driver is unable to stop in time to avoid a rear-end collision, he or she may attempt a last-minute lane change without checking to see if it is safe to do so.

Turns and Lanes

One Way

Parking and Passing

Pedestrians and Trucks

Other Regulatory Signs Other regulatory signs inform drivers of many laws, such as the direction of one-way streets, the location of no-passing and no-parking zones, the proper lane for turns, the location of prohibited turns, and streets where certain vehicles are prohibited.

A sign with the words DO NOT ENTER or WRONG WAY identifies a one-way street or an expressway ramp. If you see such a sign in front of you, you are driving in the wrong direction with the possibility of having a head-on collision. The only safe course of action in this situation is to stop and quickly turn around when it is safe to do so.

If you should meet a car coming the wrong way *toward* you, get out of its way. The driver may be drunk or confused and may not get out of your way. Flashing your headlights may also alert the driver to the fact that something is wrong.

A red diagonal slash and circle over a black symbol is an international sign that prohibits such actions as U-turns, right turns, or left turns. It is also used to indicate that certain vehicles, such as bicycles and trucks, are not allowed.

Pedestrians and truck drivers must also follow regulatory signs, some of which are directed especially to them. Pedestrian signs include CROSS ONLY AT CROSSWALK and NO HITCHHIKING. Truck drivers must follow special regulatory signs. Some of these tell truckers the height of viaducts and the weight a bridge will carry.

INFORMATION AND GUIDE SIGNS

On roads other than expressways, directions, mileage distances, and other information that is not legally binding are also given on white signs with black letters.

On expressways, however, information, distance, and direction signs are green. Blue signs alert motorists to facilities along the highways, such as food, gas, or lodging. Brown signs are used for public parks and recreation areas. Route signs have unique shapes and colors that vary depending on the type of route.

Reading Route Signs   The type of route sign depends on whether the road is an Interstate, state, or county highway. When you are following a numbered route, you will find a sign before every turn. After the turn, look for a confirming route sign. If you do not find the sign after you have driven a short distance, you may have left the route. Ask at the next

service station for a map and for the easiest way to return to the route (see ''Reading Maps,'' in Chapter 20).

Often drivers who are following a highway through an unfamiliar city tend to make serious driving errors they would not otherwise make. Some of these errors are changing lanes without looking, stopping suddenly without warning, and turning from the wrong lane. Drivers must be very careful to avoid making these errors.

Roads Without Signs   There are roads, mostly in rural areas, that present an even greater challenge to driving skills and judgment because they have no signs or pavement markings. On such roads, a driver has to rely only on a knowledge of the law and safe driving principles to detect hazards and make wise decisions about speed, car position, and distance.

WARNING SIGNS

Bright yellow or orange warning signs alert drivers to possible or actual danger ahead. Often the driver cannot see the danger easily. Words and pictures give the message.

After reading the sign, the driver should be alert for the problem and prepare to reduce speed, if necessary. When you drive on strange roads, warning signs help you greatly.

Construction Signs These orange signs are generally diamond shaped with black symbols or lettering. The most important action a driver can take in a construction zone is to slow down. Watch for sharp turns, reduced space and traction, workers, and slow-moving equipment. Be ready to stop if a worker signals with flags or signs.

No-Passing Sign A yellow NO PASSING sign is placed on the left side of the road at the start of a no-passing zone. These signs remind you of the pavement markings that prohibit passing. You may not begin or complete passing after reaching this sign.

Railroad-Crossing Sign This round yellow warning sign with black cross bars means "railroad crossing ahead." It is placed about 100 feet from the crossing in cities. Because of the higher speeds in the country, these signs are placed about 750 feet from the crossing.

Diamond-Shaped Warning Signs These yellow, diamond-shaped signs warn drivers of the following situations:

1. Intersections

2. Traffic controls

3. Change in direction

4. Poor road conditions

5. Reduction in width of road

6. Hazards

School-Warning Signs   Another type of warning sign takes the shape of an old schoolhouse. The yellow pentagon-shaped (five-sided) school sign has two designs: one for school zone and one for school crossing. School zone is the area where school buildings or grounds are next to the highway. School crossings are those crossings used by students going to and from school, but they may be located some distance from the school. A SCHOOL-ZONE sign is placed before a school zone. Sometimes as an additional warning sign, it is placed before a school crossing sign.

Drivers must be extra careful in areas with school warning signs because children are more likely to be there and because their actions are unpredictable. Small children may run into the street without looking. They may ride their bicycles on the wrong side of the street. In these areas, drivers must always be extra alert for possible trouble rather than wait for it to develop and then try to react to it.

Some school crossings on busy streets have traffic signals. On less heavily traveled streets, a STOP sign may be placed in the center or near the edge of the street. A full stop is always required at school STOP signs whether or not students are present.

At some school crossings, crossing guards or student safety patrols help students across the street. If the intersection does not have a traffic light, drivers should watch for the guards who may signal the drivers to stop.

School Zone

School Crossing

Pavement Markings

Pavement markings direct and warn drivers. The markings can be either yellow or white.

Yellow center lines indicate two-way traffic while white lines mean one-way traffic.

YELLOW CENTER LINE MARKINGS

Broken yellow lines in the center of a road mean that passing is allowed when no traffic is approaching from the opposite direction.

A solid yellow line next to a broken yellow line indicates that no passing is allowed on that side.

On two-lane roads, double solid yellow lines mean no passing in either direction. On roads of four or more lanes, double yellow lines indicate the center of the road.

WHITE LINE MARKINGS

Broken white lines separate lanes of traffic going in the same direction. These lines may be crossed with care. Solid white lines are used to channel traffic and prevent lane changes near intersections. They should not be crossed. Often white lines appear with arrows. Arrows indicate the lane from which a turn may be made. If you are in a lane marked with a curved arrow and the word ONLY, you must turn in the direction of the arrow. If both a curved arrow and a straight one are in your lane, you may either turn or go straight.

OTHER PAVEMENT MARKINGS

In no-parking zones, curb markings will either be yellow or white, depending on the local law. No-parking zones are usually near fire hydrants, close to intersections, or close to driveways.

Solid white lines along the edge of the pavement provide a guide for driving when visibility is poor.

Obstructions will have yellow warning lines when traffic is moving in the opposite direction. If the obstruction is between lanes going in the same direction, the lines will be white.

Stop lines, crosswalks, and parking space lines on streets are all white.

Railroad crossings and school warnings are written in white on the pavement.

Vocabulary

basic speed law, 23
flashing signals, 18
information signs, 25
lane signals, 18
minimum speed law, 23

pavement markings, 28
pedestrian-actuated signals, 19
pedestrian signals, 18
progressive-signal system, 19
regulatory signs, 22
right-of-way, 22

school zone, 27
traffic-actuated signals, 19
traffic control signals, 18
warning signs, 26
yield, 22

Summary

1. Drivers need to know what to do as well as what not to do at traffic lights. Red always means stop. Yellow means the light is about to change, and a driver should not enter the intersection if he or she can stop. Green means check cross traffic, move with caution, but be prepared to stop, if necessary.
2. Flashing red lights always require a full stop. At flashing yellow lights, a driver must reduce speed and be prepared to stop, if necessary.
3. Traffic-light systems may be timed at regular intervals or may be activated by pedestrians and by traffic from cross streets.
4. Shapes and colors of signs tell drivers specific information about traffic conditions ahead.
5. International signs, such as YIELD and NO BICYCLES, are becoming more common in the United States.
6. Regulatory signs carry the full force of the law and control speed, turns, lanes, stop, yield, parking, and passing.
7. Looking and yielding are two very important actions required of all drivers at STOP and YIELD signs.
8. Warning signs prepare drivers for such problems ahead as construction, no-passing zones, railroad crossings, intersections, poor road conditions, and hazards.
9. When approaching SCHOOL ZONE and SCHOOL CROSSING signs, drivers must slow and watch for children.
10. Route signs warn drivers in advance of a turn and then follow up with a confirmation sign.
11. Yellow center line markings always mean two-way traffic. White lane lines indicate traffic flowing in the same direction. Broken lines may be crossed; solid lines may not.

Driving Situations

1. You are approaching this intersection and want to turn left. Which lane should you be in? Why are the lane signals located on this street?

2. What is wrong in this picture? Why is it important to know the different kinds of pavement markings?

3. What is wrong in this picture? What should be done about it? What might happen if no one took any action to correct the problem?

4. You are driving on a street and suddenly see these signs. What do the signs tell you? What action should you take?

Chapter Review Questions

Traffic Control Signals

1. Explain how a progressive-signal system and a traffic-actuated signal affect you as a driver. (19)
2. Describe the correct action to take when approaching flashing red and yellow lights. (18)
3. Why is it important to look for children standing near the pedestrian button of a pedestrian-actuated light? (19)
4. What do red, green, and yellow traffic light arrows mean? (18)
5. What important action should a driver take when he or she starts to cross an intersection on a green light? (18)

Signs

6. What are four kinds of regulatory signs? (24)
7. What is the important difference in driver actions at STOP and YIELD signs? (22, 23)
8. Give the names and meanings of each sign below. (20)

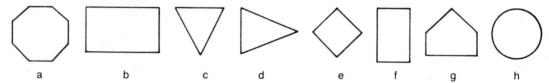

| a | b | c | d | e | f | g | h |

9. What three colors are used on information signs? (25)
10. What are three legal stopping places at STOP signs? (22)
11. What is the general meaning of each of these colors on traffic signs: red, yellow, orange, green, brown, blue, black, and white? (20)
12. Why is it necessary to watch more than the street when driving in school zones? (27)
13. How are international signs different from American signs? (21)
14. Under what circumstances could driving at the speed limit be a violation of the law? (23)
15. What are five different types of warning signs? (26)

Pavement Markings

16. What do white and yellow pavement markings mean? (28)
17. What is the difference between the actions a driver may make at solid lines and at broken lines? (28)
18. What other pavement markings beside lane markings might a driver see? (29)

Projects

1. Name some other diamond-shaped warning signs for each category.
2. Check pavement lines in your town or area. Report to the proper agency any non-standard lines or areas where lines could improve safety standards.
3. Find out if your state and neighboring states allow right turns on red.
4. Find out the speed limits for the different speed zones in your state, and compare them with neighboring states.

Chapter 2 · Test

(Write the correct answers on a separate sheet of paper.)

True-False

1. You may go in the direction a red arrow points after stopping and yielding to traffic. (18)
2. A pedestrian-actuated signal is unlikely to change if no one is present. (19)
3. In some situations, you may be required to yield at a green light. (18)
4. The law requires drivers approaching a flashing yellow light to stop. (18)
5. Traffic lights in a progressive-signal system are tripped by cross traffic. (19)
6. All regulatory signs contain red. (22)
7. The shape of traffic signs is intended to give drivers a message. (20)
8. A school-zone sign requires approaching drivers to stop. (27)
9. Information signs on highways other than expressways may be blue or green. (25)
10. Route markers are all the same shape. (25)
11. The meaning of international signs is explained only with pictures. (21)
12. A railroad-warning sign is round. (26)
13. A full stop is always required at a YIELD sign. (23)
14. Once you stop at a STOP sign, you then have the right to go. (22)
15. All warning signs are diamond-shaped. (26)
16. Yellow center lines indicate two-way traffic. (28)
17. No-parking zones are always marked with diagonal warning lines on the pavement. (29)

Answer the Question

18. color _____
    kind _____

19. color _____
    kind _____

20. color _____
    kind _____

21. color _____
    kind _____

22. color _____
    kind _____

23. color _____
    kind _____

24. color _____
    kind _____

25. color _____
    kind _____

Chapter 3

Learning Basic Car Control

Objectives
1. Identify each item on the instrument panel and briefly describe its function.
2. Locate and describe the function of each device used to control the car.
3. Locate and describe the function of each device for visibility, communication, and comfort.
4. Describe the correct position for sitting behind the wheel and the importance of this position.
5. List in order the steps in a pre-ignition check.
6. Draw a diagram of a shift indicator and label the gear positions.
7. List the correct procedures for starting the engine, putting the car in motion, and stopping an automatic-shift car.
8. List the correct procedures for starting the engine, putting the car in motion, and stopping a stickshift car.
9. List in order the steps for leaving a parked car.

Introduction

At the turn of the century, automobiles had few instruments or controls to aid drivers. As a result, cars broke down more frequently. Common problems were overheated engines, brake failures, and empty gas tanks.

Today, cars are equipped with instruments, lights, gauges, switches, buzzers, safety devices, and vehicle controls. These various devices allow drivers to keep their cars running efficiently and safely, to communicate with other road users, to protect the cars' occupants, and to help prevent theft.

Drivers should learn where these instruments are located on any cars they drive. Knowledge of these controls will enable drivers to operate them efficiently. While the location and operation of the devices may vary somewhat from car to car, this chapter explains their purpose and common location.

The chapter also provides directions on how to start both automatic and stickshift cars, how to put them in motion, and how to stop them.

Instruments, Devices, and Controls

Instruments, devices, and controls give the driver information on the way certain parts of the car are working.

THE INSTRUMENT PANEL

The car's instruments are located on the panel in front of the driver. The ignition must be turned on before the lights or gauges will register. Gauges warn the driver that something is going wrong, while lights provide a warning only after something has already gone wrong. For cars that have only warning lights, the driver should make sure the bulbs are working by checking to see if they light up when the key is turned.

Fuel Gauge (1)   This gauge shows the amount of gasoline remaining in the tank. Drivers gain the following advantages if they fill the gas tank when the gauge reads half full:

■ They will be less likely to run out of gas.

■ There will be less air in the tank to deposit water into the gasoline. Consequently, less water will be in the gasoline to cause gasline freeze in winter.

Speedometer (2)   The speedometer tells the driver how fast the car is traveling. The only sure way to know your speed is to glance often at the speedometer. Since 1975, car speedometers show the speed in both miles per hour and kilometers per hour.

Odometer (3)   This device, generally attached to the speedometer, shows the total number of miles a car has been driven. Some cars also have trip odometers that can be set back to zero to record the number of miles on any trip.

Temperature Indicator Light or Gauge (4)
This light or gauge warns the driver if the
water circulating in the engine gets too hot.
If this indicator registers hot, stop at the
nearest safe spot and wait until the engine
cools off. Then have the cooling system
checked.

Alternator Light or Gauge (5)   If the alternator is not making enough electricity to run the
car, the battery will have to send part of its
stored electricity to the engine. When the battery discharges a large amount of electricity,
this light will come on to warn the driver that
the system is not working properly. If the
light remains on or the gauge reads ''discharge'' while the engine is running, have the
electrical system checked.

Oil-Pressure Warning Light or Gauge (6)
This light or gauge warns the driver if oil is
not circulating properly in the engine. How-

ever, this gauge does not indicate how much
oil you have. The amount of oil is measured
by the *oil dipstick* located in the engine.

If the warning light comes on while you are
driving, stop immediately. Call for a tow
truck. Have a mechanic check the oil pressure system. Driving with low oil pressure
can cause serious engine damage very
quickly.

Brake System Warning Light (7)   Most cars
have a brake system warning light. If this
light comes on while you are braking, half or
all of the braking system is not working properly. If this light comes on, have a mechanic
correct the problem without delay.

To make sure the bulb is working, see if
it lights when the parking brake is on. (The
light is also a reminder to release the parking
brake.)

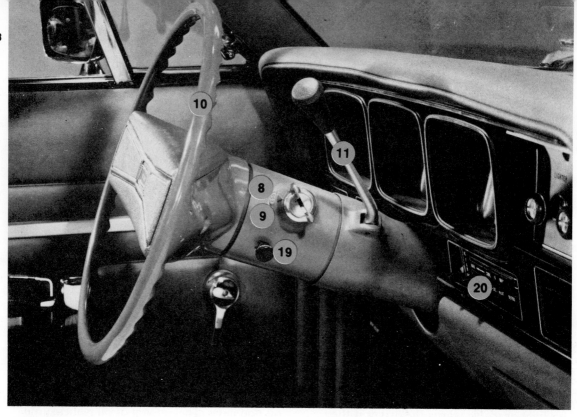

CAR CONTROLS

A driver uses the following controls to actually operate the car. In order to drive smoothly and dependably, a driver needs to get the "feel" of the controls since they vary from car to car.

Ignition Switch   Usually located on the steering column, this switch, when turned, starts the engine. On recent cars, turning the key to the "Lock" (8)   position locks both the shift or selector lever and the steering wheel. The "Accessory" (9)   position allows the driver to turn on the radio and other electrical equipment without turning on the engine.

If the key is still in the switch when the door opens, a buzzer sounds. This reminds the driver to remove the key and thereby reduce the chances that the car will be stolen.

Steering Wheel (10)   The steering wheel turns the front wheels of the car. Power steering requires less effort than manual steering.

Manual Shift Lever   In a stickshift car, the driver shifts the gears. The shift lever may be mounted either on the right side of the steering column or on the floor.

Selector Lever (11)   Though the gears are shifted automatically in a car with automatic transmission, the selector lever allows the driver to choose forward or reverse gears. The selector lever is located in the same positions as the manual shift lever.

Seat Adjustment Lever   Every car has a small lever, located at the lower left front or side of the driver's seat, that allows the seat to be moved forward and back.

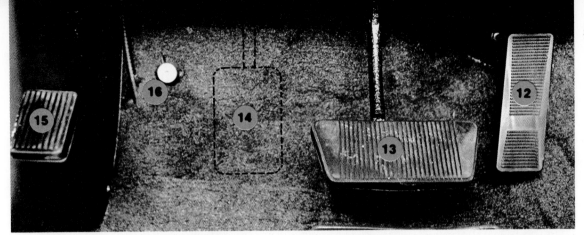

Accelerator (12)   The accelerator controls the flow of gasoline to the engine. As the driver's foot presses down on the accelerator, the flow of gas increases the speed of the engine. After starting a car, don't drive very fast until the engine warms up, especially in the winter months.

Automatic Choke   The accelerator also activates the *automatic choke.* The choke is the device that during starting controls the amount of air to the carburetor. A closed choke reduces the amount of air entering the carburetor. A mixture rich in gasoline is necessary to start the car easily. When the engine is cold, the driver must close the choke by pressing the accelerator to the floor once before starting the engine. After the engine has warmed, a tap on the accelerator will open the choke and reduce engine speed.

Caution: Closing the automatic choke when the engine is warm could make starting difficult.

Foot Brake (13)   Pushing down on the foot brake pedal forces a device against the drums or discs on each wheel. This rubbing creates friction that slows down and stops the wheels.

Pressing down on the foot brake also causes the brake lights to glow on the back of the car to warn drivers to the rear. Pumping the pedal up and down lightly makes the brake lights flash without actually braking.

Power brakes reduce the amount of pressure the driver applies to the pedal, but they do not necessarily shorten the distance needed to stop.

If you change cars, try out the brakes and drive more slowly than normal until you get used to the new brakes.

Caution: If the engine dies, power steering will not get its normal power assist, and extra effort is needed to steer. Power brakes still operate for about 4 pumps.

Clutch (14)   In a stickshift car, the clutch is located to the left of the brake pedal. Pressing in on this pedal allows the driver to shift gears.

Parking Brake (15)   In most cars, the driver sets the parking brake with a foot pedal and releases it with a hand lever. The purpose of the parking brake is to keep the car in place while parked. This brake can be used in an emergency, however, if the foot brake should fail.

DEVICES FOR VISIBILITY, COMMUNICATION, AND COMFORT

These devices are located on the instrument panel, on the steering column, or on the seat. Some of these are labelled in the diagrams on previous pages.

Light Switch　This switch controls not only the headlights but also taillights, parking lights, side marker lights, instrument panel light, license plate light, and dome light.

The dome light should be off while the car is moving because this light keeps your eyes from adjusting to the outside darkness.

The parking lights should never be used alone when the car is moving. Because other drivers may think the car is standing still, driving with parking lights only is illegal in many states.

Dimmer Switch (16) and High Beam Indicator (17)　On most cars, a floor button called a dimmer switch is pressed with the left foot to turn the headlights from low beam to high beam and back. In some foreign cars, this switch is attached to the turn-signal lever.

Located on the instrument panel, the high beam indicator light glows when the high beams are on.

Turn Signals and Indicators (18)　Located on the left side of the steering column, the turn-signal lever is moved down for a left turn and up for a right. Moving the lever turns on the signals in front and back of the car.

The turn-signal indicators in the instrument panel are generally two small green lights. One or the other flashes to show which turn signal is on. Turn signals automatically stop flashing after the car makes a turn.

On most cars, the turn-signal lever may be held down in a lane-change position, and once the hand is removed, the signal is canceled. When signaling a lane change in older cars, the driver must cancel the signal by moving the lever to the "off" position.

Cruise Control　This device available on some cars allows the driver to set the car's speed automatically for expressway driving. The system is activated by pressing a button on the turn-signal lever and then removing the foot from the accelerator. The system is released by lightly depressing the brake pedal or by pushing the button in again. This device should not be used in bad weather, in heavy traffic, or near the top of hills.

Inside and Outside Rearview Mirrors   Used as a team, these mirrors give the driver a good view of traffic to the rear. The inside mirror reflects only the view seen through the rear window. The left outside mirror gives the driver a view of the lane to the left and rear of the car.

Even with both mirrors, you will have to turn your head and glance over your shoulder when changing lanes to make up for the blind spots at both rear corners.

Sun Visor   When the sun is low, sun visors, located above the windshield, help cut the glare so the driver can see.

Emergency Flasher Control (19)   This switch is located on the steering column near the ignition switch. When it is pushed in, front and rear turn-signal lights flash on both sides at the same time to warn oncoming traffic that the vehicle is a hazard. Many states prohibit the use of emergency flashers while the car is moving.

Horn   This essential safety device is found in different locations on the steering wheel of each car model. Check to see how the horn works on each car you drive so you won't have to hunt for it in an emergency.

Windshield Wipers and Washer   The same switch generally operates both the washer and wipers.

The washer allows the driver to clean the windshield for better visibility. On very cold days, the washer fluid may ice up unless the fluid contains enough antifreeze.

Heater, Air Conditioner, and Defroster (20) These three work together to warm or cool the car and to keep the inside windshield clear of moisture on wet or cold days. Recently, rear window defrosters have become common.

Seat Belts and Shoulder Harnesses   Almost all cars have seat belts and shoulder harnesses for driver and right front passenger and seat belts for all other positions. Since 1975, the shoulder harness has included an *inertia reel* that allows the wearer to move about without restriction. In case of a sudden stop or collision, the reel holds the harness in place and keeps the wearer from hitting some part of the car.

The shoulder harness should never be used without also fastening the seat belt.

Head Restraints   These devices help prevent whiplash injuries to the driver and right front seat passenger in case the car is rear-ended.

Preparing to Drive

Before getting into a car, check for objects outside the car. Check tire pressure. Clean the windshield and side windows if they are dirty. Clear the back window ledge of any books or packages. They block the inside mirror and in a sudden stop might hit passengers or the driver.

When seated behind the wheel, close and lock all doors. Place the key in the ignition switch. Sit with your back firmly against the back of the seat. Place your left foot on the floor to the left of the foot pedals. Place your right foot on the accelerator with the heel resting on the floor at the base of the pedal. Move the seat forward or back so the position is comfortable, your knee is slightly bent, and you can reach the steering wheel, brake, accelerator, and clutch easily.

Next, adjust the inside mirror so it reflects the entire rear window. Adjust the outside mirror so you can see the area to the rear and left side of the car. Adjust the head restraint so it comes to the middle of your head.

Fasten both your lap belt and shoulder harness and see that all passengers have also fastened their belts. Your shoulder harness should be adjusted so you can place your fist between the belt and your chest. Wear the lap belt *snug and low.*

PRE-IGNITION CHECKS
Practice the following pre-ignition checks:
1. Check around the car.
2. Close and lock all doors.
3. Put key in ignition switch.
4. Be sure rear window ledge is clear of packages and books.
5. Adjust seat.
6. Adjust mirrors and head restraint.
7. Fasten seat belt and shoulder harness. Passengers should also have belts adjusted.

Driving an Automatic-Shift Car

The steps for starting, moving, stopping, and parking an automatic-shift car are easy to learn. However, the beginning driver should not be tempted to feel that they are not important. Developing correct habits for these basic procedures can prevent problems in the future.

SELECTOR POSITIONS

To help the driver remember the gear positions in an automatic-shift car, a *shift indicator* is mounted either on the steering column or by the floor selector lever.

P=Park.   This position locks the transmission and steering wheel so the car cannot be moved once the key is removed. Always shift to PARK before opening any doors. Never shift to PARK when the car is moving.

R=Reverse.   This gear is for backing the car. Never shift to REVERSE when car is moving.

N=Neutral.   This is the standstill position in which the transmission is *not* locked. Place the lever in NEUTRAL when the car is stopped for more than a short time in traffic. The engine can be started only when the selector is in PARK or NEUTRAL.

D=Drive.   This position is for normal forward driving.

L=Low (1 or 2).   This position may be used for hard pulling in low traction situations, such as mud, sand, or deep snow, and for climbing or descending a long or steep hill. In most cars, shifting to LOW gear should be avoided at speeds over 40 mph (64 km/h).

Starting the Engine

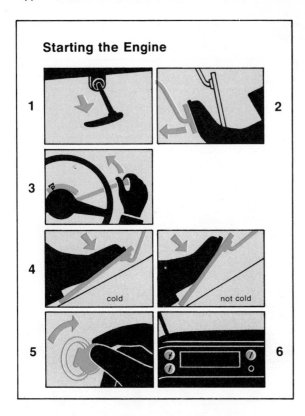

cold   not cold

STARTING THE ENGINE

The following procedure is used to start the engine:

1. Make sure the parking brake is "on."
2. With your right foot, press down on the foot brake. Before shifting into any gear, you should press down firmly on the foot brake.
3. Make sure the selector is in PARK or NEUTRAL; otherwise, the starter will not work. This limitation is a safety feature to keep automatic-shift cars from being set in motion unexpectedly.
4. Now move the right foot to the accelerator. If the engine is cold, press the accelerator to the floor *once* and release it to set the automatic choke. If the engine is not cold, simply press the accelerator slightly and hold it. (Check this against the starting procedure in the owner's manual.)
5. Now turn on the ignition switch. Turn the key only until the engine starts.
6. Once the engine is running, check the gauges. Be sure there is enough gas and that the electrical and oil pressure systems are operating.

Caution: Never try to start the car when the engine is running. Expensive damage to the starter can result. If the engine has not started, the alternator light will be red, or the gauge will show discharge. You can check to see whether the engine is running by pushing down gently on the gas pedal.

PUTTING AN AUTOMATIC-SHIFT CAR IN MOTION

Once the car has been started, the driver should use the following procedure to start the car moving:

1. With the engine idling in PARK or NEUTRAL, step on the brake pedal with the right foot.
2. Move the selector lever to DRIVE, and leave it there for normal driving.
3. Release the parking brake, but keep pressure on the brake pedal, or the car may creep forward.
4. If you are planning to leave the curb, put on your turn signal so drivers behind you will be alerted.
5. Now check traffic in both rearview mirrors and check over your shoulder to see if any vehicle is about to pass you.
6. When the way is clear, remove your foot from the brake pedal, and place it on the accelerator. Gently feed the car gasoline.
7. Check for traffic over your left shoulder again before moving into traffic.
8. Cancel the signal, if necessary, once you are in traffic.
9. After you get up to cruising speed, let up a little on the accelerator. As you drive along, adjust your speed.

Putting Car in Motion

Stopping the Car

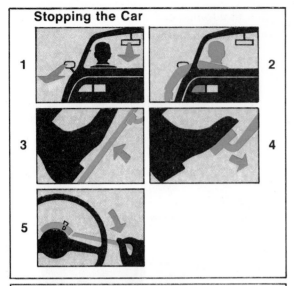

Leaving a Parked Car

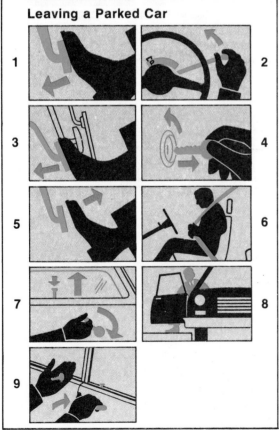

STOPPING THE CAR

Use the following steps when stopping a car with automatic transmission:

1. Make a habit of checking traffic in both mirrors before you slow down to stop.
2. Signal for a stop.
3. Slow the car down by letting up on the accelerator.
4. To stop the car, move your foot to the brake pedal, and press down gradually. Brake early enough to be able to ease up a little on the brake just before coming to a complete stop. This procedure will keep the car from dipping down in front as it comes to a complete stop.
5. Leave the selector lever in the DRIVE position if you expect to start up again immediately. Keep pressure on the foot brake until you are ready to start in order to prevent the car from creeping forward.

LEAVING A PARKED CAR

This procedure applies to both automatic-shift and stickshift cars.

1. When you stop the car to park it, keep pressure on the brake.
2. Move the lever to PARK or in a stickshift car to REVERSE.
3. Set the parking brake.
4. Turn off the ignition switch, and remove the key.
5. Release the brake pedal.
6. Unfasten lap and shoulder belts. Check to make sure the lights are turned off.
7. Close the windows and lock the doors.
8. Get out of the car on curb side, if possible.
9. Lock curb-side door. Keep keys in your hand to avoid locking them in the car.

Driving a Stickshift Car

Driving a car with manual transmission requires fine coordination of clutch, accelerator, and gearshift lever.

USING THE CLUTCH AND SHIFTING

Always hold the clutch down while moving the stickshift lever from one gear position to another. The lever and the clutch should work together as a unit. At times you will use the clutch alone, but *not* the lever alone.

Keep your foot off the clutch pedal when you have finished shifting. The habit of "riding the clutch," or driving in THIRD with the left foot on the clutch pedal, causes needless clutch wear.

Stickshift cars have a manual shift lever either on the steering column or on the floor. In the three-speed type of shift pattern, the four positions for this lever may be thought of as the four corners of an H with REVERSE in the upper left corner. The four-speed shift is used in many foreign cars and on some American cars. The fourth gear is intended for use on open highways at higher speeds.

STICKSHIFT LEVER POSITIONS

First is used to start the car moving up to a forward speed of 10 to 15 mph. It can be used for driving on very steep hills.

Second is used to bring the car up to a forward speed of 15 to 25 mph. Also it may be used for steep hills and for driving in mud, sand, snow, or ice.

Third in a three-speed transmission is used for steady forward driving at speeds above 25

mph. In a four-speed transmission, THIRD is used to accelerate to speeds up to 35 mph.

Fourth is used for speeds above 35 mph.

Neutral is the crossbar of the H, where the lever should be when the car is standing still and when starting the engine.

Reverse is used for backing the car. Never shift to REVERSE when the car is moving.

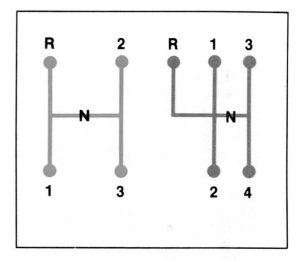

STARTING THE ENGINE

The following procedure is used to start a stickshift car:
1. Make sure the parking brake is on.
2. With your left foot, press clutch pedal down to the floor.
3. Put stickshift lever in NEUTRAL.
4. Depress accelerator part way and hold. (If engine is cold, first press accelerator to floor once and release.)
5. Turn on ignition switch.
6. Turn key only until engine starts.
7. Check gauges.

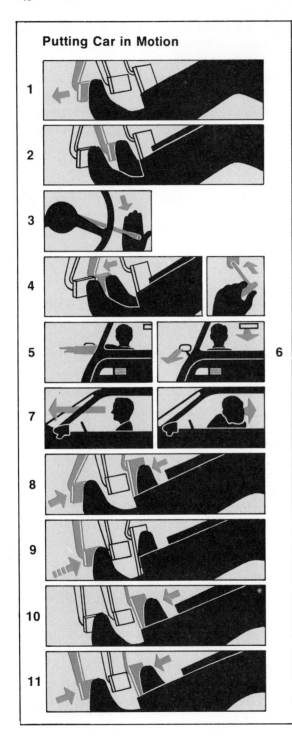

Putting Car in Motion

1
2
3
4
5 6
7
8
9
10
11

PUTTING A STICKSHIFT CAR IN MOTION

Once the engine is running, use the following steps to put a car in motion:

1. Press the clutch pedal down to the floor with your left foot.
2. Place your right foot on the brake pedal ready to use.
3. Move the stickshift lever from NEUTRAL to FIRST.
4. Now depress the foot brake and release the parking brake.
5. Signal to leave the curb.
6. Check traffic in the rearview mirrors.
7. Check traffic ahead. Check traffic to the rear by looking over your left shoulder.
8. Next, accelerate slightly and release the clutch slowly. If you release it suddenly, the car will jerk forward, or you might kill the engine. As you release the clutch, feed gas gradually. When you have released the clutch a little way, you will feel the engine catch hold and begin to pull the car. The point where the engine catches is called the *friction point.*
9. As you release the clutch, hesitate a little at the friction point.
10. Press down slightly on the accelerator.
11. Gradually, increase pressure on the accelerator as you let the clutch up all the way.

STOPPING FROM FIRST OR SECOND GEAR

The following procedures are used to stop from FIRST, SECOND, or REVERSE:

1. Check traffic in rearview mirrors.
2. Signal for a stop.
3. Press clutch pedal down.
4. Release accelerator.
5. Apply foot brake gently.
6. Shift to NEUTRAL after car has stopped.

SHIFTING FROM FIRST TO SECOND

At 10 to 15 mph, use the following steps to shift from FIRST to SECOND:

1. Press the clutch down.
2. Release the accelerator.
3. Move the stickshift lever into SECOND. A very slight pause as you direct the lever from NEUTRAL into SECOND will help you shift smoothly.
4. Once in SECOND, give the engine a little gas as you slowly release the clutch. Hesitate a moment at the friction point.

SHIFTING TO THIRD

When your speed reaches 15 to 25 mph, shift into THIRD.

1. Press down on the clutch.
2. Release the accelerator.
3. Pull the gearshift lever into THIRD.
4. While releasing the clutch, feed a little gas.

STOPPING FROM THIRD

When stopping from THIRD, use the brake pedal first without pressing down on the clutch. By keeping the car in gear, you are using the engine to slow down and to help the brakes slow the wheels. In an emergency, applying the brakes without using the clutch at all will stop the car.

1. Check traffic in rearview mirrors.
2. Signal for a stop.
3. Let up on accelerator.
4. Brake gradually.
5. At 10 mph, press down on the clutch to avoid stalling the engine.
6. Shift to NEUTRAL.

DOWNSHIFTING

The engine has greater pulling power in lower gears than in higher ones. Therefore, if you have slowed down to about 10 mph and want to regain speed, you must downshift from THIRD to SECOND.

Depress the clutch and then move the stickshift lever from THIRD to SECOND. Accelerate as you let up on the clutch pedal, pausing at the friction point. After you have reached 15 or 25 mph, depress the clutch again and shift back to THIRD.

This downshifting procedure can be used successfully when the car needs extra pulling power to climb a long, steep hill. Shift to SECOND just before the engine begins to labor. Don't wait until the car has almost stopped.

Lower gears also help a driver going down a long steep hill. Using SECOND makes the engine work to slow the car down so that the driver does not have to use the brakes so much all the way down the hill.

Once you have brought the car to a full stop, shift to FIRST before you start up again. Never shift to FIRST when the car is moving.

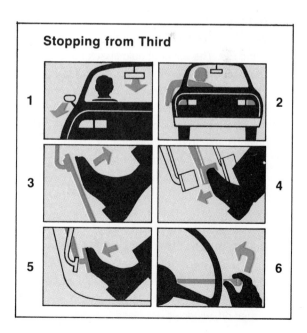

Stopping from Third

Vocabulary

accelerator, 39
alternator, 37
alternator light, 37
automatic choke, 39
brake system warning light, 37
clutch, 39
defroster, 41
dimmer switch, 40
downshifting, 49
emergency flasher, 41
foot brake, 39
friction point, 48
fuel gauge, 36
head restraint, 41
high beam indicator, 40
ignition switch, 38

manual shift lever, 38
odometer, 36
oil pressure warning light, 37
parking brake, 39
rearview mirrors, 40
riding the clutch, 47
seat adjustment lever, 38
selector lever, 38
shift indicator, 43
shoulder harness, 41
speedometer, 36
sun visor, 41
temperature indicator light, 37
three-speed transmission, 47
turn signals, 40

Summary

1. Each instrument on the instrument panel gives important information to the driver about the condition of the car. The driver should check the gauges and warning lights often.
2. Car controls enable the driver to operate the car safely and efficiently.
3. Various devices, controls, and signals provide the driver with the means of seeing better and communicating with other road users as well as provide safety and comfort for the car's occupants.
4. A comfortable sitting position behind the wheel helps in the safe and efficient operation of a car. The driver is able to reach all controls and devices.
5. A driver should perform the pre-ignition checks every time before starting the engine.
6. Drivers must know the PRNDL positions on the shift indicator so that they can shift an automatic transmission car without taking their eyes off the road.
7. Drivers must be able to start the engine, to put the car in motion, and to stop in a car with automatic transmission so that these procedures will become habitual.
8. Drivers must be able to perform the above procedures in a car with manual transmission so that these procedures become automatic.
9. Before leaving a parked car, the driver should be sure that an automatic-shift car is in PARK or a stickshift car is in REVERSE, parking brake is set, ignition switch is locked, key is removed, lights are turned off, windows are closed, and all doors are locked.

Driving Situations

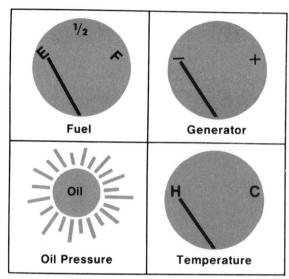

Fuel

Generator

Oil Pressure

Temperature

1. You are driving along a highway, and suddenly realize that your panel gauges look like each of the above. What might be wrong? What action should you take?

2. What errors in the use of safety devices and indicators has the driver in the above picture made? Why is the proper use of devices and indicators important?

3. You are driving an automatic-shift car in each of the above situations. What gear position should you use in each case?

4. You are driving a three-speed stickshift car in each situation. What gear should you use in each case?

Chapter Review Questions

Instruments, Devices, and Controls

1. What does the oil-pressure warning light indicate to the driver? (37)
2. How should a driver's reactions differ to warnings from the alternator gauge and the oil-pressure gauge? (37)
3. Name the two kinds of warning given by the brake warning light. How can a driver determine which warning is being given? (37)
4. What six car lights are controlled by the light switch? (40)
5. What is the function of the dimmer switch? Where is it located? (40)
6. What functions does the parking brake serve? (39)

Preparing to Drive

7. What steps should be taken prior to starting the engine? (42)
8. How should the lap belt and shoulder harness be adjusted? (42)
9. What is the proper position for the head restraint? (42)

Driving an Automatic-Shift Car

10. Why should a driver avoid turning the ignition switch when the engine is running? (44)
11. Why is it necessary for a driver to check the gauges after starting the engine? (44)
12. Why is it important to give a signal when you change lanes or leave the curb? (45)
13. What are the steps for putting an automatic-shift car in motion? (45)

Driving a Stickshift Car

14. List the steps for starting a car with manual transmission. (47)
15. What does "riding the clutch" mean? Why is this a bad habit? (47)
16. Why should a stickshift car be downshifted to SECOND when driving down a steep hill? (49)
17. When stopping in THIRD, why should you depress the brake pedal first? (49)

Projects

1. Check the owner's manual for your family car, and locate each of the instruments, devices, and controls. Also check the proper way to start this car.
2. Check a number of different car makes and models. Report on which controls appear to be located in much the same place on all cars and which are in different places.
3. Check a number of different car makes and models. Report on the various types of switches and controls for lights, windshield wipers, heater, and air conditioner. Which types of switches seem most practical?
4. Observe five experienced drivers as they are performing the pre-ignition checks, starting the engine, pulling away from the curb, and stopping the car. How many follow the procedures outlined in this chapter?

Chapter 3 • Test

(Write the correct answers on a separate sheet of paper.)

True-False

1. The parking brake could be used to stop the car whenever you don't feel like using the brake pedal. (39)
2. In many states, it is illegal to drive with only the parking lights on. (40)
3. The odometer measures the number of miles a car has been driven. (36)
4. If the car is equipped with seat belts and shoulder harnesses, the driver may use the shoulder harness without the seat belt. (41)
5. If the temperature warning light or gauge shows "hot," you should immediately drive to the nearest service station for repairs. (37)
6. Once the engine stops running, the driver of a car with power brakes and steering can no longer control the car. (39)
7. The rearview mirrors give the driver a complete view of traffic to the rear. (41)
8. The oil pressure light or gauge indicates when the oil should be changed. (37)
9. If you open the car door and hear a buzzer, the key is still in the ignition switch. (38)
10. After getting into a car, the driver should adjust the seat before adjusting the mirrors. (42)
11. LOW gear on automatic-shift cars should be used only for driving down a steep hill. (43)
12. The automatic transmission should never be shifted to PARK when the car is moving. (43)
13. The driver of a three-speed stickshift car should downshift to SECOND whenever speed in THIRD falls below 10 mph and the driver wants to regain speed. (49)
14. Friction point is the point where the engine catches as the clutch is released. (48)
15. When stopping the car from THIRD, you should depress the brake pedal first. (49)

Answer the Question

16. While you are driving, you notice the brake warning light is on. What does this tell you? (37)
17. When should a driver use the emergency flasher? (41)
18. How does the turn-signal lever work in a lane change? (40)
19. What is the proper adjustment of the head restraint? (42)
20. In what two gears will the engine of an automatic car start? (43)
21. How can a driver determine whether the engine is running? (44)
22. In what position should you place the lever when you leave the car? (46)
23-25. List in proper order the first three steps for putting an automatic car in motion. (45)

Chapter 4

Vehicle Control Within Natural Laws

Objectives

1. Explain how friction allows the tires to control the car.
2. List vehicle and road factors that determine the amount of traction available for car control.
3. List ways that tires send messages to drivers.
4. Explain how friction can affect a car's energy of motion.
5. Define stopping distance.
6. List the factors that affect a driver's ability to stop the car.
7. List two factors that affect car control on curves.
8. List three factors that affect the force of impact in a crash.
9. Explain the difference between the car crash and the passenger crash.
10. List devices on cars that protect people in crashes and what part each plays.
11. Explain the role vehicle size plays in injury and survival rates in crashes.

Introduction

Drivers need to know how the laws of nature affect their cars in order to respond correctly to driving situations. Many people learn to operate a car without this knowledge. As a result, when they are faced with certain driving situations, they may not respond correctly. They may fail to steer or brake in the most effective way.

The laws of nature are impossible to ignore, and drivers must control their vehicles within these laws. Gravity is one of the most important laws of nature. Gravity is the force that gives both cars and people their weight. In driving a car, a person notices the force of gravity most on hills. It pulls the car down the hill.

A driver must also deal with other laws: friction, energy of motion, and force of impact. Because of these forces, a driver can control a car when going straight or turning. These forces also determine what will happen if a car hits an object.

Information in this chapter will help you understand how and why a car responds the way it does to the driver's commands. This knowledge will enable you to make wise decisions and controlled responses when you are driving.

Friction

Many drivers assume that the steering wheel, brake pedal, and accelerator control the car. These controls only send the driver's reactions to the steering system, brakes, and engine. The four patches of rubber that touch the road actually control the car.

The tires make the car speed up, turn corners, and stop. However, a tire is limited in how much it can grip the road and still control the car. When one surface touches and moves across another surface, the force that resists the movement is called *friction* or traction. This natural law allows the tire to grip the road. The more friction there is between your tires and the road, the more control you have over your car.

When a driver presses the gas pedal and increases the speed of the rear wheels, friction allows the rear tires to grip the road and thereby increase the speed of the car. If the driver accelerates too fast or turns the steering wheel too sharply, the tires will begin to spin or skid, and their grip on the road will be reduced. This reduced friction may make steering impossible.

When a driver presses the brake pedal, all four tires must grip the road to slow down or stop the car. If the driver presses the brake pedal too hard and locks the wheels while the car is moving, the tires will lose their grip, and the car can go out of control in a skid. When a car skids, the driver loses most of the friction that allows him or her to steer the car.

Car control depends on the driver making only those maneuvers that will not cause the tires to lose traction with the road. When you push the accelerator or brake, or turn the steering wheel, the tires use friction to grip the road to accelerate, stop, or turn.

A driver's control of a car depends on the four spots of the tires that grip the road.

FACTORS INFLUENCING TRACTION

Two factors determine the amount of traction available: tread and road surface. Smart drivers consider these factors in making wise driving decisions.

Tread   The grooved surface of a tire is called *tread*. A good tire with wide, deep gripping tread will give a driver better traction in most kinds of weather and road conditions. Badly worn or bald tires do not grip wet or slick roads well.

Road Surface   Dry pavement provides the best traction. Crushed rock and gravel roads tend to keep the tires from getting a solid grip on the road. Stopping on wet pavement takes much longer than on dry road. Snow and ice present even greater problems. Ice can stretch stopping distance up to ten times as long as on dry pavement.

WHAT A CAR CAN TELL ITS DRIVER

You have read how tires help the driver control the car. Equally important are the messages the car sends to the driver. He or she can hear or feel the car's messages. These messages help a driver adjust his or her responses in order to control the car.

Feel   At high speeds or on slick surfaces at low speeds, the car may not respond well to the driver's steering, gas, or brake commands. This reaction is called *lack of vehicle response.*

Rough and bumpy roads cause the car to send messages through the steering system to the driver. The vibrations are saying, "Traction is not so good down here on the road. Ease up on the accelerator."

What should drivers do when they hear the engine speeding up suddenly and the tires spinning? They should let up on the gas pedal, allow the tires to get a new grip on the road, and then accelerate gently on the next try.

Sounds   On dry pavement, if the tires begin to lose traction or if the car begins to slide, the tires will howl as a warning. However, do not expect to hear these sounds on wet roads, ice, or snow. Tires sizzle on wet roads and, in most instances, run silently on ice and snow. With the radio on or with the windows rolled up, the driver might not hear these sounds.

Friction and Energy of Motion

When the energy of motion is built up, it takes longer for a car to come to a stop.

The energy an object has because it is in motion is called *energy of motion* or kinetic energy. The faster a car moves, the more energy of motion builds up. The more energy of motion a car has, the harder it will be to turn. Also, the faster a car moves, the longer it takes to stop, and the harder it hits.

Energy of motion builds up faster than most people think. When a car's speed *doubles* from 20 to 40 mph, energy of motion increases *four times,* which is two squared. If a car's speed *triples* from 20 to 60 mph, energy of motion increases *nine times* (three squared). Energy of motion increases as the square of the increase in speed.

ENERGY OF MOTION, FRICTION, AND STOPPING

What happens to the energy of motion of your moving car when you brake to slow down? When you push down on the brake pedal, the brake linings are forced against the brake drums in the wheels. With disc brakes, the brake pads are forced against the brake discs. The friction of the brakes slows the wheels and increases the friction between the tires and the road. This action causes the car to slow down or stop.

Friction causes heat, as you can feel by rubbing your hands together. The more friction there is between the brake shoes and drums, the more heat there will be in the brakes. As you press the brake, the car's energy of motion will become lower. But heat in the brakes will increase. So the car's energy of motion is changed to heat energy in the brakes.

STOPPING DISTANCE

Once a dangerous situation develops, friction does not immediately change energy of motion into heat energy. It takes time for this change to occur. Two time factors affect the length of total stopping distance: the amount of time it takes the driver to react to a traffic problem and the time it takes for the car to come to a stop. While this process is taking place, the car continues to move.

Perception Time   The length of time that it takes for a driver to identify a dangerous situation is called *perception time.* This can vary greatly, depending on visibility, driver competence, and fitness. Sometimes, more time and distance are used identifying a danger than are needed to brake to a stop. Shortened perception time is the reason it is important to have good visual habits, to be alert, and to have a good fund of driver knowledge. *Perception distance* is the distance covered in this time.

Reaction Time   The length of time required to make a decision and move the foot from the accelerator to the brake pedal is called *reaction time.* A person's reaction time is normally about 3/4 second in most situations, but

it can be much longer than this. Drivers who are tired, ill, or impaired take longer to react in emergencies. Many fail to take any action at all before the car crashes. The distance covered during reaction time is called *reaction distance.*

Braking Distance   How far a car travels from the time the brakes are applied until the car stops is called *braking distance.* Like energy of motion, braking distance increases with the square of the speed. A car going 40 mph will require about four times the braking distance as one going 20 mph.

Stopping Distance   Total *stopping distance* equals a driver's perception and reaction distances plus the vehicle's braking distance. At 55 mph, the total stopping distance can cover 211 feet. Drivers can keep total stopping distance to a minimum by thinking ahead and by carefully matching speed to driving conditions. The chart below shows the typical stopping distances for speeds from 20 to 55 mph on dry pavement.

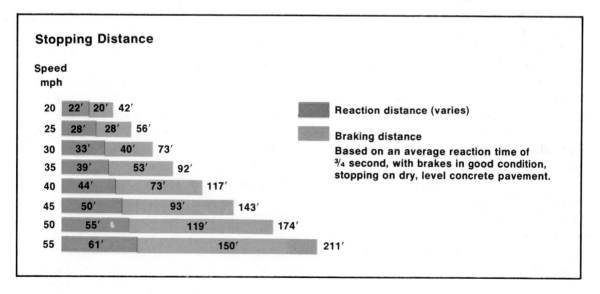

Stopping Distance

Speed
mph

Speed			
20	22'	20'	42'
25	28'	28'	56'
30	33'	40'	73'
35	39'	53'	92'
40	44'	73'	117'
45	50'	93'	143'
50	55'	119'	174'
55	61'	150'	211'

Reaction distance (varies)

Braking distance
Based on an average reaction time of
³/₄ second, with brakes in good condition,
stopping on dry, level concrete pavement.

FACTORS THAT AFFECT BRAKING DISTANCE

Although the laws of nature affect all vehicles in the same way, a driver should never assume that he or she can always stop in the same distance as the vehicle ahead. Several factors affect a vehicle's ability to stop.

Condition   Two similar cars may differ in braking distances due to differences in the condition of brakes, shock absorbers, and tires.

Speed   The higher the speed, the longer the braking distance, and the more difficult it is to keep the car under control while stopping.

Hills   Hills both increase and decrease braking distance. The force of gravity pulling the car downhill makes the car go faster and lengthens braking distance. Gravity, however, helps a driver who must stop suddenly while going uphill. Once the driver removes his or her foot from the accelerator, the car slows down quickly because gravity is pulling it toward the bottom of the hill.

Road Surface   Tires grip better on dry roads than on wet or icy roads. Pavement provides more traction than gravel.

THE STOP-SWERVE DECISION

When a dangerous situation occurs ahead, most drivers hit the brakes and stop. In many cases, this action is correct. Sometimes, though, drivers apply their brakes and slide into an object when they could have swerved around it.

When a driver is faced with an emergency at speeds over 30 mph, he or she can swerve around an object in the path ahead in less distance than the driver needs to stop. Only a small part of the total energy of motion built up in a moving car is used up in a lane change. Coming to a stop requires the brakes to change all of the built-up energy of motion into heat energy. However, the decision to swerve or stop also depends on whether the driver is sure no car is in the lane he or she will be entering.

How Much to Swerve?   How sharply a driver may need to swerve around an object depends on two factors: closeness to the object and speed.

As the picture at the right shows, the closer a car gets to a car ahead, the sharper the driver must swerve to get around it and the less stopping distance the driver has. If the driver is very close to the car and must swerve, the gap in the next lane must be large in order for this driver to swerve safely into the lane.

The farther the driver is from the car ahead, the less sharply the driver needs to turn the steering wheel and the greater stopping distance the driver has. The driver will be better able to maneuver into the next lane if that driver is further from the car ahead.

Car colors in all model photographs represent:
Yellow: The action car.
White: The other cars moving around action car.
Neutral: Parked cars.

Speed also influences how much the steering wheel may safely be turned. *The higher the speed, the less the driver should turn the steering wheel.* When a car is going 10 mph, the driver will turn the wheel much more than if the car were going 25 mph. At 55 mph the wheel is turned much less than if the car were going 25 mph.

However, remember that most steering actions taken in traffic do not require the driver to decide between stopping or swerving. This maneuver should be used only as a last resort. Swerving should not be practiced in traffic but in a protected area.

The closer you get to a vehicle the harder it is to get around it, and the farther back the car behind must be.

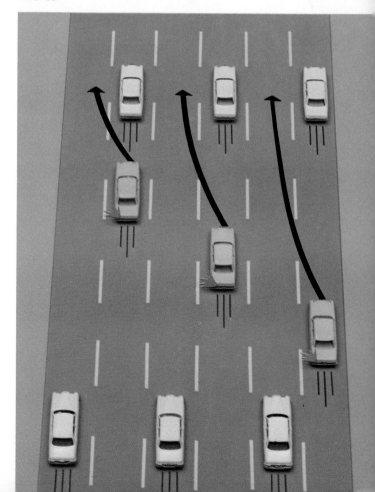

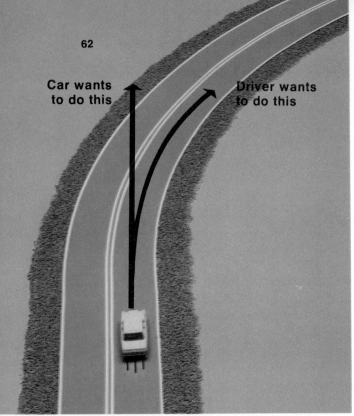

Car wants to do this

Driver wants to do this

The higher the speed the more the vehicle resists turning a corner or taking a curve.

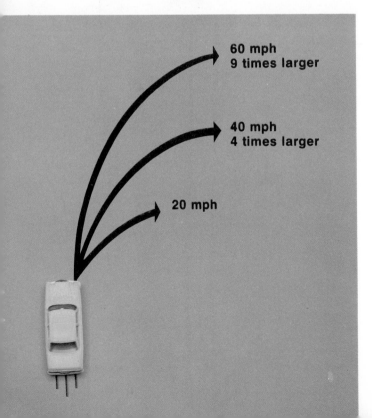

60 mph
9 times larger

40 mph
4 times larger

20 mph

CURVES

When a driver rounds a curve or turns a corner, two forces—energy of motion and friction—act on the car. Energy of motion causes a car in motion to continue to move in the same direction and at the same speed until an outside force is applied.

As shown in the illustration to the left, the car wants to go straight, but the driver wants to turn. The friction of the tires as they grip the road helps the driver make the turn. The energy of motion tends to keep the car moving in the same direction. If the friction is great enough, the car rounds the curve. In order to reduce the energy of motion, the driver must brake to slow the car down. If the tires lose their grip, the law of motion causes the car to skid in the direction it is moving. No driver has been able to overcome the laws of nature. Therefore, drivers must control their vehicles within natural laws.

Factors Affecting Car Control in Curves   The following factors affect the way a car behaves in a curve.

1. **Sharpness of Curve** The sharper a curve, the more force is needed to hold the car on the road at a given speed. Highway engineers can make curves safer by making them larger or more gradual. As the lower illustration shows, a curve designed for 40-mph must be four times larger than that of a 20-mph curve. A 60-mph curve must be nine times greater than a 20-mph curve.

2. **Bank of Curve** A curve that is higher at the outside than on the inside is called a *banked curve.* This curve will help overcome a car's tendency to tilt or slide toward the outside of the curve. Banking helps you hold your car on the road, as the highway engineers intended.

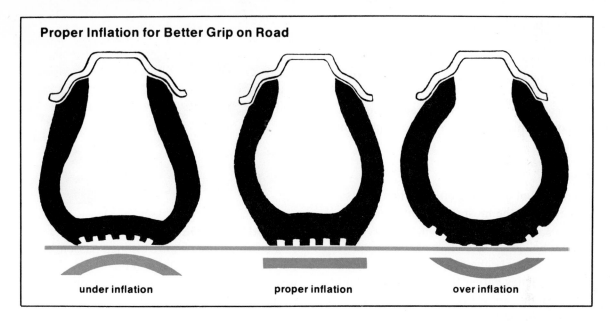

Proper Inflation for Better Grip on Road

under inflation   proper inflation   over inflation

3. **Speed** The driver who decides to take a curve posted for 20 mph at 40 mph may not realize that the amount of friction needed to keep the car on the road will be four times as great as the engineer intended. In all probability, the car will leave the road. At many highway curves, speed signs are posted just below the curve sign.

A driver has no control over how sharp or banked a curve is. But every driver can do something about adjusting speed. Good drivers do not wait until they are on a curve to reduce their speed. They slow down well ahead of the curve.

Tireprints Change in Turns The friction between the tire and the road can change in a curve. Turning sharply can cause part of a bias-ply tire to lift off the road. In a turn, the amount of rubber in contact with the road is reduced at the same time the need for traction is much higher.

When a driver turns sharply right, the car leans to the left. Strong side forces cause the right side of the tire to lift off the pavement. The sharper the turn and the higher the speed, the more the car will lean and the less the right tire will grip the road.

On the other hand, radial tires tend to grip the road better in a turn than bias-ply tires. The whole tire flexes and leaves a full tireprint. Thus, the driver has more traction and better control. If radials are turned too sharply, they can also lose their grip on the pavement.

The amount of air in a tire determines the size of the tireprint on both bias-ply and radial tires. The lower the tire pressure, the more the tire will lift off the pavement in a sharp turn or curve. Checking tire pressure is very important because pressure affects car control.

Force of Impact

Another law of nature is important in collisions. The force of a body hitting something is called the *force of impact*. Three important factors affect the force of impact: weight, speed, and distance between the impact and final stop.

SPEED

The speed of a moving object when it hits something is the most important part of its force. Like energy of motion, the force of impact builds as the square of the speed. Thus, a car traveling 60 mph will hit any object nine times harder than one going 20 mph. The resulting impact felt by the passengers in that car will be nine times greater than it would be in a 20-mph crash. This fact explains why passengers are more frequently killed in high speed crashes.

WEIGHT

At a given speed, a truck weighing 40,000 pounds will hit an object 10 times harder than would a 4,000 pound car. The heavier a body, the more energy of motion it has. The greater the energy of motion, the harder it will hit.

DISTANCE BETWEEN IMPACT AND STOP

The distance covered by the car between the time it first hits an object and its final stop can vary greatly. If a moving car hits something solid like a large tree, the car will stop very suddenly because the tree will not give. The resulting impact will be very great. If the car hits something less solid like a chain link fence, it will take longer to stop because the fence will bend. The impact will be far less damaging.

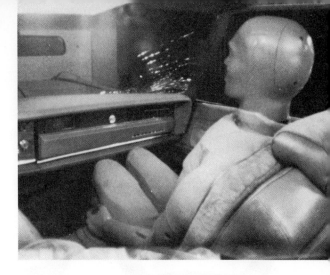

CAR AND PASSENGER CRASHES

In a crash involving unrestrained passengers, two crashes occur. The first one takes place when the car hits an object. The second crash occurs when the passengers hit something inside the car.

Car Crash Two factors determine how suddenly a car will stop in a crash. The first is whether the object the car strikes is solid or whether the object gives. A second relates to the crush area of the car ahead of the passenger compartment. If the car has a short hood, the front has little metal to use up the car's energy of motion. Therefore, the force of impact will reach the passenger area. If the hood is longer, the front of the car has more metal to absorb the crash. The car will stop over a slightly longer distance, and the passenger's impact will be less severe.

Passenger Crash If a driver slams on the brakes while traveling 50 mph, the passengers will be thrown forward. They will not be injured, though, because the braking distance will be over 100 feet (30 meters). But if the car hits a solid object at that speed, it will stop in about 6 feet (2 meters). Even if they try, the passengers will not be able to hold

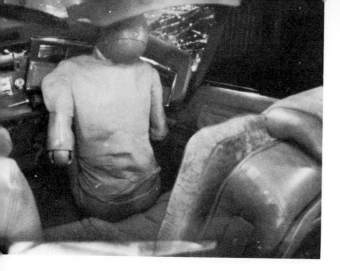

themselves back. They will smash against the inside of the car at 50 mph and come to a stop in less than 2 feet unless they are wearing seat belts.

DEVICES TO PROTECT PASSENGERS

Cars are now built with safety devices to protect passengers against injury in a crash.

1. **Seat Belts and Shoulder Harnesses** Nothing prevents the passenger crash better than seat belts and shoulder harnesses. They enable the passenger to travel at exactly the same speed as the car, because when the seat belts are buckled, the passengers become part of the car. Wearing seat belts and shoulder harnesses reduces chances of death and serious injury because the second crash takes place against the seat belts.

2. **Front and Rear Crush Areas** These include the front and rear-end structures of the car. The bending of metal in the crush area often absorbs much of the car's energy of motion. The crush areas stretch out the stopping process and increase the chance of survival in crashes. The smaller the car the smaller the crush area and the lower the chance of survival in a serious collision.

3. **Side Door Beams** They look much like guardrails seen along highways. The beams are fastened inside car doors to protect passengers in side collisions.

4. **Energy Absorbing Windshield** This contains a thick plastic sheet between two layers of glass. The windshield acts like a safety net and keeps passengers from being thrown through it.

5. **Energy Absorbing Steering Wheel and Column** Both the wheel and steering column are designed to bend and give under impact. These cushion the force of impact when the driver hits the steering wheel in a crash.

6. **Padded Dash and Interior** Areas inside the car that passengers could hit are padded to absorb the energy of motion. In addition, knobs and controls are recessed so that they will not injure people in a crash.

7. **Head Restraints** Head restraints are placed behind the front seat to help prevent injuries to the driver and right front seat passenger when their car is hit from behind.

8. **Door Locks** These help keep doors from popping open in crashes and rollovers. Passengers thrown through open doors are much more likely to be killed or injured.

Vocabulary

banked curve, 62
braking distance, 59
crush area, 65
energy of motion, 58
force of impact, 64

friction, 56
passenger crash, 64
perception distance, 59
perception time, 59
reaction distance, 59

reaction time, 59
stopping distance, 59
tireprint, 63
traction, 56
tread, 57

Summary

1. Friction is the force that allows the tires to grip the road.
2. Two important factors that determine the amount of traction are tire tread and road surface.
3. Tires send messages to the driver through the sound and feel of the car.
4. Friction of the brake linings against the drums and the wheels against the road slows down the car's energy of motion.
5. Stopping distance is the total time it takes to stop a car and includes perception distance, reaction distance, and braking distance.
6. Vehicle condition, speed, hills, and road surface affect braking distance.
7. Sharpness and bank of a curve as well as the car's speed affect the car's ability to take the curve.
8. Weight of the vehicle, speed of the vehicle, and the distance between impact and stop affect the force of impact.
9. The car crash occurs when the car hits an object while the passenger crash occurs when the passengers hit the inside of the car after a crash.
10. Front and rear crush areas, steering wheel and column, safety belts, padded interior, and head restraints all work to protect people in crashes.
11. The smaller the car the lower the chance of surviving a serious crash. Crush areas ahead of the passenger area as well as in the body and frame play an important role in protecting the passengers.

Driving Situations

1. You want to accelerate, but all that happens is that the wheels just spin and the engine speeds up. What should you do? What physical force is important in recovering your control?

2. You are traveling 50 mph and suddenly realize that a car is stopped in your lane. How much longer would it take to stop than if your speed was 25 mph? What should you do in this situation?

3. You are approaching a curve at 20 mph. The sign says that the curve should be rounded at 10 mph. If you take the curve at 20 mph, how much larger should it be? What action should you take to round the curve safely?

4. You are driving the yellow car and have slammed on the brakes to avoid a head-on crash. The wheels are sliding. You want to head for the shoulder. What should you do?

Chapter Review Questions

Friction

1. Why don't the steering wheel, brake pedal, and gas pedal actually control the car? (56)
2. What two important factors influence the amount of traction that tires have on the pavement? (57)
3. How does friction affect the ability of the tires to control the car? (56)
4. Describe two ways a car can send messages to the driver. (57)

Energy of Motion and Friction

5. When a driver doubles the speed of a car, what happens to braking distance? to energy of motion? to the size of the curve needed? to the force of impact in a crash? (58, 59, 64)
6. How does friction help a car? (58)
7. List three factors that influence braking distance. (60)
8. Why does perception time vary among drivers? (59)
9. How does the amount a steering wheel may safely be turned change as speed increases? (61)
10. What effect does tire pressure have on the shape of tireprints in turns? (63)
11. In a curve, why does a car want to go in a straight line? What is needed to make the car follow the curve? (62)
12. What factors influence the car's control on a curve? (62)

Force of Impact

13. When a car crash occurs, what prevents the passenger crash? (65)
14. What three factors determine how hard a car will hit an object in a collision? (64)
15. Why are front and rear crush areas in a car important to passenger protection and survival in crashes? (65)
16. What two safety features require the active attention of drivers to protect them in crashes? (65)

Projects

1. Select a team of students to survey the percent of cars in the school parking lot that have tires worn below 3/32 inch. Tires are considered to be bald beyond this point. Discuss the dangers of being on the road with cars with badly worn tires.
2. Survey the number of each size car in the school parking lot, including full size, intermediate, compact, and subcompact. Write a report on the survey, and discuss the kind of protection each crush area gives the passengers.
3. Station a student at each exit to the school parking lot. Determine the percent of students who have the seat belts attached. Report to class on percentage of student's using seat belts. In the report, discuss the issue of whether federal or state governments should by law require everyone to wear seat belts as in Australia.

Chapter 4 ▪ Test

(Write the correct answers on a separate sheet of paper.)

True-False

1. Gravity has no effect on the braking distance of a car going down hill. (60)
2. Once a car crash takes place, a passenger crash is unavoidable. (65)
3. If the brakes are locked and the tires are sliding, it is impossible to steer the car. (56)
4. The steering wheel, gas pedal, and brake pedal control the car. (56)
5. Steering movements should be smaller as the car goes faster. (61)
6. The safety devices installed in cars protect cars from crashes. (65)
7. When a driver presses on the brakes, friction changes the car's energy of motion into heat energy. (58)
8. The car crash and the passenger crash take place at the same instant. (65)
9. The main purpose of tires is to give the car a soft ride. (56)
10. For proper car control, a curve designed for 60 mph should be twice as large as a curve designed for 30 mph. (62)
11. If two persons' perception times are the same, their stopping distances will be the same. (59)
12. Impact and stop are two words that mean the same thing when you discuss force of impact. (64)
13. Energy of motion allows the tires to grip the road. (58)
14. The amount of air in the tire determines the amount of tire on the road. (63)
15. Energy of motion affects stopping, cornering, and impact. (58, 62, 64)

Answer the Question

16. When the rear wheels lock in a panic stop, what action should a driver take? (57)
17. What are some factors that affect braking distance? (60)
18. How does gravity affect a car's braking distance both going up and down hills? (60)
19. When a driver comes upon an object in the road, what two factors determine how sharply he or she can swerve? (61)
20. What are two protective devices in a car that will not work unless the driver uses them? (65)

Chapter 5

IPDE and Driving Strategies

Objectives

1. Describe the five Smith System driving rules.
2. List four parts of the traffic environment a driver must look for and respond to when driving.
3. List five methods that you can use to communicate with other drivers.
4. Describe how stored knowledge helps drivers make accurate predictions.
5. List six driving factors that must be judged correctly in order to make wise driving decisions.
6. List five things to evaluate about the other driver when making predictions.
7. Describe two important things to consider when making driving decisions.
8. Describe how to learn decision-making when riding in a car as a passenger.
9. List three factors that determine how much action a driver can take.
10. Describe a space cushion.
11. List four requirements for a safe path of travel.
12. Explain the meaning of minimizing, separating, and compromising.
13. List the ABC's of formation driving.

Introduction

Most drivers who are involved in crashes can handle a car quite well. But the blame for most crashes cannot be placed solely on defective cars, unsafe roads, bad driving conditions, congestion, or the other person. The blame often must rest on the missed clues and bad decisions made by the drivers themselves.

Unlike airline pilots who fly in a highly controlled system, millions of individuals must drive in a system with fewer controls. Many drivers who eventually wind up in a crash often don't know why or how it could have happened. But the driver with an organized system of operation is the one who usually stays out of trouble.

This chapter will present a system that will help you learn how to see more and gain more meaning from what you see. It will help you to analyze traffic situations and make wise decisions in time to take safe actions.

This chapter will also provide strategies you can use to handle driving situations that are sure to occur. You will also learn how to get along with other road users as well as how to look out for yourself in different kinds of traffic situations now and throughout your whole lifetime of driving.

The IPDE Process

Being able to see well does not ensure that drivers will detect all of the critical clues in traffic or will take proper actions once they see those clues. Seeing, thinking, and responding properly to traffic situations is called the IPDE process.

Everybody uses some kind of process or system to drive. Drivers with an unorganized system will have more close calls and collisions. The driver with a more organized system that deals with all possibilities in traffic will be more successful.

To process traffic information properly, a driver must first *identify* problems. The second step is to *predict* what might happen. The third step is to *decide* on a safe action to take. The fourth and final step is to *execute* the plan by taking some kind of controlled action.

IDENTIFYING

A driver who sees a bicycle coming out of a driveway identifies it as a potential problem. Not all parts of the driving scene are that easy to identify.

Identifying involves more than just seeing. A driver must know what to look for, when to look, where and how long to look. This is called *searching* or *scanning*.

The Smith System Harold Smith, along with the Traffic Safety and Highway Improvement Department of the Ford Motor Company, developed a system of good seeing habits for drivers. The Smith System includes five rules that are easy to remember:
1. Aim high in steering.
2. Keep your eyes moving.
3. Get the big picture.
4. Make sure others see you.
5. Leave yourself an out.

Be alert for a child coming from between parked cars. Look near, far, left and right. Make mirror and head checks to the rear.

Rule 1: Aim High in Steering   To see things in time, it is best to look way ahead. In city traffic, look more than one block ahead. On expressways and highways, look more than a half mile ahead. Take advantage of hills and curves to get a glimpse of conditions in the distance.

Rule 2: Keep Your Eyes Moving   Eyes moving means taking selective glances near and far, right and left, as well as making occasional checks to the rear. Always return your eyes to the straight-ahead position after taking a glance to the side, rear, or at the instrument panel.

Take Quick Glances   Most beginners do not realize how much they can see in a second. To check this, shut your eyes and then open and close them in an instant to see what is in the picture above. The eyes can see a great amount of detail in a second. Drivers who stare focus on details longer than they should and miss seeing other vital details.

Rule 3: Get the Big Picture   The big picture is a result of aiming high and moving the eyes. It is a mental process of piecing together all of the details seen ahead, to the sides, and to the rear. The big picture will be useful in making predictions and decisions needed for a safe path of travel.

Seeing Requires Attention   To identify a potential hazard or a helpful driving clue, you must first sense it by seeing, hearing, smelling or feeling. Doing this requires full driver attention. Distractions can be dangerous because they can keep you from applying the IPDE process effectively. When you are driving, keep your mind totally on the driving task. When you are a passenger, avoid becoming a distraction.

Know What to Look For   Moving your eyes is of no value if you do not know what to look for. A driver must pay attention to the traffic environment, which includes:
- Traffic controls: lights, signs, and pavement markings.
- Road features: intersections, hills, curves.
- Other road users and their actions: vehicles, pedestrians, and cyclists.
- Your own vehicle: instruments, controls, speed, and position.

Rule 4: Make Sure Others See You   Not only should drivers make sure they are seen, they should make sure that other drivers understand their plans.

Communicating   This involves decoding and understanding the messages other drivers are intentionally and unintentionally sending out. As a driver, you must be an effective sender of messages that are easy to understand. As a receiver, you must see and interpret the messages that are sent in the form of lights, signals, car position, horn, eye contact, and body movements.

Talking Lights   The lights on your car are used to communicate with other drivers. It is important for you to understand the language of lights.

- **Taillights on** "I am here." In all kinds of weather and lighting conditions, taillights tell other drivers where you are. But if your taillights are burned out or dirty, they can no longer talk.
- **Brake lights on** "I am stopping or standing." "I see something that may cause me to slow or stop." "You are too close."
- **Turn-signal lights on** "I plan to turn or to change lanes."
- **High beam-low beam** "I am approaching." "I want to pass." "Please dim your headlights."
- **Emergency flashers** "I cannot move." "I am in trouble."
- **Back-up lights on** "I plan to back up." "I want that parking space."

Car Position   Car position can help or mislead the other driver. A slight movement toward the center line could indicate preparation for a left turn. A movement toward the right side of the lane could warn of a turn to the right.

Horn   Some drivers fail to use the horn when they should. Others consider it a substitute for the brakes. Properly used, a light tap on the horn may say, "I am here." A loud blast of the horn may be needed in the event of great danger.

Eye Contact   When the other driver is in a position to move into your path, check the eyes to see if the driver is looking at you. If not, get a driver's attention with a tap of the horn and be prepared to stop. If the driver is looking at you, there is some assurance that he or she may not move into your path, but don't count on it.

Body Movement   Body movements can also be a clue to actions the other drivers intend to take. If an oncoming driver is looking to the left, that driver might be planning to turn left. A head check could mean a lane change. Another driver might motion you to go forward, but be sure that it is safe before you move.

Rule 5: Leave Yourself an Out   This means leaving escape paths open. The skilled driver has developed the ability to put the vehicle into the traffic stream and position it in a matter of seconds. There is nobody in front of the car, nobody alongside it, and nobody behind it. The driver does this by adjusting constantly to keep a space cushion all around the car.

PREDICTING

The traffic picture is constantly changing. Cars start, speed up, change lanes, turn and stop. Vehicles and pedestrians cross your path of travel. Changing traffic lights also determine your movements. In order to have a safe plan of action, you must always predict what is likely to happen ahead.

Predictions depend on accurate knowledge of what other road users might do and what your own car can be expected to do. How accurate your information is will influence the quality of decisions you make.

Judgments   Judgment is learned from the time you are born. As a pedestrian and bicyclist, you already had some experience making judgments.

Without making accurate judgments, a driver would be unable to make accurate predictions, wise decisions, and to take safe driving actions. Since predictions involve the actions of other road users, you must be able to judge speed, distance between vehicles, time, and space beside your car. You must also be able to judge traction and visibility.

Learning to make good judgments is an essential driving skill. Use every opportunity to develop your ability to judge traffic and road conditions whenever you are a passenger or a driver.

Predict that the light will stay green for several more seconds.

Predict that stopping will take longer so braking must be done sooner.

Predict that the semi-trailer truck will swing into your path.

Your Own Vehicle Your own vehicle needs speed, time, and space to complete any maneuver. These three factors are important for making safe predictions and judgments.

Picture yourself in your car at a STOP sign waiting to turn right. You must predict what traffic approaching from your left will do. You must also predict how long it will take to turn and speed up to the flow of traffic. On dry pavement, your prediction is that you can speed up quickly. Ice on the pavement changes the prediction and also the driving decision. Your predictions should lead to a safe path of travel at all times.

Predicting Actions of Other Drivers It is easy to be fooled by another person in traffic. For that reason, you should assume the worst will happen. Then you will be prepared instead of surprised. Consider the following factors to help you predict what might happen:

1. **Path** Where will the other driver go? How much space will that driver need?
2. **Action** What action will he or she take?
3. **Timing** When will that driver act?
4. **Threat** How much of a threat is that driver, cyclist, or pedestrian to your safety?
5. **Point of Conflict** Approximately where will your paths cross?

In this situation, would you swerve to the left, slow down, or stop?

DECIDING

There are no tasks more important for a driver than making wise decisions in time to take safe actions. As drivers follow a selected route, they must decide how to adjust their path, position, and speed. They must make all these decisions in a short time because new problems keep occurring. New factors emerge that can cause drivers to change their minds about a decision just made.

Alternatives and Consequences Drivers usually have more than one alternative in any driving situation. Good decision-makers consider all possible alternatives before making a final choice within the brief time available. The basis for this choice is the collection of all available information about the situation through the IPDE process.

The purpose of decision-making is to gain favorable outcomes or results. To do this, drivers must consider the consequences of each possible choice, often in a split second.

Decisions Take Time Many driving decisions can be made in seconds and split seconds, but some take longer. Perhaps you have seen a driver suddenly stop talking in the middle of a sentence to prepare for handling a sudden and unexpected emergency. That driver needed extra time to figure a way out of a sticky situation.

Decisions take longer when
- The situation is complicated.
- You do not have a pre-plan.
- You have several choices.
- You are tired, confused or impaired.
- The area and the situation are new to you.
- You are distracted or preoccupied.

Practice Decision-Making As with other steps in the IPDE process, knowledge is the key requirement for sound decision-making.

A poor decision is being made by this driver who intends to turn around near a hilltop. An approaching car may come over the hill.

There are no pat answers for every driving situation that occurs, but drivers can develop pre-planned actions for many situations. As a passenger, practice decision-making and compare your decisions to those of the driver.

EXECUTING

A driver must make decisions to take the best path and position at the right speed. To control path, position, and speed, the driver can execute only five possible actions: brake, accelerate, steer, accelerate-steer, and brake-steer. The precision and timing with which these are done strongly influences the outcome in any driving situation.

The decision a driver makes depends on three important factors: speed, space, and traction. A sharp turn or quick stop is impos-

Be aware of an oncoming driver's problems as well as your own. Stay back when trouble develops ahead.

sible at high speed, under poor traction conditions, or in limited space.

Pathway   One important way of taking action with a car is to steer it through a planned path of travel. Speed, steering, and braking skill play an important role in the action.

Position   How you position your car within the lane and relative to other cars is another important driver action. By carefully positioning the car in traffic, drivers can achieve a space cushion ahead, to the rear, and to the sides.

Speed   This is the third and most important action. It can be your friend as you move quickly to your destination, or it can be your enemy when it is too fast for conditions. A great many collisions and fatalities are due to driving too fast for conditions.

The faster your speed, the more space you will need to maneuver. The correct strategy is to choose a safe speed and be alert for changes in traction, visibility, space and traffic flow that might require a reduced speed. *The speed limit may not always be the safe speed.*

Driving at the right speed for conditions has the following advantages:

- There is more time to think and act.
- Less distance and space are required to control the car.
- It is easier to keep control of the car in an emergency.

Drivers do not have control over the conditions they must face, but they do have control over their speed.

Oncoming car may threaten you onto the shoulder.

Always try to keep a space cushion around your car.

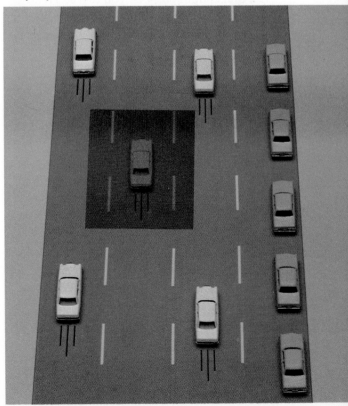

Safe Path of Travel

Some drivers assume that the road ahead will always be clear and safe. They are in for surprises because it is not reasonable to expect trouble-free driving all the time. As you practice driving, your most important objective will be to assure a safe path of travel, a path that is free of hazards when you use it.

As you apply the IPDE process, you will be looking for clues that tell you whether or not you have a safe path of travel. Four important requirements help make a safe path of travel: traction, visibility, traffic flow, and space.

TRACTION

The first requirement for controlling a car is traction between tires and pavement. Without it, a car would be uncontrollable. But traction is not without limits. You should evaluate traction continuously as you drive. To do so, three important questions must be answered:

1. Will available traction allow me to carry out my present plan of action?
2. Will available traction allow me to keep my car in the intended path?
3. Will available traction allow me to handle any emergency that might develop?

The poorer traction becomes, the lower your speed must be. It will take longer to stop, speed up, or make maneuvers. Traction can change quickly in a very short distance. If you are alert and always keep an eye open for changing traction conditions, you will not be caught by surprise and better able to control your car.

VISIBILITY

A second requirement for a safe path of travel is visibility. Two important visibility factors are:

1. **Sight Distance** Sight distance refers to how far you can see ahead. Weather, hills, curves, other vehicles, and a dirty windshield can all reduce sight distance. A good driver is constantly and accurately

Slow down under poor traction conditions.

Good visibility is vital any time of day.

Slow down, and stop if necessary, under certain traffic conditions.

Take special care to move slowly in reduced space conditions.

deciding on a proper speed by how far he or she can see.

2. **Field of Vision** This relates mainly to intersections but also includes alleys, driveways, or any other point where another road user may cross the path of travel. Trees, parked cars, and buildings can all reduce the field of vision at intersections. The narrower the field of vision, the lower the speed must be.

Again, as with other conditions, the key thing to look for is change. When conditions are less than ideal, speed must be reduced.

TRAFFIC FLOW

The third requirement for a driver to consider is traffic flow. This vital question must be answered by every driver in traffic: "Can I keep on going with my car?" Again, the important thing to look for is change. This is why it is so important to aim high in order to see far ahead as you drive.

SPACE

A fourth requirement for a safe path of travel is space. Wise drivers always allow *more than enough space* for their cars to pass safely through a given point. Many collisions occur when the space a driver thought was wide enough suddenly becomes too small or completely shut off. These factors contribute to reduced space conditions:

1. **Change in Width of Roadway** Be alert to conditions such as standing water, snow, or absence of road shoulders which can reduce the width of the road or street.

2. **Roadside Hazards** Bridge railings, posts, overpasses, and construction can all reduce the width of the driving space. Pedestrians, bicyclists, animals, and parked cars can also move from the roadside and suddenly reduce available space.

3. **Traffic Conditions** Another driver can suddenly swerve from his or her lane in an attempt to pass, change lanes, or evade another vehicle.

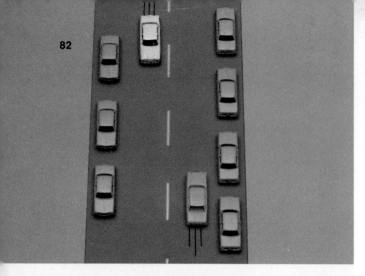

Strategies

Following are techniques that can be used to manage time, speed, and distance to your own advantage.

MINIMIZING A SINGLE HAZARD

You can *minimize* or reduce a potential hazard by putting more distance between you and a hazard. Suppose you are driving past a car that has just parked. In a second or two, you can expect the door to open. You minimize the hazard by moving to the left a few feet so that you will miss the door if it were to open suddenly.

SEPARATING HAZARDS

Often in traffic, two or more hazards will threaten a driver at the same time. Some drivers unwisely take things as they come and accept the risk of handling several hazards at once.

In the middle picture, a driver in the parked car may pull out. If speeds are not changed, you, the cyclist, and the oncoming car will reach the parked car at the same time. By slowing, you can allow the car and the bicycle to pass through one at a time. You can then handle each hazard separately with all the space you need. *Separating* is achieved by adjusting speed until the hazards and the risks are reduced.

COMPROMISING SPACE

At times, handling traffic problems one at a time is not possible. In the bottom picture, you are driving past a line of parked cars. A large truck is approaching. Space is limited. So you reduce speed and *compromise* on space by giving more space to the greater danger, the truck.

Stay out of formations, if you can. Give yourself plenty of time and space to maneuver.

ABC'S OF FORMATION DRIVING

Formations are groups of cars going different places on the same road at the same time. Formations often develop at red lights. They also develop where one or two cars are moving so slowly that they hold up traffic to the rear.

It is important to remember that you have some control over what happens to you in a formation of cars. You can reach your destination more easily and more smoothly if you follow the ABC's.

Allow   Don't slow up traffic by holding a side-by-side position with another car. Other drivers have a right to go on their own way. Mature drivers will not block traffic. They will allow.

Blend   Good drivers blend with the rest of the formation. They are dependent on each other for safety. A dangerous movement on the part of anyone could endanger many, if not all, members of the formation. Establish friendly relations with the rest of the forma-

tion by being a steady driver. When you must change lanes, do so smoothly.

Control Your Feelings   As the number of cars in a formation increases, competition for space begins to develop. Drivers become more aggressive and take more chances. Calm acceptance of your role in the formation will help you to keep a cool head.

Drop Out If Necessary   Drop out of a formation when you see pressures building and the collision potential increasing. You might also move ahead through a loosely packed formation and thus improve your security in traffic.

Expect Change   Because the potential for change is constant in formations, attention must also be constant. When driving in a formation, you should watch for two important factors: changes in speed and changes in lane position of other vehicles. Changes are most likely to take place near intersections and interchanges as well as near large parking lot entrances and exits.

Vocabulary

communicating, 73
compromising, 82
formation, 83
minimizing, 82

potential hazard, 73
scanning, 72
searching, 72

separating, 82
space cushion, 74
strategy, 82

Summary

1. The organized system of aiming well ahead (Aim high in steering), scanning the roadway for clues (Keep your eyes moving), and attaching the proper meaning to what is seen (Get the big picture) is vital to making wise decisions in traffic. The other two important rules are make sure others see you, and leave yourself an out.

2. Traffic controls, other users, roadway features, and your own car are four important parts of the traffic environment that must be checked continually.

3. Communicating is vital for the safe, smooth flow of traffic. It can be done with lights, horn, eye contact, car position, and body movements.

4. Predicting depends on accurate stored knowledge of what other drivers might do and what your own car can be expected to do.

5. Judgment of speed, time, distance, space, traction, and visibility provide needed information for making wise driving decisions.

6. A driver should evaluate the other driver's path of travel, when and where an action might be taken, how much of a threat the other driver may be, and where your paths may cross in order to predict how much of a threat the driver might be.

7. When drivers carefully consider all of the alternatives open to them and the consequences of each possible choice, wiser decisions are likely to be made.

8. Decision-making can be learned by applying the IPDE process while a passenger or observer in a car. It need not be limited to behind-the-wheel experiences.

9. How much action a driver can take depends on the car's speed, space, and traction.

10. A space cushion is the space around a vehicle which allows a driver to take as much action as is needed when it is needed.

11. The four requirements for a safe path of travel are adequate width or space, traction, visibility, and clear space ahead for traffic flow. To achieve a safe speed, drivers must adjust to changes in these four elements.

12. Three strategies that are used to reduce dangers are minimize, separate, and compromise. To minimize, move away from a hazard by changing car position and/or adjusting speed. To separate, adjust speed to handle several hazards one at a time. To compromise, allow the greatest amount of space to the greatest danger.

13. The ABC's of formation driving are allow, blend, control your feelings, drop out if necessary, and expect change.

Driving Situations

1. What detail requires driver attention?

2. What is the clue of developing trouble?

3. What action should be taken at this time?

4. What action might be taken here?

Chapter Review Questions

The IPDE Process

1. What are the five Smith System driving rules? (72)
2. What are the four parts of the driving environment that drivers must check in traffic? (73)
3. What are five ways a driver can communicate with other drivers? (74)
4. What are two predictions a driver must make and how does stored knowledge help to make accurate predictions? (75)
5. What six kinds of judgments must a driver make about other drivers? (75)
6. What five things must you evaluate about other drivers? (76)
7. What two important factors must be considered while making driving decisions? (77)
8. How can judgment be learned while you are riding in a car? (75)
9. What three factors limit how much action can be taken when driving? (79)

Safe Path of Travel

10. What are the four elements that are required for a safe path of travel? (80)

Strategies

11. What is meant by minimizing, separating, and compromising? (82)
12. List the ABC's of formation driving. (83)

Projects

1. Keep track of driving errors you see other drivers making, and note how many are manipulative and how many are due to faulty information processing.
2. While riding in a car, count the number of traffic details that require decisions for each mile driven in city traffic and on rural roads.
3. Stand on an overpass of a busy roadway and observe the performance of drivers. What percent pay little or no attention to their space cushion?
4. Talk to an accident investigation officer. Determine whether faulty decision-making or faulty car handling is the chief cause of most accidents.

Chapter 5 · Test

(Write the correct answers on a separate sheet of paper.)

True-False

1. Searching and seeing can be done without conscious attention. (72)
2. All predictions made in traffic concern other drivers. (75)
3. Decision-making can be learned only while one is driving. (78)
4. The speed limit may not always be the safe speed. (79)
5. To separate hazards is to handle them one at a time. (82)
6. Drivers have little control over what happens to them when they drive in formation. (83)
7. The "aim high" rule of seeing requires a driver to look through the top half of the windshield. (73)
8. Knowledge of driving principles and laws help drivers to make more accurate predictions. (75)
9. Knowing the consequences of a given choice is an important part of decision-making. (77)
10. Use of the horn should be strongly discouraged in traffic. (74)
11. In selecting a safe path of travel, drivers should choose the lane with the best traction, visibility, space, and traffic flow. (80)
12. Compromising is done by giving the greatest space to the greatest danger. (82)

Answer the Question

13. What part of IPDE tells what might happen? (72)
14. What part of IPDE helps a driver to see problems? (72)
15. What part of IPDE tells the driver to take controlled action? (72)
16. What part of IPDE tells the safe action to take? (72)
17. Which Smith System rule helps to piece together all the details seen ahead, to the sides, and to the rear? (73)
18. What do we call the "language of lights?" (74)
19. What requirement, other than traction, space, and traffic flow, is important for a safe path of travel? (80)
20. What is the most important action a driver can take when space, visibility, or traction present a problem? (80)

True-False

1. A driver can obtain the most information by keeping the eyes moving. (9)
2. Most traffic collisions could have been prevented if one of the drivers involved had taken the proper action. (10)
3. A solid yellow line in your lane next to the center line means no passing. (28)
4. A driver does not need to come to a full stop at all STOP signs. (22)
5. The emergency flasher must be used to alert other drivers when driving in rain or fog. (41)
6. The brake system warning light comes on when the engine is running and the parking brake has not been released. (37)
7. When a car's speed doubles, its braking distance doubles. (59)
8. Car control is determined mostly by tire contact with the pavement. (56)
9. The identifying part of the IPDE process requires the driver to stare at each detail of the traffic scene. (73)
10. In order to make correct decisions in traffic, a driver must consider the consequences of each possible alternative action. (77)

Answer the Question

11. A driver collects information from the driving scene and also uses what other kind of information to predict accurately? (9)
12. What are the three major elements of the HTS? (4)
13. What action can be taken against a driver who is convicted of violating too many traffic laws? (10)
14. Which instrument indicates how many miles a car has been driven? (36)
15. What should a driver do if the oil-pressure warning light comes on while the car is moving? (37)
16. What gear position should be used for climbing or descending steep hills? (43)
17. What two physical factors determine the amount of traction available to the driver of a moving car? (57)
18. What three distances make up a car's total stopping distance? (59)
19. What factor that a driver can control determines the space needed to execute a safe maneuver? (79)
20. For what four road conditions are warning signs generally used? (26)

Chapter 6

Basic Car Maneuvers

Objectives

1. Explain the technique and procedure for proper steering when driving forward.
2. List in correct order the steps for making a lane change.
3. Explain the procedure for making turns at intersections.
4. Describe the correct posture, steering, seeing, and speed control procedures for backing a car.
5. Diagram and explain how to make a turnabout at a right and a left alley or driveway.
6. Diagram and explain the steps for making a three-point turnabout and a mid-block U-turn.
7. List the steps for angle and parallel parking.
8. List the procedures for parking uphill and downhill with and without a curb and explain the reasons for the procedures.
9. Explain two methods for starting an automatic-shift and a stickshift car on a hill.

Introduction

Before interacting with others in the highway transportation system, new drivers must learn to control the car while performing basic maneuvers. These basic maneuvers, such as turning at intersections, are essential tools needed by all drivers in many traffic situations. They serve as stepping stones for more advanced maneuvers where correct decisions and the way they are carried out may determine one's safety.

Although some of these basic maneuvers like steering and turning may appear very simple, they often lead drivers into serious difficulty. Failure to start or complete a turn in the correct lane, or making a lane change without checking over the shoulder, cause many collisions. By learning and practicing correct maneuvers, you can avoid most of these difficulties.

Just as important as the proper execution of the maneuvers, is the knowledge of when and where to perform these maneuvers. For example, a perfectly executed turnabout or parking maneuver may be dangerous when carried out near a curve or at the crest of a hill.

In learning any maneuver correctly, new drivers must first have a clear idea of the procedure used to execute that maneuver. This chapter will describe the proper procedure to use for most of the maneuvers commonly performed in traffic.

Steering and Turning

The success of every driving maneuver depends upon proper placement of the car on the road. Therefore, drivers must have excellent steering control in addition to knowledge of correct procedures for different maneuvers.

HAND POSITIONS

To steer properly, a driver's hands should hold the steering wheel firmly on each side in a position that feels comfortable.

Imagine that the steering wheel is the face of a clock. One of the most comfortable and safest hand positions for steering control is the 10 and 2 position. Some drivers prefer other balanced hand positions, like 9 and 3. Regardless of the hand position, the steering wheel should be held with the knuckles of the hands outside the rim of the wheel. This position will keep the spokes from hitting the hands and thus allow the driver to turn the wheel.

TRACKING

Steering the car on its intended path is called *tracking.* When first learning to correct steering errors, new drivers may over-correct by turning the steering wheel too much. This mistake can be overcome by looking well down the road and making only slight steering corrections as needed. Watching the steering wheel or looking at a fender or hood ornament can cause steering control problems.

Once correct steering adjustments are learned, they become automatic. The driver then finds it easier to concentrate on the all important IPDE process.

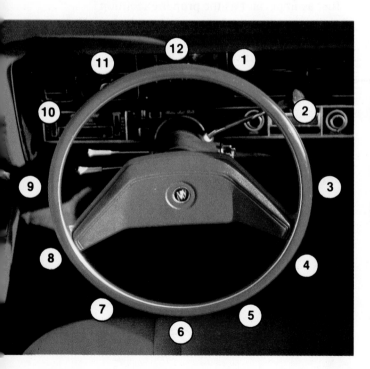

HAND-OVER-HAND STEERING

Hand-over-hand steering makes turning easier and smoother. Start to turn with the hand that is located on the side opposite to the way you are planning to turn. Place this hand near the top of the steering wheel and pull down almost to the bottom. The other hand reaches over the first one to get a new grip and pull down again. Continue this procedure until the car has turned the corner. Most cars will straighten after a turn if the driver just relaxes the grip and lets the wheel unwind through the palms. At slow speeds and with certain cars, drivers may have to unwind the wheel to straighten the car.

CORRECT SIGNALING

Correct signaling is so important that it should be learned before you put the car in motion. Even though you use turn-signal lights, you need to know the hand and arm signals to use at certain times.

Hand signals may show up better in bright sunlight than turn-signal lights. At night, however, turn-signal lights show up better than hand signals. Often it is wise to signal with your hand as well as your turn signal.

Right

Left

Stop

MAKING LEFT AND RIGHT TURNS

After the driver decides to make a left or right turn, the first step is to get into the correct lane. To do this, a lane change may be necessary. A lane change should be made about a block before the turn.

Follow these steps when changing lanes:

1. Check traffic ahead and through both rear-view mirrors.
2. Make a head check (quick glance over your shoulder), signal and, if clear, move into correct lane.
3. Cancel signal and adjust speed.

Procedure for Making Turns The numbers in the diagram correspond with the following:

1. About half a block before the turn, signal and start slowing by applying soft pressure to the brake pedal.
2. Increase eye scanning movements and be alert for pedestrians and bicyclists.
3. Check front and rear traffic as well as both directions on the cross street.
4. Slow down to about 10 mph (16 km/h) just before the crosswalk.
5. For a right turn, be about four feet from the curb if there are no parked cars, and make a final traffic check to the left before turning the wheel. Begin turning when front wheels are even with the bend of the curb around the corner.
6. For a left turn, be in the lane nearest the center line. Make a final traffic check and start turning just before the center of the intersection.
7. Stay in the same lane throughout the turn, sighting the turn path, and continue scanning for pedestrians and bicyclists.
8. Halfway around the corner, accelerate gently and allow the steering wheel to return to the straight-ahead position.

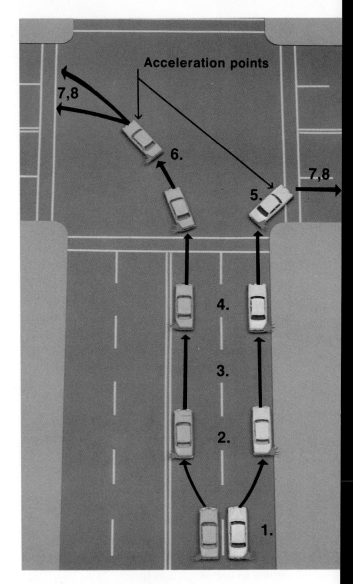

Turning in a Stickshift Car In sharp turns, or for other reasons to go very slowly, you will need to downshift to a lower gear. This means shifting from THIRD to SECOND or from FOURTH to THIRD. Shift gears and let the clutch come back out before starting the turn. This will keep both hands free for steering and will slow the car as it enters the turn.

Backing and Turning Around

Success in backing a car depends on correct posture, seeing, steering, and speed control. When these actions are done successfully, a new driver is ready to undertake the maneuvers necessary for turning a car around.

BACKING

In order to see as much as possible while backing, turn your body to the right and put your right arm over the back of the seat. Look through the back window. Place the left hand on the steering wheel at the 12 o'clock position. Release the brake gradually, but keep your foot covering the brake. Most automatic-shift cars will creep without acceleration, and this speed is usually fast enough for controlled backing. Turn the steering wheel in the direction you want the car to go.

To make a sharp turn, use hand-over-hand steering. When backing around a corner to the right, check first for traffic and pedestrians. There must be ample space on the left side because the front wheels will track far to the left of the rear wheels. The extra space must be to the right of the car when backing around a corner to the left. When backing left, make quick checks over the left shoulder between looks through the rear window.

During all backing maneuvers, make quick traffic checks to the front and sides, then continue looking back until the car is stopped. Never put your head out the window or open the door while backing.

When backing in a stickshift car, you control the car's speed by using the clutch. Release the clutch just to the friction point and hold it there. This will ensure controlled speed. When stopping, push the clutch in and brake to a stop.

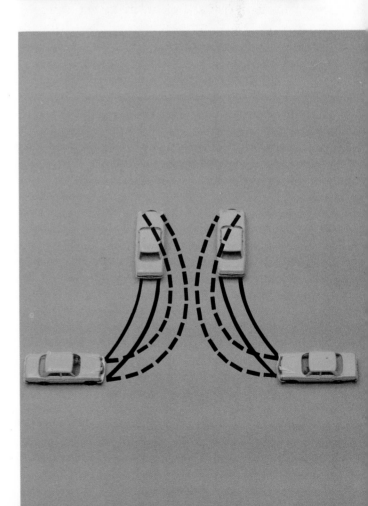

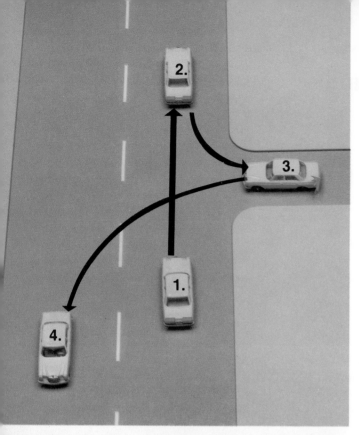

TURNING THE CAR AROUND

In many cases the best, safest, and often quickest way to turn a car around is to drive around the block. This is easily done by making three right turns, followed by a left turn. However, on a dead-end street or in some other spots, you will have to turn the car around. Usually the safest type of turnabout is backing into an alley or driveway on the right. You then enter the street forward.

For All Turnabouts

- Select a site that provides at least 500 feet clear visibility in each direction.
- Do not make turns near hills, curves, or within 200 feet of an intersection.
- Be sure local traffic ordinances permit the turn you plan to make.
- Be sure there is enough space.
- Check for traffic and pedestrians before and during the time you are turning around.
- In a stickshift car, maintain control of speed with the clutch at the friction point.

The steps in the four following turnabouts correspond to the numbered car positions in the pictures.

Alley or Driveway (Right Side)

1. Check rear traffic, and signal for stop.
2. Recheck traffic, and back slowly right to position 3. Stop with wheels straight.
3. Signal left, check traffic, and drive forward toward position 4.

Alley or Driveway (Left Side)

1. Use left turn procedure to drive to position 2. Stop with wheels straight.
2. Check all traffic, especially from right, and back slowly right to position 3. Stop with wheels straight.
3. Drive forward toward position 4.

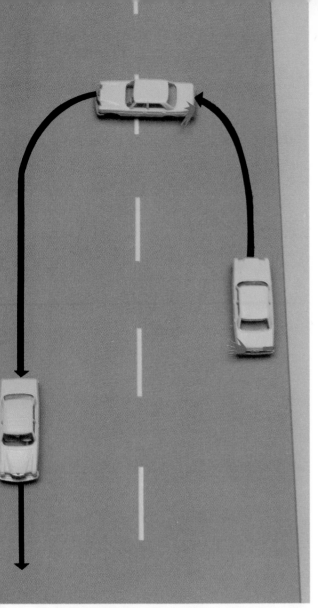

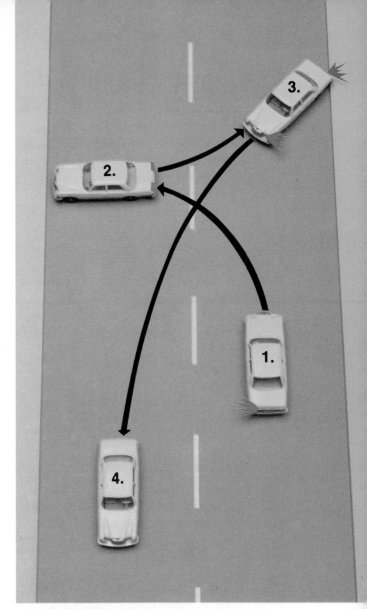

Mid-Block U-Turn

1. From stopped position at right, check traffic, signal, and turn sharply left while moving slowly to position 2.
2. Recheck for traffic and for space to finish turn. Continue moving slowly toward position 3.

Three-Point Turnabout

1. From stopped position at far right, check traffic, signal, and turn sharply left while moving slowly to position 2. Stop with wheels straight.
2. Recheck traffic, turn wheels sharply right while backing slowly to position 3. Stop with wheels straight.
3. Check traffic again. Move slowly steering left toward position 4.

Parking and Starting on a Hill

Most communities permit two common kinds of parking: angle (diagonal) and parallel. A third type is similar to angle parking but it is done perpendicular to the curb. All of the instructions for parking procedures refer to parking on the right side of the street. They are reversed for parking on the left on a one-way street or parking lot.

ANGLE PARKING

Once you have spotted an open space, follow these steps for angle parking.
1. Check rear traffic, signal a right turn, and begin to brake. Keep as far left as the traffic lane permits.
2. Flash brake lights to warn drivers behind.
3. When you can see straight down the right stall line, turn wheels sharply right and slowly enter the stall.
4. Straighten wheels when centered in the space and stop before striking the curb. (Hold clutch down in a stickshift car.)

To enter a perpendicular (90°-angle) parking space, begin to turn right when the front bumper is even with the left taillight of the vehicle to the right of the space. Continue same steps as for angle parking.

Leaving an Angle Parking Space
1. Check rear traffic and creep straight back.
2. Control speed in an automatic-shift car by keeping foot on brake. Hold clutch at the friction point in a stickshift car.
3. When your front bumper is even with left car's rear bumper, begin turning right.
4. Back into nearest lane, straighten wheels, and stop. Shift to a forward gear and proceed.

Perpendicular Parking

PARALLEL PARKING

The key to successful parallel parking is speed control. To park, you need a space about six feet longer than the car. As you back into the parking space, make sure that the left front corner of your car will not get in the way of passing traffic. The following steps correspond to the positions in the picture at left:

1. Flash brake lights, signal, and stop two to three feet away from the front car with rear bumpers even (Position 1). Shift to REVERSE, check traffic, and back slowly while turning to the right. Aim toward the right rear corner of the space. (Look over right shoulder.)
2. Straighten wheels and back straight when the front seatback of your car is even with the rear bumper of the front car (Position 2).
3. Turn sharply left when your front bumper is even with the front car's back bumper (Position 3). Continue to back slowly.
4. When your car is almost parallel to the curb and before you touch the car behind (Position 4), straighten wheels and stop.
5. Slowly pull forward, centering the car in the space (Position 5).

When leaving a parallel parking space, you are responsible for avoiding a collision. Follow these steps:

1. Back straight until almost touching the car behind. Turn wheels left just before stopping.
2. Signal left, check traffic over left shoulder, and move forward slowly.
3. Check right front fender for clearance.
4. Turn wheels to right when halfway out of parking space, centering car in lane, and gently accelerate. In a stickshift car, control speed with friction point.

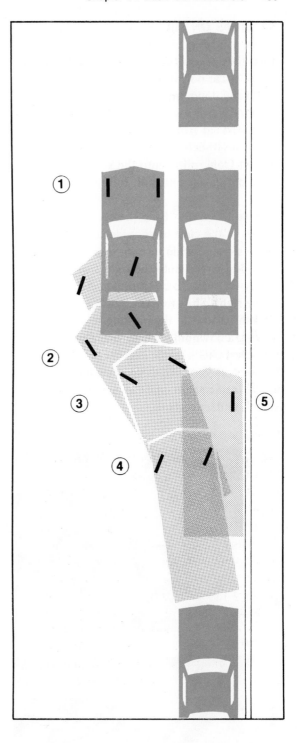

PARKING ON HILLS

When a car is parked on a hill, the driver must take precautions to make sure it stays there. A car not properly parked on a hill could roll down into traffic. On hills with curbs, the front wheels are turned so the curb keeps the car from rolling. Where there is no curb, the wheels must be turned to prevent the car from rolling into the street.

To park a car on a hill, follow these steps.

Headed Downhill Stop the car within six inches of the curb or shoulder. Let the car creep slowly, while turning sharply to curb or shoulder. Creep until the right front tire rests gently on the curb or front wheels are turned to the right. Shift to PARK (REVERSE in a stickshift) and set the parking brake. When leaving a downhill parking space with a curb, you must check traffic and back away from the curb as you turn the wheels left. Stop and check traffic again, shift to DRIVE (or FIRST), signal, and leave curb.

Headed Uphill with a Curb Approach parking space close to the curb. Just as you stop, turn wheels sharply left. Shift to NEUTRAL, and let car creep back slowly until back of right front tire rests gently on curb. If parking on a one-way street on the left side, turn the wheels sharply to the right. A good way to remember the correct direction for turning is to always turn away from the curb. Secure the car for uphill parking.

Headed Uphill with No Curb Pull over to the side of the road (completely off the pavement, if possible). Just before stopping, turn wheels sharply right. Secure the car as indicated above. Since there is no curb to hold the car, turning the wheels toward the shoulder enables the car to roll off the side of the road if it is pushed or released, rather than down the hill into traffic. When leaving an uphill parking space without a curb, follow procedure for starting on a hill.

Downhill with no curb

Uphill with a curb

Downhill with a curb

Uphill with no curb

STARTING ON HILLS

Many times drivers find it necessary to stop on a hill. In cities with many hills, drivers would hardly be able to drive at all if they had not mastered the ability to stop on a hill and then start forward without rolling back.

In an automatic-shift car, there are two methods for starting on hills without rolling back. One is to use your left foot on the foot brake after you have stopped, then accelerate gradually and gently release the foot brake with the left foot when the engine begins pulling. A smooth start depends on coordinating these two actions.

The second method involves the use of the parking brake on very steep hills.

1. As soon as you stop, set the parking brake firmly.
2. Move right foot to accelerator and accelerate so the engine is pulling against the parking brake.
3. Check traffic and signal if you are turning.
4. Release parking brake and accelerate to driving speed.

When stopping on a slight grade, merely release the foot brake and quickly accelerate before the car starts to roll back.

Using the parking brake is also the best method in a stickshift car when stopping on a steep hill.

1. Set the parking brake as soon as the car is stopped.
2. Shift to FIRST.
3. Accelerate to a fast idle and bring clutch pedal out to the friction point.
4. When it is time to move, accelerate more, and let the clutch pedal clear up while releasing the parking brake *at the same time.*

For very slight grades, you can learn to coordinate the clutch and accelerator to catch the car before it rolls back. To do this, re-lease the clutch gradually to the friction point after stopping and shifting to FIRST. When it is time to move, the right foot moves quickly to the accelerator and feeds gas. At the same time the clutch is released, and acceleration is increased. When first learning this method, a slight rollback will not hurt. With practice, the maneuver can be made without rollback.

Vocabulary

angle parking, 98
hand-over-hand, 93
lane change, 94

mid-block U-turn, 97
parallel parking, 99
perpendicular parking, 98
three-point turnabout, 97

Summary

1. The steering position used for controlled steering must be comfortable for the driver. A commonly used position is 10 and 2, as on the face of a clock. Some people prefer a 9 and 3 position. The wheel should be held from the outside of the rim.

2. To change lanes, check traffic through rearview mirrors and over shoulder, signal, and move into correct lane if the way is clear.

3. Prepare for a turn at an intersection at least a block away by moving to the proper lane. Signal and start slowing while making traffic checks. Turn into the same lane by using hand-over-hand steering.

4. When backing a car, put the right arm over back of seat. Look back through the rear window. Steer with left hand starting at the 12 o'clock position. To back right, steer right; to back left, steer left.

5. A turnabout from an alley on the right is started by backing into the alley. After checking traffic and signaling, drive forward into the proper lane. For a turnabout on the left, turn left into an alley or driveway, check traffic, and back slowly to the right into nearest lane. Proceed forward.

6. When making a three-point turnabout and mid-block U-turn, begin from a stopped position at far right. Check traffic, signal, and move car slowly while turning sharply left with hand-over-hand steering. The three-point turn has one backing step not needed in the U-turn.

7. When looking for an angle parking space, stay well away from the parked cars. Check traffic, signal, and turn sharply into the space when you can see the right lane line. For parallel parking, the car must be moved very slowly with the steering wheel turned sharply at the proper times and the eyes looking both back and front.

8. In order to keep a parked car from rolling downhill, the wheels should be turned to rest against the curb. If there is no curb, wheels must be turned so car will not roll off the road if pushed or released.

9. Starting on a hill can be done either by using the left foot on the brake pedal or by using the accelerator and releasing the parking brake at the same time. In a stickshift car, shift to FIRST, hold clutch at friction point, then release parking brake and accelerate when time to go.

Driving Situations

1. Why is it important for a driver to check behind the car before backing out of a place?

2. What procedure must the driver follow before entering the traffic lane? If there is a collision, who is at fault? Why?

3. The driver above needs to make a turnabout. Which method should the driver choose? Why?

4. How must the cars parked downhill have wheels turned? The uphill cars? Why is this important?

Chapter Review Questions

Steering and Turning

1. What is a commonly used hand position for comfortable and controlled steering? What other position is preferred? (92)
2. Why should the hands be kept on the outside of the steering wheel? (92)
3. What seeing and steering procedures should a driver follow to make the car track correctly? (92)
4. Explain and compare the steps to follow for making a right turn and a left turn starting with a lane change. (94)
5. How and when should downshifting be done in preparation for a turn? Why? (94)

Backing and Turning Around

6. Explain the posture and speed control procedure for backing in a straight line. (95)
7. What is the best way to turn a car around? (96)
8. When backing around corners to right or left, where must the driver check for ample space? Why? (95)
9. What factors should be considered before a driver does a turnabout? (96)
10. Explain the procedure for making a turnabout from a driveway on the right side. (96)

Parking and Starting on a Hill

11. Explain the procedure for leaving an angle parking space. (98)
12. Explain the maneuver to follow at each position of the parallel parking procedure. (99)
13. How should the wheels be turned when parked on a hill with a curb? How should the wheels be turned when there is no curbing? (100)
14. How is the left foot used when starting on a hill? What other method might be used? (101)
15. How can a stickshift car be started from a stop on a very slight upgrade? (101)

Projects

1. Find out from the local police whether more collisions result from angle parking or parallel parking. Which causes the most damage?
2. Watch drivers as they turn corners in your town. How many start and finish their turns in the correct lane?
3. When riding with your friends or parents, notice how they hold the steering wheel. What hand position do they use? Do they use hand-over-hand for turns?
4. From local police records, determine how many collisions occur as a result of left and right turns. Which type is more numerous?
5. From local police records, determine how many collisions occur as a result of turnabouts. Which types cause the most damage and injury?

Chapter 6 · Test

(Write the correct answers on a separate sheet of paper.)

True-False

1. Drivers should guide by a fender to keep the car tracking in the intended path. (92)
2. A turnabout from a driveway on the right is started by pulling into the driveway. (96)
3. A driver should check rearview mirrors and make a head check (quick glance over the shoulder) before changing lanes. (94)
4. When turning right, the driver should start to accelerate after the turn is completed. (94)
5. When backing around a corner to the left, the front of the car will track farther to the right. (95)
6. It is the responsibility of the driver leaving a parallel parking space if there is a collision. (99)
7. When backing straight, speed is normally controlled by the accelerator. (95)
8. A car is held at the curb when parking uphill by turning the steering wheel away from the curb. (100)
9. When starting from a stop on a steep grade, it is best to use the parking brake. (101)
10. Downshifting in a stickshift car should be done before entering a turn. (94)

Answer the Question

11. Safe backing depends on what actions? (95)
12. What type of steering should be used when turning corners? (93)
13. How is speed controlled when backing in a stickshift car? (95)
14. How much space is needed in order to parallel park? (99)
15. When backing around a corner to the right, how is the steering wheel turned? (95)

Chapter 7

Interacting at Intersections

Objectives

1. List the average amount of time it takes to cross a street, turn right, or turn left from a stopped position.
2. Tell the distances that cars traveling at various speeds can cover in 6 seconds.
3. Describe the correct procedure to use when crossing or joining traffic from a STOP sign where your view is reduced.
4. List the checks that must be made before turning left at a traffic light with oncoming traffic.
5. List the different kinds of protected left turns.
6. List the right-turn conflicts that can develop in city traffic.
7. Describe the procedures for right and left turns at a red light.
8. Describe the difference between a controlled and an uncontrolled intersection.
9. Describe the correct procedure to use when approaching and crossing an uncontrolled intersection.
10. List at least six situations where drivers must yield the right-of-way.
11. Describe the correct actions to take at the different kinds of controlled railroad crossings.
12. List three safety precautions that drivers should take as they approach railroad crossings.

Introduction

The possibility of a crash is greater at an intersection than at any other place on a street or highway. Intersections are dangerous because the paths of many drivers cross here. In a recent year, about 40 percent of all collisions and 25 percent of all fatal collisions took place at intersections. A driver crosses or turns at an intersection about every 10 seconds on an average trip in town and about one each minute in the country.

At each intersection, drivers must make safe decisions if collisions are to be avoided. The driver is the key figure in intersection safety. Application of the IPDE process can prevent crashes at intersections.

Safe IDPE performance depends on knowledge. Drivers must know what to look for, where to look, and when. They must also understand what they see, as well as what actions they can take. This chapter will present information on how to make wise decisions at intersections.

Controlled Intersections

Drivers approaching intersections with traffic lights, STOP signs, or YIELD signs are required by law to obey these traffic controls and to yield the right-of-way to through traffic. Intersections where lights and signs assign the right-of-way are called *controlled* intersections. Uncontrolled intersections have no signs or lights. Because intersections are dangerous, drivers need to develop three skills for crossing and turning into moving traffic at controlled intersections.

JUDGING TIME

Judging the time needed to make these maneuvers is the first skill. A driver needs to know how long it takes to turn right, to turn left, and to cross traffic on a typical street.

The amount of time required to make these maneuvers at controlled intersections appears in the illustration below. Driver inexperience and poor traction can increase the amount of time needed to turn or to cross an intersection.

JUDGING SPEED AND DISTANCE

The second skill a driver must have for crossing and turning is the ability to judge how far another car will travel while the driver is turning a corner or crossing an intersection.

The table below shows the distance a car can cover in 6 seconds at various speeds. These distances are shown as fractions of a city block to make it easier to judge distance and to decide when it is safe to go. You may find it easier to judge cars as going slow, moderate, or fast rather than trying to estimate exact speeds.

CHOOSING A GAP IN TRAFFIC

The third skill a driver needs is the ability to choose a gap or space between approaching cars in order to cross or join traffic. The gap must be longer than the amount of time it takes to make the turn so that the turn can be made safely with room to spare. A driver who needs 6 seconds to complete a right turn must have at least an 8-second gap between cars approaching from the left in order to enter the traffic flow safely. Cars must be farther away when a driver turns than when he or she crosses because the driver needs additional time to accelerate and adjust to the speed of other vehicles. *The higher the speed of the approaching vehicles, the longer the gap must be.* A car traveling 30 mph (48 km/h) will cover a whole city block in 6 seconds while a driver uses up 6 seconds just completing a turn. So the approaching car must be more than a block or at least 8 seconds away for the driver to start a turn.

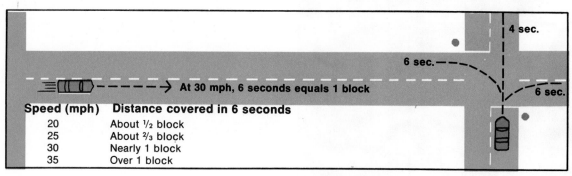

At 30 mph, 6 seconds equals 1 block

Speed (mph)	Distance covered in 6 seconds
20	About ½ block
25	About ⅔ block
30	Nearly 1 block
35	Over 1 block

BLOCKED INTERSECTION

When a driver's view of an intersection is blocked by parked cars or other obstructions, following the procedures below should help the driver cross and enter traffic safely.

Crossing Traffic

1. Look through the windows and under the parked cars. Keep glancing left and right while creeping forward.
2. If the street appears clear, move to Position 2. Here, a driver can still stop clear of cars from the left.
3. When the left is clear, glance right. Then, move to Position 3 where you could still stop safely for a car from the right, and stop only momentarily.
4. When clear from the right, go.

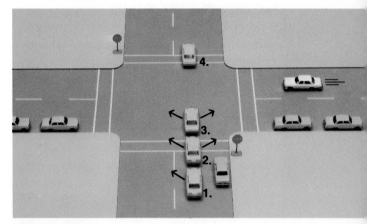

Crossing traffic

Joining Traffic with Right Turn

1. Begin moving forward and steering into right turn at same time.
2. Glance left for traffic and right for turn path. In Position 2, a driver can see farther without blocking traffic.
3. When clear, go. At Position 3, check mirror to determine how much to accelerate to adjust to traffic.

Turning right

Joining Traffic with Left Turn

1. Glance left and right through the windows and under the parked cars.
2. Stop at Position 2 if traffic is coming from left.
3. If the lane to the left is clear, move, stopping only momentarily, at Position 3 where you could still stop safely for a car from the right.
4. When clear from right, go. At Position 4, check mirror to determine how much to accelerate to adjust to traffic.

Turning left

PROTECTED LEFT TURNS

At controlled intersections, a driver can make a *protected* or *unprotected* left turn, depending on the kind of traffic signal. Protected left turns are made when special left-turn lights or green arrows allow drivers to turn without oncoming traffic. Three kinds of protected left turns are:

■ **Left-Turn Arrow**   A green arrow is added to the red, green, and yellow lights.

■ **Left-Turn Light**   At some locations with left-turn lanes, a separate left-turn light is mounted near the lane. A sign may read LEFT TURN SIGNAL.

■ **Delayed Green Light**   At the beginning of a signal cycle, the green light will be delayed for the oncoming traffic. When your green light comes on, oncoming drivers will remain standing. This is your cue to make your left turn. Move cautiously in unfamiliar situations.

UNPROTECTED LEFT TURNS

An unprotected left turn is made at an intersection with a traffic signal that does not have any special lights or lanes.

Positioning   When the light turns green, move into the intersection ahead of the crosswalk but not beyond the center of the intersection. Keep your wheels straight until you actually begin your turn. Put your car close to the center line so you will not block cars that want to pass on your right.

While preparing for a left turn, check four places to assure a safe path of travel:

1. **Traffic Light**   Check for a green light before moving ahead.
2. **Inside Lane**   On four-lane streets, check speed, distance, and number of oncoming cars in inside lane.
3. **Outside Lane**   On four-lane streets, check outside lane for cars moving rapidly toward the intersection. Standing cars or trucks in the inside lane can hide cars or motorcycles in the outside lane.
4. **Turn Path**   Check the exact path your vehicle will take. Look for pedestrians in or near the crosswalk.

Keep wheels straight until you begin left turn. Watch for an oncoming car that may be hidden by standing cars.

RIGHT-TURN CONFLICTS

Even though a right turn appears to be less dangerous than a left turn, conflicts can develop. The three following conflicts can lead to collisions:

First is the pedestrian conflict. When approaching an intersection and planning to turn right, check to the right for pedestrians who might be in or near the crosswalk.

Watch traffic ahead for turning cars and pedestrians.

A second conflict can develop in the rear if the first car changes speed or stops for pedestrians. To alert drivers behind, signal one-half block in advance of the turn. Slow gradually. Abrupt stops invite rear-end crashes.

Third, a four-lane street can lead to a conflict with an oncoming left-turning vehicle. Time your right turn so you do not complete it just as an oncoming car is finishing a left turn unless the lanes are wide and the speeds are low.

TURNS ON RED

In many states, turns on red are permitted where no signs are posted to prohibit this action. Check your state's laws on turns to be sure that you are obeying the law.

Right on Red   When planning to turn right on red, you must come to a full stop. After yielding to traffic from the left and to pedestrians, complete the turn into the right lane.

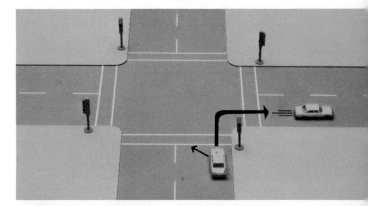

Left on Red   Left turns on red are permitted only when turning from a one-way to another one-way street. Follow the same stopping procedure as right turns on red. Yield to traffic from the right.

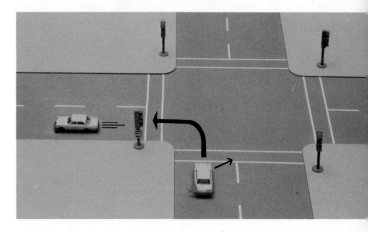

Uncontrolled Intersections

Uncontrolled intersections, which have no signs or lights to regulate the flow of traffic, are possibly more dangerous than controlled intersections. When a driver has a choice of driving on roads with or without controls at intersections, the safest choice is to drive on those with controlled intersections. However, sometimes a driver cannot avoid driving on side streets with uncontrolled intersections.

UNCONTROLLED INTERSECTION PROCEDURE

Quick reactions and panic stops are not enough to avoid trouble at uncontrolled intersections. Using the IPDE process with the following procedures can help drivers cross uncontrolled intersections safely:

1. At mid-block, **Identify**
- the exact location of the intersection.
- whether intersection is controlled or uncontrolled.
- the sight distance to the right and to the left.
- any traction problems that may require you to slow near the intersection.

2. Approaching an uncontrolled intersection, **Predict**
- where to begin checking for cross traffic.
- how much to reduce speed to match sight distance.
- what possible actions other drivers or pedestrians might take.
- whether traffic to the rear can stop.

3. Nearing the corner, **Decide**
- when to begin braking.
- when to glance to left first, then right. (A long look to the left can cause the driver to be late looking right.)
- whether to keep pressure on foot brake.
- whether to stop or go.

4. Then **Execute** a decision to
- stop if car is coming from either direction.
- go if the way is clear. Take a second glance in each direction, and accelerate through the intersection.

IDENTIFY UNCONTROLLED INTERSECTIONS

One reason for collisions at uncontrolled intersections is the driver's failure to identify the intersection as uncontrolled. Each driver assumes that the other driver will stop or, on a quiet street, assumes that no one will be there. Just because one street is wide and the other is narrow is no reason to assume that the intersection is controlled.

Another reason for intersection crashes is the driver's failure to identify an intersection ahead. Look for these clues:

- Street signs and street lights.
- Parked cars on cross streets.
- Power lines and rows of fences in the country.
- Fire hydrants.
- Mailboxes.

At an uncontrolled intersection such as this, look to your left for one-way traffic.

Yielding the Right-of-Way

Good drivers know that they have no guarantee of safe passage through intersections. No driver ever has the legal right-of-way. Yielding the right-of-way means *allowing cross-street traffic to pass through the intersection.* The photographs on these pages show situations in which drivers are required to yield the right-of-way. Below are some points to consider in right-of-way situations:

1. Failure to yield the right-of-way is one of the most frequent violations in fatal crashes.
2. The right-of-way is given to you by another driver. Never assume the right-of-way until you are sure that the other driver is going to yield.
3. Traffic laws tell who is required to *yield* the right-of-way, not who *has* it.
4. The safer action to take is to yield the right-of-way even though the other driver is supposed to yield to you. This is less dangerous than to take the right-of-way and not get it.
5. A green light or STOP sign on a side street does not guarantee you safe passage through the intersection.
6. No one is authorized to take the right-of-way if doing so is a threat to life or property.
7. Even when another driver is required to yield the right-of-way, you can be responsible for a collision if your actions contributed to it.
8. If you pull out and force another car to slow down, wait, or stop for you, you have not yielded.

YIELD at a STOP sign
- to all traffic on the through street.
- to pedestrians in a crosswalk (marked or unmarked).

YIELD to emergency vehicles
- to emergency vehicles sounding a siren or using a flashing light
Stop close to curb, clear of intersection. Wait for vehicle to pass

YIELD at a four-way stop
- to the car that first comes to a stop.
- to the vehicle on your right if you both arrive at the same time
- to pedestrians in a crosswalk.

YIELD at a traffic-light change
- to vehicles still in the intersection.
- to pedestrians still in the intersection.

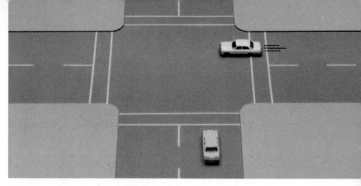

YIELD at an uncontrolled intersection
- to a vehicle that has entered the intersection.

YIELD coming from an alley or driveway
- to pedestrians before reaching sidewalk.
- to vehicles before entering street
  (Make two stops.)

YIELD at a YIELD sign
- to vehicles from your right.
- to vehicles from your left.
- to pedestrians.

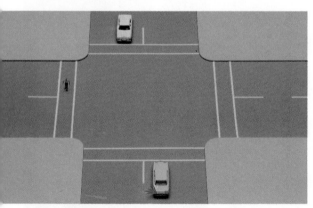

YIELD at an uncontrolled intersection
- to oncoming traffic when you turn left.
- to pedestrians in a crosswalk.

YIELD when turning at a green traffic light
- to pedestrians in the crosswalk where you turn left
  or right. (Pedestrians have the green light too.)
- to oncoming traffic that is at all close.

Railroad Crossings

A railroad crossing is a particularly dangerous kind of intersection. One of every three railroad-crossing collisions results in a death. How can a driver miss seeing something as big as a train? Amazingly, 60 percent of the drivers involved in railroad-crossing collisions live within two miles (3 kilometers) of the crossing. In addition, 60 percent of the collisions happen in daylight.

Unlike most other intersections, railroad crossings are almost always marked. Some crossings have large white X-shaped lines painted on the road. Most crossings have a round yellow warning sign. It is usually placed about 100 feet (30 meters) from crossings in towns and about 700 feet (213 meters) from crossings in the country.

CONTROLLED CROSSINGS

Only about 20 percent of the railroad crossings are protected by lights, gates, or STOP signs. Even so, four of each ten fatal railroad-crossing collisions occur where a flasher or gate is in operation. The following rules apply to the different kinds of controlled crossings:

- **Flashers**   A full stop must be made when railroad flashers are on. The vehicle must remain stopped until the track is clear.
- **Crossing Gate**   A full stop must be made when the gate is down. The vehicle must remain stopped until the gate is raised. It is illegal to drive around the gate even if no train is visible.
- **Stop Sign**   A full stop is required. The driver may proceed if the track is clear.

Some states require all buses and vehicles with flammable contents to stop at every railroad crossing. If you are following one of these vehicles, be prepared to stop.

UNCONTROLLED CROSSINGS

Eighty percent of all railroad crossings in this country are uncontrolled. These kinds of crossings are marked with crossbuck, a large, white X-shaped sign standing by the crossing, and/or yellow warning signs but do not have gates or flashers.

RAILROAD-CROSSING PROCEDURES

When approaching railroad crossings, remember that the train always has the right-of-way. The driver should take the following actions quickly and accurately at a crossing:

1. Make sure no train is coming before you start to cross. Promptly check the field of vision at the crossing. The shorter the sight distance, the lower your speed must be. At night, change headlights to high beam to see if a train is at the crossing.
2. Turn the radio and air conditioner off and open the side window. Listen for a whistle or other train sounds.

3. Reduce speed so that you can stop safely before reaching the crossing. With a stick-shift car, shift to a lower gear before starting to cross to keep the engine from stalling. When you start across the tracks in an automatic or stickshift car, keep your speed up to at least 10 mph (16 km/h). Then, if your engine should stall on the tracks, your car will have enough momentum to carry it safely across.
4. If several cars are crossing at the same time, don't cross until the car ahead is far enough on the other side to leave room for your car *beyond the tracks.* Otherwise, you may be stopped right on the tracks!
5. Never cross behind a train that has just passed until you are sure the crossing is clear both ways. A second train, hidden by the first, may be coming on another track.

Summary

1. The average time required to cross a street is 4 seconds and to turn right or turn left is 6 seconds.
2. The distance covered in 6 seconds at 20 mph is 1/2 block, at 25 mph is 2/3 block, at 30 mph nearly 1 block, and at 35 mph over 1 block.
3. To enter a through street where visibility is reduced, continue to glance left and right, and plan position changes as you move from a stopped position to a point where visibility improves.
4. Before making a left turn at a traffic light with oncoming cars, check the traffic light, inside lane, outside oncoming lane, and turn path.
5. The different kinds of protected left turns are green arrows, special left-turn lights, and delayed green cycles.
6. Right-turn conflicts should be expected with pedestrians in the crosswalk, with traffic to the rear, and with oncoming left-turning cars.
7. Right and left turns on red after a stop must be handled in the same way as STOP signs. Left turns on red can be made only from a one-way to another one-way street.
8. At controlled intersections, traffic is controlled by means of STOP signs, YIELD signs, or traffic lights. At uncontrolled intersections, there are no signs or lights, and approaching drivers must control the intersection.
9. When approaching an uncontrolled intersection, reduce speed and check for approaching traffic to left and right.
10. Drivers must yield to traffic at uncontrolled intersections if entering from a parked position or an alley, to an emergency vehicle, to pedestrians, and to vehicles already in the intersection.
11. If railroad-crossing lights are on flashing, stop. Proceed only when the track is clear. At a railroad STOP sign, come to a full stop. When a crossing gate is lowered, stop and wait until the gate is raised.
12. When approaching a railroad crossing, reduce speed, listen, look in both directions, and plan to stop if a train is approaching.

Driving Situations

1. You are driving the yellow car approaching an uncontrolled intersection. You and the other car are the same distance from the intersection. What should you do?

2. You are driving the yellow car and are planning to turn right at an uncontrolled intersection. What should you do?

3. You are approaching an intersection where a car is stopped for a traffic light. Where should you stop? What could happen in this situation?

4. The light has just turned green, and you plan to turn left. What four checks should you make? What are some problems in this situation?

Chapter Review Questions

Controlled Intersections

1. How many seconds are usually required to turn right, to turn left or to cross at an intersection with a STOP sign? (108)
2. If a car is approaching from your left, for which of the turns that you might make must that car be farthest away? (108)
3. How much distance will an approaching car cover while traveling 35 mph (56 km/h)? (108)
4. When crossing a two-way street where parked cars block visibility, which way should a driver look first? (109)
5. How far forward in general should a driver who intends to turn right position the car from a STOP sign to get a better view of the street? (109)
6. List the checks that must be made when turning left at a traffic light. (110)
7. What are three different kinds of left-turn signals that can be used to provide a protected left turn? (110)
8. What three conflicts can develop during a right turn? (111)
9. Describe the procedures for turning right on a red light. (111)

Uncontrolled Intersections

10. What is meant by an uncontrolled intersection? (112)
11. List the steps a driver must take when approaching an uncontrolled intersection. (112)

Yielding the Right-of-Way

12. List six situations where a driver is required to yield the right-of-way. (114-115)
13. Why isn't a driver guaranteed safe passage through an intersection? (114)

Railroad Crossings

14. List three things a driver must do when approaching a railroad crossing. (117)
15. When flashers are in operation at a railroad crossing, what are drivers required to do? (116)

Projects

1. Contact your local police department or sheriff to obtain information on intersection collisions in your area or city. Make a report to the class.
2. Take a traffic count at several busy intersections noting the number and kinds of violations. You may want to report your findings to the local newspaper.
3. Develop a list of intersections where visibility is limited. Send a copy to your police department or city council.
4. Make a check of all railroad crossings in your local area to be sure that all crossbucks are visible and readable. Report your findings to the class.

Chapter 7 · Test

(Write the correct answers on a separate sheet of paper.)

True-False

1. A conflict with an oncoming left-turning car can develop while a driver is turning right at a green light on a four-lane street. (111)

2. Traffic laws establish who has the right-of-way at intersections. (114)

3. If a car coming from your left at 35 mph (56 km/h) is 1/2 block away, you can safely make a right turn. (108)

4. It is illegal to drive around a lowered railroad-crossing gate. (116)

5. A car from the right must be farther away when you are turning left than when you are crossing the street. (108)

6. When approaching an uncontrolled intersection, you should brake until you are sure that you will not have to stop. (112)

7. Most railroad crossings are not protected by gates or flashers. (117)

8. At a four-way stop, the car that stops first goes first. (114)

9. You wish to turn right onto a through street where parked cars block your view. You should point your car right as you pull forward to a position where you can see. (109)

10. The fourth lens on a traffic signal is usually for a green arrow. (110)

11. You should slow down and proceed cautiously when railroad-crossing flashers are operating. (116)

12. Drivers should take several left-right looks as they cross a through street where parked cars reduce the field of vision. (109)

13. If a street is wide and smooth, you can be sure that the intersection is controlled. (113)

14. You should not stop on railroad tracks in a line of traffic. (117)

15. A driver should not pull left of the center line while waiting to make a left turn at a green light. (110)

Answer the Question

16. In which situations might you have to yield the right-of-way even though you have a green light? (115)

17. In which situations can a driver make a turn on a red signal if such action is legal in that state? (111)

18. Which action takes the shortest amount of time: turning left, turning right, or crossing an intersection? (108)

19. What is the difference between a controlled intersection and an uncontrolled intersection? (108, 112)

20. Why should a driver never move beyond the center line while waiting to make a left turn? (110)

Chapter 8

Following and Meeting Traffic

Objectives

1. Describe the extent and cause of the rear-end collision problem.
2. List five disadvantages of tailgating.
3. Name four things to look for when following in traffic.
4. List four IPDE requirements for safe following.
5. Describe the 2-second rule and its advantages.
6. List some locations where rear-end collisions might occur.
7. List three ways a driver can communicate with traffic to the rear.
8. List three things a driver can do to reduce the chance of being hit from behind.
9. List the conditions that could cause the oncoming car to cross the center line into your lane.
10. Explain what a driver can do to reduce the danger of oncoming traffic.

Introduction

Most driving is done while following cars, being followed, and meeting oncoming vehicles. The potential for crashes is always there. The death toll would be much higher if most drivers were not competent and alert. Most head-on and rear-end collisions are the result of human failure.

One fourth of all crashes are rear-end collisions. In 1974, 3,900,000 rear-end collisions took place in this country.

During the same period, head-on collisions took the lives of 5,700 Americans. Though the head-on was only 2.6 percent of all crashes, it accounted for 7 percent of all the fatalities. Clearly, the head-on is one of the most deadly crashes.

Collision-free driving is not easy, but millions of drivers have such records. The skills they use can be learned. This chapter is about the things you can do to be an accident preventer rather than an accident maker.

Following

There is no substitute for adequate following distance to prevent rear-end collisions. Quick reaction and good brakes cannot always be relied on to keep drivers out of trouble. Both of these factors operate within limits and cannot be speeded up or improved as speed increases. An adequate following distance gives drivers both time to react and distance to stop safely.

TAILGATERS

Some drivers do not maintain a safe following distance in traffic. Every day we see many drivers tailgating and getting away with it. This may give beginning drivers the idea that it is a safe practice. If a driver is tailgating and there should be a misjudgment, a mo-ment of inattention or an emergency, then time and space are squeezed down to impossible limits. The result is a rear-end collision.

Disadvantages of Tailgating The first step that all drivers must take toward following safely in traffic is to view tailgating as a disadvantage. They must not believe they are saving time by easing up to the car ahead. The most time that can be saved by tailgating is about two or three seconds.

Even though the risk of a collision may be small at any one time, over the long term the odds are that tailgaters will be involved in a collision. Experienced traffic officers know that there are two kinds of tailgaters: those who have had rear-end collisions and those who are going to have them.

An inattentive driver struck this cab even though proper signals were shown. Be sure that the situation is stable ahead before shifting your eyes off the road.

What Tailgaters Give Away   Tailgaters give away more than stopping distance. The closer they get to the car ahead:

- The less distance they can see ahead.
- The sharper and harder the turn must be to steer around a vehicle.
- The wider the space must be to change lanes.
- The less chance they have of swerving safely in an emergency.
- The less chance they have to stop in time without hitting the car ahead.

Advantages of Space   In traffic, you may not always be able to do what you want when you want. You can, however, increase the amount of time that you need. By increasing your following distance, it is possible to make safe moves when you want to. Tailgating, on the other hand, limits you only to braking when things begin to stack up in the lane ahead.

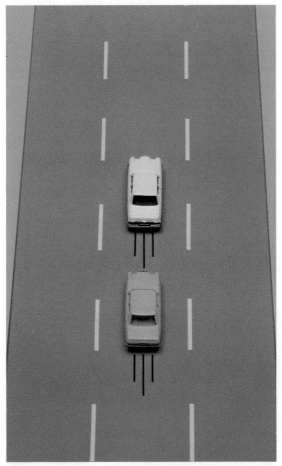

Following another vehicle closely leaves no room to maneuver.

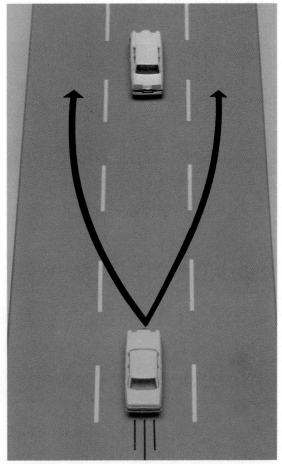

A longer following distance leaves room to steer around a vehicle.

WHAT TO LOOK FOR WHEN FOLLOWING

The following clues should alert the driver to start braking.

Brake Lights   These are the number one clue to watch for in traffic. Even brake lights in the next lane can be a sign of trouble. Experienced drivers respect brake lights and react promptly by covering the brake pedal when they see brake lights ahead.

Shrinking Distance Ahead   Be sure to ease up on the gas if you see the distance between you and the car ahead shortening. This means the car is going slower than you are. The

At intersections, slow down and be alert for drivers who might suddenly stop because they cannot turn.

slower car ahead might stop quickly and involve you in a rear-end collision.

Back Bumper Kick Up   When the rear bumper of the car ahead suddenly kicks up, the driver has slammed on the brakes, and the car will slide to a stop in a second or two.

Intersections   Intersections often trigger sudden stops that a driver might not predict. Because a driver starts a turn is no guarantee that he or she will finish the turn. Look ahead of the turning car to see if something in its path might cause it to stop. Traffic lights, improper turns, sudden lane changes, and pedestrians are just a few of the reasons for sudden stops. Be extra alert at intersections.

IPDE REQUIREMENTS FOR FOLLOWING

If tailgating is not a good following action, what are the driver's important requirements for a safe following distance?

Time is the first requirement. Often, the time required to identify a problem, to predict what might happen, and then to decide on the right action takes longer than executing; in this case, stopping the car.

Distance is the second requirement. The distance between you and the car ahead gives you room and time for the IPDE process. When the distance is too short, drivers may only have time for part of the IPDE process. In most rear-end collisions, drivers run out of time and distance.

Field of Vision is a third important requirement. The driver must be able to see possible problems to the sides as well as ahead that could require a sudden stop. A field of vision is best maintained by not getting too close to the vehicle ahead.

Space to the Side, which is part of the *space cushion,* is the fourth requirement. A space cushion on the side gives the driver another choice besides stopping. Tests have shown that at speeds above 30 mph (48 km/h) a driver can swerve to the next lane in less distance than the driver can stop. By keeping open space to the side, a driver may be able to avoid a rear-end collision.

A tailgater's view is so blocked that the driver cannot see the dangers ahead.

By leaving a space cushion around your car, you will not get boxed in traffic. Always leave yourself an "out."

Using the 2-second rule helps you keep a good following distance between you and the car ahead. Here you would start counting as the rear end of the car ahead reaches the edge of the shadow.

You would end your count as the front of your car reached the shadow. If you reached that spot before finishing your 2-second count, your following distance is too close.

TACTICS FOR FOLLOWING

When following in traffic, you do not have to be at the mercy of what takes place ahead. You can take positive actions to avoid hard stops and rear-end collisions.

2-Second Interval   Leaving a 2-second interval between you and the car ahead is a good guideline. When the back bumper of the car ahead reaches the shadow of the overpass, begin counting "one thousand one, one thousand two." If your front bumper reaches the shadow before the count of "two," you are too close.

If you are too close, ease up on the gas pedal and increase the following distance. The 2-second system is good because it allows a safe distance for speeds up to 50 mph.

Increase your following time to 3 seconds or more when
■ You are being tailgated.
■ The car ahead of you is tailgating.
■ Traction is poor.
■ Your speed is over 50 mph.

Pick a Safe Time to Look Away   Imagine yourself checking the mirror or looking for a house number for about 2 seconds. Suppose the driver ahead slams on the brakes while you are still looking away. By the time your eyes return to the road, it may be too late to stop. How can you prevent this?

First, be sure the situation ahead is stable before you look away.

Second, take several split-second looks rather than one long look.

Third, ask a passenger to help with street names, house numbers, or other navigation duties.

Look Ahead of the Car Ahead   Looking only at the rear bumper of the car ahead is an invitation to trouble. Look over, through, and around the car ahead. On hilltops and in curves check ahead for speed, for following distance, and for possible problems that could be developing. Watch brake lights in adjacent lanes that serve as an early warning of a stop or slow down.

Locations to Watch   Knowing where sudden stops are likely to be made can alert you to where danger is the greatest. These areas are near:
■ Traffic light controlled intersections.
■ Lanes next to parked cars.
■ Parking lot entrances.
■ Interchanges where cars enter and leave.
■ Sanded intersections on ice-covered streets.

Look ahead of the car ahead. See possible problems when the driver ahead sees them.

Attention   Attention is vital in any activity where accurate judgment and quick reactions are required. Following other cars in traffic is just such an activity. A momentary distraction is enough to cause a collision because the car ahead can stop in a second or two.

The Space Grabber   Suppose you are following with a 2-second interval when a driver in the next lane swerves into your following space. You can easily become angry at a time like that. You may consider "guarding" your space by reducing the space ahead. But this is a dangerous game.

The space grabber costs you only a second or two. When a space grabber swerves into your space, drop back and again establish a safe gap ahead of your car.

Tailgater Ahead   When tailgaters are seen ahead, it is wise to increase following time to 3 seconds or more. A line of tailgaters can lead to a chain reaction rear-end collision.

Being Followed in Traffic

As a driver, you should be aware of actions you can take to prevent a tailgater from hitting you.

DRIVER AHEAD IS RESPONSIBLE TOO

When a rear-end collision occurs, the driver doing the hitting is likely to be held at fault. But a driving error made by the lead driver may help cause a rear-end crash. A driver should take great care to keep his or her car from being hit from the rear.

COMMUNICATING

A driver can communicate with the driver to the rear in several ways. First, and easiest, is with your brake lights. Flash the brake lights when you see that you might have to slow down or stop. Second, signal for all

A driver directly ahead of you will move slightly to one side so that you can see brake lights of a driver way ahead.

turns and lane changes. Third, move aside to give the trailing driver a first-hand view of the signal of the driver ahead of you. This is especially good when the driver in front of you is signaling for a left turn.

WHAT A TAILGATER TAKES AWAY FROM YOU

Imagine driving car B in the situation shown in the illustration below. Your following distance is 2 seconds, but car C is tailgating. Then imagine A hitting the brakes hard for an emergency stop. You brake hard and keep from hitting A, but C hits you in the rear. Anytime you allow a driver to tailgate your car, you are permitting that driver to dictate how hard you may use your brakes.

How to Reduce the Danger   When tailgated, it is best to increase your following distance

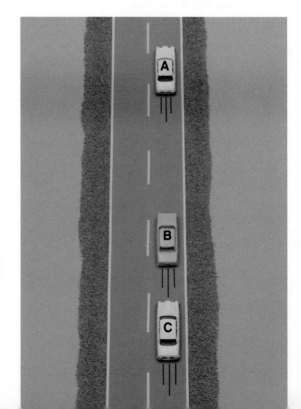

so that stops can be made more easily over longer distances. This will give the driver behind a chance to stop safely too.

YOU AND YOUR BRAKES

Good car control is not just being able to stop in time. It is getting stopped in a way that lets others stop safely too. You can put the driver to the rear on the spot by suddenly slamming on the brakes. One series of tests done with new cars under ideal conditions resulted in very short stopping times. At 20 mph, cars were stopped in $1^1/_4$ seconds. At 45 mph, 2 seconds were required. At 60 mph, the time was 3 seconds.

To keep from being hit from behind
- **Signal early** for turns, stops, or lane changes.

A new car can stop so quickly that the driver behind has a drastically short time to react and stop. Stopping times in the chart below are for new cars under ideal conditions.

- **Keep rear lights** clean and working.
- **Make stops gradual** enough to give following drivers time to stop.
- **Flash brake lights** to warn drivers behind before you slow down or stop.
- **Keep pace** with traffic when conditions are favorable.
- **Get the big picture to the rear** by means of your inside and outside mirrors so you always know how close rear traffic is.
- **Before changing lanes,** be sure to make a head check toward the direction you wish to move.
- **Get rid of tailgaters** by helping them pass safely.
- **Raise hood and turn on emergency flashers** if your car stalls in traffic and cannot be moved.
- **Think ahead** Late decisions and sudden actions mean trouble for everyone.

When another vehicle follows you too closely, signal early and make gradual stops.

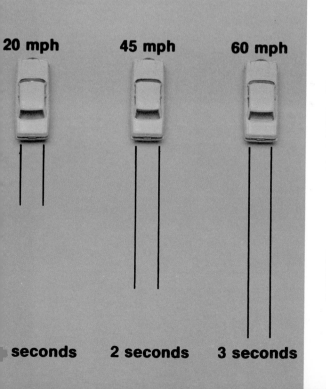

Oncoming Traffic

Usually, meeting cars in traffic causes no great problem. But you can never be sure that an oncoming driver will not come over into your lane for one reason or another.

LOOK FOR OTHER DRIVERS' PROBLEMS

If drivers wait until they see an oncoming car beginning to cross over the center line, it could be too late. Skilled drivers look for reasons that might cause the oncoming driver to swerve into their lanes. Being aware of the reasons could provide the extra seconds needed to prevent a collision.

Why They Cross   Some reasons why drivers might cross the center line are
- **Loss of control** Blowout, drop off edge of road, skid, caught in loose gravel or snow along edge of road, strong cross wind.
- **Reduced space** Parked car, snowdrift, standing water, object in the road, narrow bridge, barricade.
- **Making a maneuver** Passing, turning left, turning around, going too fast in curve, making wide right turn into your path.

- **Driver impairment** Drunk, asleep, poor vision, confused, distracted.
- **Visibility** Driver blinded by sun, headlights, or inability to see pavement lines due to adverse conditions.
- **Traction** Unexpected spot of poor traction on the pavement.

DO YOU HAVE ROOM TO MEET?

Weather and traffic conditions can greatly reduce the amount of room normally adequate for meeting other vehicles. Snowdrifts and standing water can hide center lines and cut down on driving space. Farm equipment can be much wider than it appeared in the distance. Wide loads like mobile homes can leave very little room.

As an oncoming vehicle approaches, predict what speed and space adjustments you must make, if necessary, according to these conditions:
- **Space** How much will the driver need?
- **Stability** Does the vehicle appear to be steady as it approaches? Will it continue on a safe course?
- **Pathside** Will things along both pathsides continue to be stable?

When space looks too narrow for your car, reduce speed or stop to let other vehicles through.

Look for problems that might cause the oncoming driver to swerve into your lane.

When your lane is blocked, wait for oncoming traffic to clear.

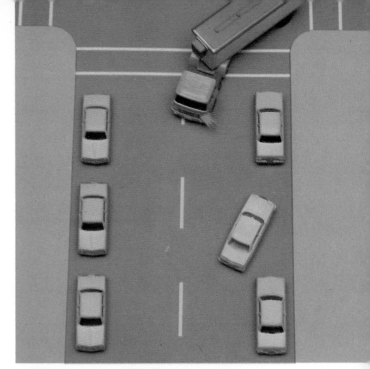

CHOOSING A MEETING POINT

Good drivers look things over and decide just where it is best to meet. Here are some guides in choosing a meeting point:

- Avoid meeting at the exact point a problem must be handled. Try to handle a problem ahead of time.
- Choose to meet where you have the most space and, if possible, the most adequate swerve space. Stop if the space looks too narrow.
- If meeting in reduced space cannot be avoided, put the biggest space between you and the greatest danger. For example, a driver would choose to drive near a parked car and give more room to an oncoming truck.

WHEN YOUR LANE IS BLOCKED

The driver whose lane is partly or completely blocked does not have the right to swing out into the other lane and force oncoming traffic to stop or wait. When your lane is blocked, you must wait.

MEETING ON NARROW STREETS

Parked cars can choke off too much of the space on a street for safe meeting. The space you wish to take must look wider than your car and the oncoming car for you even to consider meeting it in a tight space. In many instances, it may be best to pull over in a gap between parked cars and wait.

ACTIONS TO TAKE

These actions can be taken to reduce the danger of oncoming traffic:

- **Headlights in daytime** make your vehicle easier to see.
- **Move to the right** so the oncoming driver will see you sooner. This reduces the amount of swerve needed to dodge trouble.
- **Reduce speed** With heavy oncoming traffic, the speed limit could be too fast. At lower speeds, stops can be made more quickly
- **Evasive action** Signal, brake, and swerve at the same time when a car begins to cross into your lane.

Vocabulary

field of vision, 127
following distance, 124

stopping time, 131
tailgating, 124
2-second interval, 128

Summary

1. Nearly one fourth of all crashes are rear-end collisions. Most of these are caused by following too closely and inattention.
2. The closer a tailgater gets to the car ahead, the harder it is to (1) see around a vehicle, (2) steer around it, (3) change lanes, (4) swerve safely, and (5) stop in time.
3. When following, look for brake lights, shrinking distance, back bumper kick up, and sudden stops near intersections.
4. Time, distance, field of vision, and space to the side are required for a driver to perform the IPDE process safely.
5. The 2-second interval is the most reliable way to set a safe following distance because it allows adequate reaction distance for most conditions.
6. Danger of a rear-end collision is greatest at traffic light controlled intersections, lanes near parked cars, parking lot entrances, interchanges, and ice-covered intersections.
7. A driver can communicate with traffic to the rear by flashing brake lights, signaling for all turns and lane changes, and moving aside to let trailing driver see signal of vehicle ahead.
8. By looking ahead, signaling early, and planning easy stops by flashing brake lights, a driver can warn drivers to the rear who will have a chance to stop in time and avoid hitting you.
9. Some reasons why drivers might cross over to your lane are loss of car control, reduced space, bad maneuver, driver impairment, loss of visibility, and poor traction.
10. Driving with headlights on, moving to the right, and reduced speed are actions that drivers can take to reduce the hazard of an oncoming threat.

Driving Situations

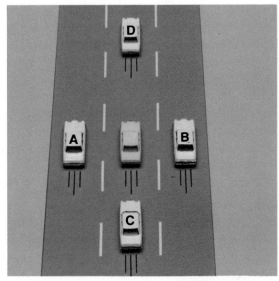

1. You and the oncoming car are timed to meet on the bridge. What is the danger? Who should yield? What should you do?

2. You are driving the yellow car. What is the problem? What should you do?

3. You are driving the yellow car. A driver behind is tailgating you. What problem is that driver creating for you? What should you do?

4. You are driving the yellow car. Car A is tailgating the car ahead. What is the danger? What should you do about it?

Chapter Review Questions

Following

1. What is the extent and cause of the rear-end collision problem in this country? (123)
2. What are four disadvantages of following too closely in traffic? (125)
3. What are four important factors to look for when following other vehicles? (126)
4. What are four IPDE requirements for following safely? (127)
5. Explain how to use the 2-second rule when following. (128)
6. What are four conditions or situations where the following interval should be increased to 3 or more seconds? (128)
7. What three things can a driver do to avoid hitting the car ahead when it is necessary to glance away from the road? (128)
8. What three traffic locations tend to trigger rear-end collisions? (129)

Being Followed in Traffic

9. What are three ways a driver can communicate with traffic to the rear? (130)
10. What is the major disadvantage of being tailgated? (130)
11. What three things can a driver do to reduce the chance of being hit from behind? (131)

Oncoming Traffic

12. What five conditions might cause an oncoming car to cross the center line? (132)
13. How can you reduce the danger of oncoming traffic crossing into your lane? (133)
14. What three rules should you follow to select a safe meeting point on a narrow street or road? (133)

Projects

1. Learn to count seconds with the aid of the sweep second hand on a clock or watch. Say "one thousand one, one thousand two" as you count.
2. When you ride in a car, time the interval in front of your car as well as that of other drivers in traffic for one week. Report to the class whether or not the interval was adhered to during that time.
3. Ride with an experienced driver. Study about 25 drivers following behind your car. Of that number, how many followed your car too closely? Report to the class.
4. Stand near a busy street and study the following habits of passing drivers. What following habits lead to trouble? Report to the class.
5. Obtain information from police or highway patrol about rear-end collisions and head-on collisions in your town or county. What are the official reasons given for rear-end and head-on collisions?

Chapter 8 · Test

(Write the correct answers on a separate sheet of paper.)

True-False

1. One fourth of all crashes are rear-end collisions. (123)
2. The closer you get to the car ahead, the wider the space needed to steer to the next lane. (125)
3. Most cars are able to stop in about the same distance from a given speed. (125)
4. Rapidly shrinking distance to the car ahead is a cue to brake promptly. (126)
5. A driver should keep open space to at least one side of the car when following another car in traffic. (127)
6. The 2-second rule applies at all speeds. (128)
7. The best way to defend against a "space grabber" is to close up the distance ahead of your car. (129)
8. Intersections are a common location for rear-end collisions. (129)
9. The most important thing a tailgater takes away from you is the choice of using your brakes as hard as you might need to. (130)
10. Flashing your brake lights is a good way to signal for stops. (131)
11. The stopping time for a new car traveling 20 mph can be as short as $1^{1}/_{4}$ seconds. (131)
12. Your best defense against a threat from oncoming traffic is to be ready to act when you see the car cross the center line. (132)
13. To reduce the danger of oncoming cars in daytime, it is best to drive with your headlights on. (133)
14. Exactly where you meet an oncoming vehicle in reduced space situations is a matter over which you have little control. (133)
15. The best way to defend against a head-on collision is to look for problems of oncoming traffic. (132)

Answer the Question

16. If traffic and road conditions are less than ideal, how much should following interval be increased? (128)
17. What important factor influences following distance? (124)
18. In order for a driver to maneuver properly, what is the safest thing the driver could have around the vehicle? (127)
19. When meeting oncoming vehicles in traffic, what is the most important thing to look for? (132)
20. What is the most important thing a tailgater takes away from you? (130)

Chapter 9

Motorcycles in Traffic

Objectives

1. Explain the driver's responsibilities toward motorcyclists in traffic.
2. Explain the limitations of motorcycles and cyclists in traffic.
3. Explain the cyclist's responsibilities toward drivers in traffic.
4. Name the items of wearing apparel and equipment that protect a cyclist.
5. Describe the procedures a cyclist should follow while learning to ride.
6. List safety rules and procedures for motorcycle passengers.
7. Explain how both the driver and cyclist can use the IPDE process for defensive strategies and tactics in traffic.
8. Describe situations in which a motorcycle might be hidden from a driver's view.
9. List defensive tips cyclists should follow.
10. Explain situations for which an extra space cushion between a motorcycle and a car is necessary.
11. Describe the effects of adverse conditions on the cyclist.

Introduction

Even though many drivers will never ride a motorcycle, they will be better drivers if they understand the capabilities and limitations of cycles and cyclists with whom they must share the road.

In recent years, more and more people have been using motorcycles as a means of transportation and recreation. The number of motorcycles has increased at a very rapid rate. The low cost of buying and operating a cycle are two of the main reasons for this increase.

In fewer than 10 percent of all motor vehicle collisions, injury or death occurs. However, injury or death takes place in about 85 to 90 percent of motorcycle crashes. This high injury and fatality rate results from the exposed position of the motorcycle rider. Unlike the driver who is protected by the car, the cyclist is in the open and fully exposed.

In order to reduce motorcycle crashes, national standards have been established regarding motorcycles. These standards call for states to require special examination or reexamination for a license to operate a motorcycle. They also require manufacturers to install a seat and footrest for the passenger, turn signal lights, and at least one rearview mirror on each motorcycle. In order to further reduce motorcycle injuries and deaths, the cyclist and the car driver must cooperate in traffic.

Car Driver's Responsibilities

Since cyclists are much less protected than car drivers, the drivers must accept an extra share of responsibility for avoiding collisions. Drivers must keep in mind how destructive a car can be to a motorcyclist. Car drivers should show cyclists the same courtesy they show other drivers. Cyclists are legally entitled to their share of the road. Even if a cyclist fails to hold the correct position in a traffic lane, a driver must take special care not to hit the cyclist. Car drivers should be aware of the following facts and limitations of motorcycles and cyclists so they will give cyclists enough space for safe operation.

INEXPERIENCED CYCLISTS

Many cyclists are using rented or borrowed machines and have not had enough practice for good control and judgment. Thus, car drivers must always be alert and anticipate cyclists' errors.

CYCLISTS WITHOUT PROTECTIVE CLOTHING

Many cyclists ride without protective clothing and equipment. A car driver must watch out for and feel personally protective about such riders.

HANDLING TRAITS OF CYCLES

Another responsibility of car drivers is to learn what handling traits motorcycles have and how they operate in traffic. Know, for instance, that the cyclist leans to the side when making a turn and does little or no turning of the handlebars. The cyclist may have difficulty handling a cycle in a turn on windy days or on rough roads. Learn to watch the cyclist's body and front wheel when he or she is making turns. Car drivers who understand the handling traits of cycles will be better prepared to operate a car when cycles are present in traffic.

IMPROPER BRAKING

Another cycle problem that drivers must be alert for is improper braking. Braking for a four-wheeled vehicle requires a single movement of the foot to the brake pedal. A cyclist, however, has to operate separate brakes for front and back wheels. The front brake, operated by a lever on the right handlebar, supplies up to 70 percent of the braking power. A foot pedal controls the rear wheel brake. Generally, both brakes should be used together, but the rear wheel brake should be applied first. This braking maneuver requires careful coordination of foot and hand for maximum braking effect. Improper braking can lead to loss of control.

POOR TRACTION

As important as good traction is for automobile control, it is far more important for a two-wheeler. A rider's balance and upright position depend on the grip of two tires on the pavement. Water, sand, oil slicks, or loose gravel on the road reduces traction and makes cycle control even more critical. Drivers who are alert for such conditions will predict sudden changes in a cyclist's position or direction and will give the cyclist extra space.

SEEING CYCLISTS

Car drivers must also train themselves to look for two-wheelers in traffic. Think small, because cycles are small, but they are not small as traffic problems. Be prepared for cyclists' mistakes, and stay well back, always giving them extra space. Cyclists can help make themselves more visible to other drivers by riding with their headlights on at all times. Many states require this by law.

Good traction is important for a motorcyclist.

To be seen, headlights should always be on.

Cyclist's Responsibilities

In addition to obeying motor vehicle laws, cyclists must operate within special rules. They must know the limits and handling characteristics of their machines.

Beginning cyclists should have many hours of practice before riding on the street. All the riding skills should be mastered. Experienced cyclists know that it takes at least 500 miles of riding to get the feel of a motorcycle. Even more than the driver, cyclists need a sound understanding of traffic dangers and defensive strategies.

SELECT THE PROPER CYCLE
When planning to purchase a motorcycle, consider first how and where you plan to use it. If you expect to operate it mostly in residential areas and in cities, you should buy a cycle that will give you excellent handling. If you plan to do trail riding or touring, you would probably select a more powerful cycle. Smaller size cycles are usually not allowed on expressways. Trail bikes are not suitable for street riding, while street bikes do not last well for off the road riding.

KNOW PARTS AND SAFETY EQUIPMENT
Cyclists must become familiar with the operating parts and safety equipment of the cycle. They must be able to locate and operate all controls automatically. The picture shows the basic controls and safety equipment. Cyclists must also be able to inspect the cycle and perform preventive maintenance. Consult the owner's manual for specific directions for your machine.

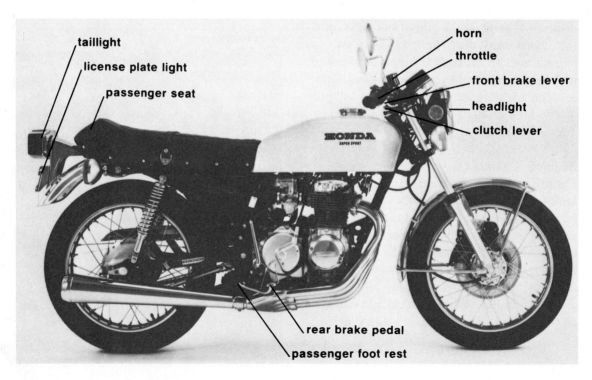

taillight
license plate light
passenger seat
horn
throttle
front brake lever
headlight
clutch lever
rear brake pedal
passenger foot rest

KNOW LAWS GOVERNING CYCLISTS

Cyclists must obey all traffic laws that apply to drivers of four-wheeled vehicles. They must also know and obey those laws that apply only to motorcycle riders. Since the laws are not the same in every state, most departments of motor vehicles have a booklet containing motorcycle laws for their state. Of special importance are laws about financial responsibility, inspection, and use of protective equipment.

USE PROTECTIVE EQUIPMENT

Motorcycle riders are not protected like car drivers. For a comparison of the protection provided by cars and motorcycles, see the chart on this page. As a result, cyclists are much more likely to be injured in a collision or fall. By wearing protective clothing and equipment, cyclists can prevent many injuries or reduce the seriousness of injuries that do occur.

Passenger Protection ● Yes ● No		
Safety Feature	**Car**	**Motorcycle**
Side collision protection (frame-door)	●	●
Rear-end crash protection (bumper-frame)	●	●
Head-on crash protection (bumper-hood)	●	●
Rollover protection (frame-top)	●	●
Lap-shoulder belts	●	●
Padded interior	●	●
Windshield washers and wipers	●	●
Automatic front-rear brake coordination	●	●
Stability in poor traction	●	●
Easy to see in traffic	●	●
Winter operation in snow-belt states	●	●

In most falls, the cyclist will sustain at least some kind of injury to hands, arms, feet, or legs. If the crash is severe, head, neck, and chest injuries often occur.

The most important piece of protective equipment is an approved safety helmet. A cyclist should never ride without a securely fastened helmet. Head injuries account for about two-thirds of all motorcycle fatalities. Almost all states now have laws requiring cyclists to wear helmets. This requirement has saved many lives each year.

Besides a helmet, cyclists need protection for their eyes. A windshield, face shield, or a pair of goggles protects the eyes from flying insects, wind, and pebbles or sand thrown from the wheels of moving vehicles.

Heavy shoes or boots and gloves help protect the cyclist against scraped hands and feet in case of a spill. Pants and jackets of heavy material will also help reduce injuries in a fall.

LEARN TO RIDE PROPERLY

All beginning cyclists should be taught proper riding techniques by a trained instructor. High schools in increasing numbers are beginning to offer classroom and laboratory instruction in motorcycle riding. Just as there are basic driving procedures to learn for operating a car, there are even more critical procedures to learn for the safe operation of a cycle. Starting, stopping, balancing, and controlling the cycle need to be mastered before the beginner rides in traffic.

LEARN TO RIDE WITH A PASSENGER

The inexperienced cyclists may be surprised to find how much harder balancing is with a passenger on the cycle. Cyclists should not carry passengers until they have had many hours of practice in a variety of traffic situations. They will notice a difference in accelerating, braking, and turning when they are carrying passengers.

A passenger should wear the same type of protective gear as the cyclist. The passenger should sit still on the seat and hold the passenger hand grips with both hands. If the cycle does not have hand grips, the passenger should hold on around the waist of the cyclist. The passenger should keep his or her feet on the footrest at all times.

The passenger should *not* try to balance the cycle. This is the cyclist's job. The cyclist should do the leaning during a turn while the passenger remains a fixed part of the machine.

A motorcycle with two people calls for double caution from the car driver. The cyclist must also use double caution as he or she has a double responsibility.

Defensive Strategies and Tactics

Both car drivers and cyclists need to use their best driving strategies and tactics in order to share the road. Because cyclists might travel in several places within a traffic lane, drivers must watch for them on all sides. The driver in the top picture did not see the cyclist to the right and thus, when the driver made the turn, he or she cut off the turning cyclist.

IPDE FOR CAR DRIVERS AND CYCLISTS

IPDE can help drivers and cyclists develop defensive strategies.

Identify   The driver must identify the spots where a motorcycle might be hidden or might come out suddenly. Be extra alert for cycles when crossing intersections and when turning or passing. The cyclist can help by being aware of spots where cycles may be invisible or where the driver might not expect them.

Predict   In predicting the actions of other users, both the car driver and the cyclist must keep in mind the different handling traits of the two vehicles. Both must be prepared for situations and conditions that are known to cause collisions. The two bottom pictures on the right give examples of situations that require the driver to predict.

Decide   All decisions will be made on a sounder basis if all operators consider the problems of the operators of other vehicles as well as their own.

Execute   Drivers and cyclists both should avoid sudden actions. Being careful not to surprise other drivers is a precaution for both to take as they execute their decisions.

DEFENSIVE CYCLING STRATEGIES

The motorcyclist, as well as the car driver, has the responsibility to practice defensive strategies all the time. The following tips will usually help the cyclist avoid trouble:

1. Position your cycle in traffic and on the open road in a way that will let other drivers see you. In general, the left-car wheel track is the safest position.

2. Avoid riding in a driver's blind spot. Stay well back and in the proper lane position so that the driver can see you.

3. Cross railroad tracks as close to a right angle as possible. This maneuver will help prevent the cycle's wheels from getting caught in the tracks and causing a spill.

4. Do not ride between lines of moving cars. This is not a legal pathway, and any time saved is not worth the risk of being "squeezed."

5. Move head and eyes frequently. The cyclist's view to the rear is limited, even with two mirrors.

6. Avoid changing lanes unless necessary. When changing lanes during a passing maneuver, move well over to use the full left lane. Use the same passing procedure as when driving a car.

7. When riding in pairs, don't ride side-by-side. The rider on the right should stay just to the rear of the rider on the left. When approaching turns, move into single-file position to make the turn in the correct lane.

8. Stay visible by using headlight and taillight both day and night. The use of reflective strips on both cycle, clothing, and helmet will add to your visibility.

2

3

4

7

CITY TRAFFIC

A major area of conflict for cyclists and car drivers is at intersections. When driving in the city, be prepared to yield to motorcycles at intersections, regardless of the legal right-of-way. Always watch for turn signals from cyclists. However, not all cyclists have turn signals and may lose steering control when giving arm signals. Be especially alert for cyclists at blind intersections.

The following are defensive strategies for car drivers in city traffic:

- Always keep an adequate space cushion between you and the cyclists.
- Avoid pulling up close behind a cyclist, especially one who is about to turn. This action may cause the cyclist to turn hurriedly and result in a fall.
- Before turning at intersections, check to see if a cyclist is about to pass on that side.
- When turning left across oncoming traffic, look for a motorcycle that may be hidden by oncoming traffic.

HIGHWAY TRAFFIC

The high speeds on the open highway add problems for both drivers and cyclists. Because of the small size of cycles, they appear to be farther away than they really are. The motorcycle's small size also complicates the passing maneuver. A driver may not see a cycle in the space ahead of the vehicle he or she is passing. Watch for cyclists when you are passing.

When planning to overtake and pass a motorcycle, don't tailgate. Stay back until you start your pass. Then move over into the next lane. Never try to pass a cyclist in the same lane even if the cyclist is riding far to the right in the lane.

Be aware of all vehicles in the intersection.

A driver should be aware of a motorcyclist when passing another car on a highway.

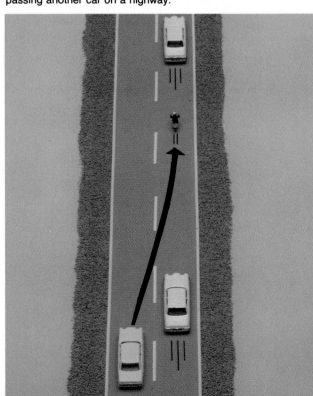

The worst traction for cyclists is immediately after the rain starts.

ADVERSE CONDITIONS

Rain, fog, darkness, or snow present special problems for both car drivers and cyclists. However, the motorcycle cannot handle bad conditions as well as an automobile. A puddle that hides a deep hole will jolt a car; the same puddle could throw a motorcycle out of control.

Motorcyclists do not have to ride very long before they find themselves riding in the rain. Just as for car drivers, the worst time for cyclists is immediately after the rain has started. As the water mixes with dirt and oil on the road, traction is greatly reduced. Since balance is important for cycle control, the reduced traction is far more critical for the cyclist.

When rain starts, a driver can turn on the windshield wipers. When road dirt splashes on the windshield, the driver can use the windshield washers. The cyclist has neither of these devices on the motorcycle. As a result, the cyclist's vision is reduced and may even be distorted.

When riding on wet or slippery roads, cyclists should try to avoid riding on pavement markings. Painted lines can be extremely slippery when they are wet. Riding in the tracks made by cars and trucks helps cyclists gain extra traction. A bumpy surface and gravel roads also cause reduced traction for cars and cycles. However, since balance is important for cycle control, the hazards are far greater for the motorcyclist.

When you drive a car, remember that bad weather makes it harder to spot a cyclist, and the cyclist may be hurrying to get out of the rain. Be extra alert and allow a greatly increased space cushion under adverse conditions.

Vocabulary

face shield, 144
front brake lever, 141
passenger hand grips, 145

protective clothing and equipment, 143
safety helmet, 144
trail riding, 142

Summary

1. Car drivers have an extra responsibility to avoid conflicts with cyclists since drivers are protected, and motorcyclists are not.
2. The small size of motorcycles and the difficulty of balance and control contribute to traffic problems. Cyclists lack adequate protection and are often inexperienced.
3. Cyclists must obey all motor-vehicle laws as well as special rules for cycles. They are responsible for controlling their motorcycles under all conditions.
4. Cyclists should use helmets, eye protectors, gloves, heavy shoes, jackets, and a windshield or face shield whenever they ride.
5. Cyclists should receive proper riding instruction and should practice many hours before entering traffic.
6. Cycle passengers should wear protective gear and sit still on the cycle. The passenger should let the driver do the balancing.
7. The IPDE process for both driver and cyclist should include defensive strategies for identifying hidden spots for cycles, predicting handling traits of all vehicles, considering others when making decisions, and avoiding sudden actions.
8. Cyclists are often hard to see when they are hidden at blind corners and between vehicles in traffic lanes, as well as when they are not traveling in the correct path.
9. Motorcyclists should drive in the left car-wheel track of the lane, avoid riding in driver's blind spots, cross railroad tracks at a right angle, avoid unnecessary lane changes, always have lights on, and not ride side-by-side.
10. Both car drivers and cyclists must always keep an extra space cushion between them, especially at intersections, in city traffic, and in adverse conditions.
11. Adverse conditions can reduce and distort the vision of a cyclist. Balance and control are much more difficult on slippery roads.

Driving Situations

1. What is the cyclist doing wrong? If the driver plans to turn right, what should he or she do first?

2. What correct procedures is the cyclist following? What defensive strategies should the driver follow? What actions should the driver predict?

3. What is the motorcyclist doing wrong? How do adverse conditions affect the cyclist's traction, vision, and control? What could a cyclist do to correct his or her errors?

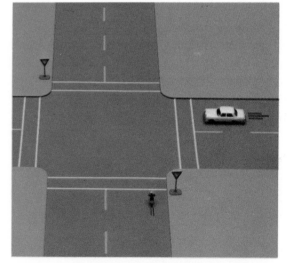

4. Which person should legally yield at the intersection, the driver or the cyclist? What should the driver predict? What should the cyclist predict? What must the car driver do?

Chapter Review Questions

Car Driver's Responsibilities

1. Why are the motorcycle fatality rates high? (140)
2. What safety advantages does a car driver have that a motorcyclist does not? (140)
3. Why is traction even more important for a cyclist than for a car driver? (141)
4. Why is braking more difficult for a cyclist than for a car driver? (141)
5. What three road conditions would present greater traction problems for the cyclist than the driver? (141)

Cyclist's Responsibilities

6. What five cyclist responsibilities will decrease a cyclist's problems in traffic? (142-145)
7. What items of wearing apparel and equipment are important for cyclist's safety? (144)
8. What is the best way for a new cyclist to learn how to operate his or her cycle? (145)
9. How do the safety features and handling traits of cars and motorcycles differ? (143)
10. What differences will the cyclist notice when carrying a passenger? (145)
11. Why should a cyclist always wear a safety helmet? (144)

Defensive Strategies and Tactics

12. What are five defensive cycling tips? (147)
13. When might a cyclist be hidden from a driver's view? (146)
14. In what situations should a motorist give a cyclist an extra space cushion? (146-149)
15. What defensive strategies for each IPDE step should drivers follow? (146)

Projects

1. Visit a local insurance company, and compare the cost of full insurance coverage for a motorcycle to the cost of full insurance coverage for a family car.
2. What special laws or regulations govern the operation of motorcycles in your state? What protective equipment is required?
3. Keep a record of the number of cyclists you see during five days. How many are wearing little or no protective gear?
4. Visit the local police station, and ask the officers what the types and causes of motorcycle accidents are.

Chapter 9 · Test

(Write the correct answers on a separate sheet of paper.)

True-False

1. Car drivers should show motorcyclists the same respect and courtesy they show other drivers. (140)
2. Motorcycle passengers do not need to wear protective equipment. (145)
3. Cyclists should cross railroad tracks at right angles. (147)
4. Braking on a motorcycle is just as easy as braking on a car. (141)
5. Drivers should constantly be identifying spots where cyclists might be hidden. (146)
6. A motorcycle protects the cyclist. (143)
7. Car drivers should predict cyclist errors whenever cycles are sharing the road. (141)
8. In city traffic, cyclists may safely ride between moving lines of traffic. (147)
9. Since cyclists are concerned with balancing and controls on the cycle, they are not responsible for identifying and predicting traffic problem situations. (146)
10. Drivers should leave extra space when following a cyclist about to turn. (148)

Answer the Question

11. What are cyclist's responsibilities in traffic?   (142-145)
12. How did national standards affect state laws regarding cyclists?   (139)
13. Why is it important for car drivers to understand the special handling traits of motorcycles? (140)
14. Why does a car offer more passenger protection than a cycle?   (143)
15. What effects might wet and slippery roads have on cyclists?   (149)
16. Under what conditions should a cyclist ride with headlight on?   (141)
17. Why should a cyclist have practiced alone for many hours before carrying a passenger? (145)
18. Why do drivers carry extra responsibility for avoiding conflicts with motorcycles in traffic? (140)
19. In addition to leaving on the headlight, how can cyclists make themselves more visible to other highway users?   (147)
20. What laws must cyclists obey?   (143)

True-False

1. When turning left at an intersection, a driver should make a final traffic check just before entering the intersection. (94)
2. When turning at an intersection in a stickshift car, you should downshift gears after starting the turn. (94)
3. When parking uphill without a curb, you should turn the wheels toward the shoulder. (100)
4. When starting uphill, the driver can use the left foot on the brake to keep the car from rolling back. (101)
5. It takes the same amount of time to cross an intersection as it does to turn left or right at the same intersection. (108)
6. A right turn on a red signal is permitted in some states after yielding to pedestrians and to traffic from the left. (111)
7. Railroad crossings protected by flashers and gates have largely eliminated fatal train-car collisions. (116)
8. A driver with quick reactions and good brakes can safely follow other vehicles in traffic more closely than 2 seconds. (124, 128)
9. When turning the car around, you should back into the alley or driveway and drive forward into the street. (96)
10. In most rear-end collisions, the driver doing the hitting is at fault. (130)
11. Car drivers must give cyclists extra space when traveling with them in traffic. (140)
12. Beginning cyclists do not need any training before riding on the street. (145)

Answer the Question

13. When turning at an intersection, at what point should the driver reach the slowest speed? (94)
14. Which will give the driver a wider range of vision when backing straight back: turn head right or left? (95)
15. At controlled intersections, what two devices assign the right-of-way? (108)
16. If you and a car on your right arrive at a four-way stop at the same time, who must yield the right-of-way? (114)
17. What are two ways a driver can communicate with the driver behind? (130)
18. How can protective clothing help a motorcyclist? (143)
19. When tailgated, how can a driver best reduce the danger? (130)
20. What three clues tell you the driver ahead is braking? (126)

Chapter 10

Driving in Towns and Cities

Objectives

1. Explain why driving in the city presents so many possible conflicts.
2. List the advantages a driver gains by reducing speed in complex traffic situations.
3. Describe how far ahead a driver should look in city traffic and how this helps a driver prepare for a changing green light.
4. Explain how to determine the potential danger from cars parked at the curb and how to deal with this danger.
5. Explain how a driver determines which lane and which position in the lane are best on two-way and one-way streets.
6. List some ways a driver can identify a one-way street.
7. Describe the proper lane for turning both left and right from a one-way into both a one-way and a two-way street.
8. Describe when and where motorists should be especially watchful for pedestrians and bicyclists.
9. List the decision-making skills that are helpful in guarding against collisions with pedestrians and bicyclists.
10. Describe the proper procedures for getting out of a car on the street side.
11. List some important factors that cause bicyclists to be involved in collisions with cars.

Introduction

Town and city traffic conditions provide a great variety of possible problems for drivers. The different kinds of city streets contain many signs, signals, pavement markings, pedestrians, bicyclists, neon lights, outside noises, and vehicles of all kinds. Drivers deal with up to 300 traffic situations per mile of city driving. On the other hand, in highway driving they probably face only about 100 traffic situations per mile. In about one out of ten situations, the driver must take some special action.

Good driving habits and cooperation with other road users can make city driving easier. Drivers who position their cars correctly on the street are less likely to get into trouble. A willingness to share the road with others and to yield the right-of-way reduces the chances of a collision.

Pedestrians and bicyclists on city streets complicate the driving task because they are more difficult to see. While the people in an automobile are relatively protected in a collision, almost every pedestrian and bicyclist struck by a car is hurt. Many are killed. So the car driver has a special responsibility to watch for and to protect them as much as possible.

Basic Procedures for City Driving

The possible conflicts with other vehicles, pedestrians, and bicyclists on city streets require that the driver be constantly aware of traffic. Inner city areas are especially dangerous because the streets are frequently used as playgrounds by children, as market places by ice cream vendors, and as places for social gatherings by adults. The more people use the streets, the greater the chance for dangerous conflicts to develop.

DECISION SPOTS IN TRAFFIC

When traffic situations become complex, drivers need extra decision time. Reducing speed is essential. Drivers can gain four important advantages by reducing speed:

1. They have more time to see all details and to *identify* their meaning.
2. They have more time to analyze the information and to *predict* what may happen.
3. They can *decide* calmly and give others more time to react to their decisions.
4. When they *execute* their decisions, they can stop and/or steer around the danger.

Look Ahead; Stay Back   Look ahead at least one-block whenever city traffic allows you to see that far. In the middle of a block, you should be looking at least to the middle of the next block.

Follow far enough back to have room to see, maneuver, and stop. With these two basic strategies working for you, most traffic situations will be routine. Rarely will an emergency develop.

Covering the Brake   In many situations, taking your foot off the accelerator and covering the brake pedal, ready to brake, is enough. Since this action reduces your stopping distance, you may not actually need to use the brake unless the situation demands it. But avoid "riding the brakes" since this keeps your brake lights on all the time and increases wear on brake linings.

A good situation in which drivers should cover the brake is while driving in the right lane next to parked cars. They should glance through the rear windows of cars at the curb to see if anyone is in the car. Brake lights, signal lights, exhaust smoke, or wheels pointed outward are all clues that warn drivers a parked car may pull out. A parked car's door could pop open into the path of a car in the right-hand lane. When the right lane is wide enough, drive at least a car door's width away from parked cars.

City Passing   Don't cross the center line to pass another vehicle in a town or city street, and don't pass at or near an intersection. It is better to wait and see if the driver ahead plans to turn soon in a few blocks. At intersections, a car from the side street may turn directly into your path if you are passing in the left lane.

Be Ready for the Green Light to Change   By looking a block ahead of the car, the driver can check the traffic signal at the next corner. This check gives the driver plenty of time to determine what to do before reaching the intersection.

If the light is green when the driver first notices it, he or she can expect it to change shortly. A traffic light that has been green for a long time is called a *stale green light.* Flash-

Be alert for a door opening at any time as you approach parked cars.

Do not pass at or near busy intersections.

On yellow, proceed past intersection if safe to do so.

Special lanes are marked for left turns only.

ing pedestrian signals warn the driver that the traffic signal is about to change. By anticipating the yellow light, the driver can plan whether to slow and stop before entering the intersection or to continue through.

That decision depends on the distance to the intersection, speed of the car, condition of the pavement, width of the intersection, presence of cross traffic, and closeness of the car behind. At any speed, there is a *point of no return* beyond which drivers can no longer stop without entering the intersection.

Checking ahead for a stale green keeps you from dashing up to traffic lights and slamming on the brakes. This also reduces the possibility of being hit from behind.

Never speed up to get through a green light before it changes. Drivers on the side street may see the light changing in their favor and enter the intersection just as the green comes on. Collisions often result from such actions.

LANE CHOICE ON MULTILANE STREETS

If you want to drive slower than traffic in the left lane or expect to turn right soon, then choose the right lane. If left turns are prohibited or special lanes are provided for left turns, the left lane could be the best choice. But if a large number of cars are making left turns from the left lane and oncoming traffic is heavy, stay out of the left lane. Generally, driving in the right lane provides protection against head-on collisions. If there are three lanes moving in your direction, choose the center lane unless you plan to turn.

CAR POSITION

Position your car in the lane so you are least likely to conflict with other road users. Don't drive too close to the pavement marking lines on either side. Below are five precautions to reduce the likelihood of being involved in a conflict. These precautions will also help a driver handle the conflict if it does develop.

- Avoid driving in another driver's blind spot.
- Avoid letting another driver stay in your blind spot. Move ahead, or drop back.
- Avoid driving side-by-side with another vehicle, if you can.
- Stay out of bunches, if possible. If caught in a bunch, move away as soon as possible.
- Keep up with the flow of traffic.

CHOOSE THE SAFEST ROUTE

One important pre-trip decision to make for any trip is to choose a safe, quick route to your destination. The time of day and density of traffic should affect your route selection. Through streets are generally better than side streets because most through-street intersections have some traffic-control devices. One-way streets are more desirable than two-way streets because one-ways have fewer left-turns and fewer chances for head-on collisions. With a little thought, you can plan a route that will reduce delays and high-risk situations.

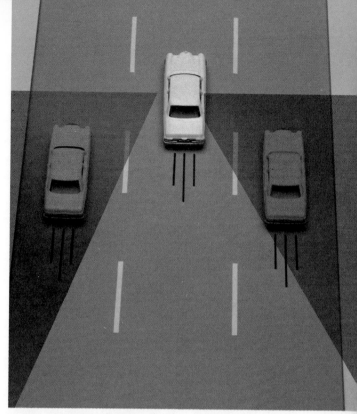

Stay out of a driver's blind spot.

Avoid "bunching" in traffic.

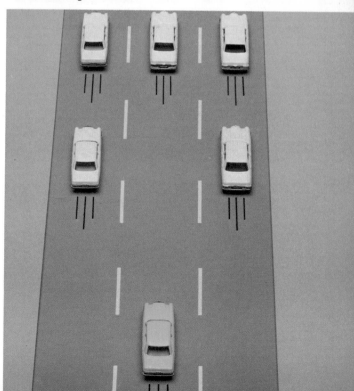

PROCEDURES IN PARKING LOTS

In most cities, many property damage collisions and some injuries occur in parking lots. The following procedures will help reduce parking-lot problems:

- Drive very slowly (15 mph or below).
- Follow the routes for traffic. Obey the traffic arrows on signs or on the pavement. Don't drive diagonally across a partly empty parking area.
- Watch carefully for children. They are less closely supervised than when they cross the street.
- Avoid tight parking spaces.
- Avoid backing into an angle space. If you back in, you will be headed against the flow of traffic when you leave.
- Drive far enough into the space so the rear of the car won't be in the way of moving cars.
- Avoid driving too far into the space and preventing the opposite car from pulling all the way into its space.
- Center the car in its space and park it parallel to the lines so it will not take up two spaces.
- Avoid letting the car door swing out and hit the next car.
- Secure the car properly and lock it when you leave.
- Keep looking in all directions when backing out of a parking space.

A defensive driver does not risk hitting a hidden car by passing a bus at a corner.

Detours will require you to slow down or stop and heed given directions.

PROBLEMS IN CITY TRAFFIC

Driving in towns and cities presents the driver with some special problems.

Parked Cars Hide Cross Traffic When approaching an intersection where a line of parked cars blocks the view, slow down or stop, if necessary, to get a good view of traffic. Do the same when buses or trucks block your view. If you are stopped beside a bus or truck, let that vehicle go first when the light turns green.

When a car coming out of an alley is partly hidden by parked cars, it may startle the driver ahead. That driver may swerve or stop suddenly. In either case, be ready to stop.

Detour in Your Lane When you see that street repairs are blocking your lane, you must prepare to stop. Slow down early enough to make a careful detour around the repair. A few cars from one direction will probably drive through the one clear lane and then a few from the opposite direction. Be patient and wait for the signal from a worker directing traffic, if one is there.

If your lane is blocked, you must yield the right-of-way to a driver from the opposite direction. Let the other driver go through first. When the way is clear, move around the obstacle before you drive too close to it. Then you can pass it without swerving sharply.

Turning at Corners Be sure to look left just before you turn *right*. You are entering a lane used by vehicles approaching from your left. Even if traffic is light, check for cross traffic.

Just before you turn *left,* check to the right. The law requires left-turning drivers to yield to cars from the right, as well as to all others in an uncontrolled intersection.

Driving on One-Way Streets

Almost all cities have one-way streets to move a greater volume of traffic with higher speed and safety. On one-way streets, the right-hand lane is used for right turns or parking. The center lanes are for cars going straight through, and the left lane for left turns or parking.

IDENTIFYING ONE-WAY STREETS

How can a driver identify a one-way street?

■ In most cities, ONE-WAY signs will be mounted on the STOP sign, YIELD sign, or traffic-light post.

■ Moving traffic and parked cars are all pointed the same way.

■ If a one-way street is properly marked, all center lane lines will be broken white lines.

■ All signs on both sides of a one-way street will face toward you. If you head down the left side of a street where the signs face away from you, you are either on a two-way or a one-way street going the wrong direction.

■ Watch for signs to tell you where a one-way street is beginning, ending, or changing.

■ Pavement markings can tell you whether the street is one-way or two-way.

ENTERING ONE-WAY STREETS

Entering a one-way street to the right requires a simple right turn from the right lane to the right lane on the one-way street. A turn into a one-way street to the left requires a sharp left turn into the first lane on the left. Be in the farthest left lane as you approach the intersection.

SPEED ON ONE-WAY STREETS

Streets with no oncoming cars can be an invitation to exceed the speed limit. Many drivers do not realize that going 5 mph (8 km/h) over the speed limit saves only a few seconds in a block.

On the other hand, the driver who drives much under the speed limit can block traffic behind and cause bunching. This could tempt some drivers to take unnecessary risks in passing.

Be in the correct lane for a turn from a one-way to a one-way street.

Watch carefully when turning from a one-way to a two-way street.

LANE CHOICE ON ONE-WAY STREETS

Which lane you select to drive in on a one-way street makes a difference in how many driving problems you will meet. Lane choice depends on how far you wish to travel and which direction you want to turn. The center lanes are best if you plan to continue on the one-way street for a number of blocks. Cars parked along the curb can cause problems and delays for drivers in the outside lanes. Also, turning cars slow up traffic in the outside lanes.

WRONG-WAY DRIVERS

Occasionally, you might meet a car headed the wrong way on a one-way street. If this happens, sound your horn, flash your headlights, and signal with your arms to warn the driver of the mistake. Also, try to get out of the car's way.

LEAVING ONE-WAY STREETS

Many drivers wait too long to change lanes for a turn. They should make their lane change one or two blocks before the turn.

Generally, a driver should leave one-way streets from the far left lane for left turns and the far right lane for right turns. If the two outer lanes are for parking, start the turn in the lane next to the parked cars. To turn left from a one-way street, get into the moving lane nearest the left-hand curb. In some one-way streets, the lane farthest left may be for left turns only. Turning right from a one-way street is the same as turning right at any intersection.

Be prepared for the driver who makes a left turn from the right half of a one-way street. In order to be able to react in this situation, stay as far from other cars when approaching intersections as traffic allows.

Protecting Pedestrians and Bicyclists

During recent years, more bicycles than auto-mobiles have been sold in this country. Most of the 12 million bicycles sold annually have been for adult use. An estimated 100 million Americans, young and old, are riding bikes for fun, exercise, and transportation. As a result, the number of bicycle deaths and injuries has increased at an alarming rate, both for young and adult riders.

Pedestrian fatalities continue to account for almost 20 percent of all traffic deaths, with about 9,000 pedestrians killed and 120,000 injured each year. Most of these deaths and injuries occur in towns and cities. Because of the great difference in weight and speed between motor vehicles and pedes-trians, drivers have a special obligation to prevent conflicts with them.

DRIVER'S RESPONSIBILITY

Over 75 percent of pedestrian fatalities are in the under-15 and over-45 age groups. Chil-dren act on the spur of the moment. They run into the street without thinking. Older pedes-trians may not see or hear very well and may not move out of the way quickly. Many adult pedestrians killed in traffic are under the influence of alcohol.

Until recently almost three-fourths of the bicycle fatalities were younger than 15 years old. With more and more adults riding, the percent of adults killed continues to increase. Today fewer than half are under 15 years old.

When and Where to Expect Pedestrians

Drivers must learn when and where to expect pedestrians in order to avoid conflicts. Look

Actions of Pedestrians Resulting in Injuries and Death	
Actions	**Percent**
Crossing at intersections	30.5
Crossing between intersections	39.5
Walking in road with traffic	3.5
Walking in road against traffic	2.6
Standing in road	4.1
Getting on or off vehicle	1.8
Pushing or working on vehicle in road	1.1
Other working in road	0.9
Playing in road	5.4
Other in road	6.1
Not in road	4.5

Statistics from *Accident Facts*, National Safety Council

for them in these places and under these conditions:

■ **Crosswalks and Intersections** Many pedestrians assume that drivers will yield the right-of-way to anyone in the crosswalk. They don't realize that drivers approaching intersections must look for all kinds of dangers and may not notice a pedestrian in the crosswalk or one jaywalking across the intersection.

Pedestrians sometimes stand in the street instead of on the curb. They may dash across the street without warning. Even when a driver can stop in time, the driver behind may not be able to do so.

A hazardous situation may develop when a driver approaches an intersection in a clear right lane as the light turns green. If cars in the center lane have not yet started moving, they may hide a pedestrian who is making a last-minute dash for the curb.

Always reduce speed as you drive past a line of standing cars.

■ **Turning Corners** At intersections with traffic signals, the green light allows the pedestrian to cross. However, it also allows cars to make right and left turns that cross the pedestrian's path. Drivers turning at intersections may be forced to stop suddenly for pedestrians. Be sure to yield the right-of-way to pedestrians in this situation. Frequently, they fail to look for turning cars.

■ **Coming out of an Alley or Driveway** Drivers leaving an alley or driveway must stop before crossing the sidewalk and yield the right-of-way to pedestrians. They must stop again before entering the street.

In many places, buildings obstruct the view of drivers coming out of an alley or driveway. A gentle tap of the horn warns pedestrians that you are about to cross the sidewalk.

Watch for pedestrians in any approach to a street where a full stop is required.

■ **School Buses and Other Buses** Most states require traffic going *both* ways on two-way streets to stop when a school bus with its red lights flashing stops to load or unload passengers. In most states, if the roadway is divided by a median strip, the vehicles approaching the bus on the other side of the median need not stop.

After stopping, you may not go ahead until the lights on the bus stop flashing and the STOP sign is withdrawn.

Look for pedestrians whenever any kind of bus stops. People getting off may run across the street. Others may rush to catch the bus. Approach any stopped bus slowly and be ready to stop.

Decision-Making Skills To guard against the sudden appearance of pedestrians and cyclists, drivers must pay close attention to their driving. They must also use the following additional techniques:

■ **Seeing Habits** The "big picture" extends beyond the curb to the sidewalk and even into front yards. Cars parked at the curb may hide children playing nearby.

■ **Car Placement** The possibility that the door of a parked car will open presents a continuing hazard to drivers. By not driving close to parked cars, a driver can reduce this hazard.

■ **Communication** Don't assume that pedestrians and cyclists are aware of your car. An early tap on the horn and eye contact with them provides greater assurance that you will not surprise them.

■ **Speed Control** Speed and stopping distances are so closely related that choosing the correct speed is an important factor in protecting pedestrians and cyclists. To determine a safe speed, take into account the visibility, traction, and placement of your car. Covering the brake reduces stopping distances in case you must stop.

Traffic from both directions must stop when a school bus stops to load or unload passengers.

Protecting the Bicyclist   A bicyclist may get in a driver's way without thinking about the difference in the speed between cars and bicycles. Also, riders can maneuver their bicycles so quickly they may surprise a driver.

Drivers must be especially alert for bike riders who

- ride into a car's path from driveways and intersections.
- ride on the left side of the street against traffic.
- run STOP signs and traffic signals at intersections.
- ride at night without lights and proper reflectors.
- turn without signaling or without any obvious regard for oncoming traffic.

Drivers can use the following techniques to protect these unalert bike riders:

1. Check the position and stability of the rider.
2. Reduce the car's speed if necessary.
3. Check oncoming traffic, traffic behind, and the passing path around the bike.
4. Pass carefully when a safe opportunity arises.
5. Make it easy for other drivers to see the bicycle and to adjust.
6. Avoid startling the rider by gently tapping the horn well in advance when overtaking cyclists who might be unaware of your presence.
7. Be sure to signal your intention to turn when you are in front of a cyclist.
8. Watch for cyclists when opening the street-side door. Also watch for them when stopping a few feet away from the curb and opening the curb-side door.

PEDESTRIAN'S RESPONSIBILITY

Emphasizing the driver's responsibility to avoid hitting pedestrians may lead pedestrians to neglect their own responsibilities to stay out of the way of moving vehicles.

Pedestrian Right-of-Way Pedestrians must yield the right-of-way to vehicles *between* intersections and must cross in the crosswalk on green or with WALK signals. If the signal changes while pedestrians are crossing, drivers must allow them to complete the crossing.

The Driver as Pedestrian The moment a driver steps out of a car, he or she becomes a pedestrian. The driver should remember that he or she no longer has the car's protective shield.

A driver is much safer getting in and out of a car on the curb side. If you must get out on the street side, follow these steps:

1. Check the inside and outside mirrors.
2. Look over your shoulder out the left side windows to check traffic. Near a corner, also watch for turning cars.
3. If no cars or cyclists are coming, open the door, but keep watching for cars.
4. Get out, close the door, and move quickly to the curb. Go around to the rear of your car, so you will be facing traffic.

Take care also if you enter a car on the street side.

1. Check traffic.
2. Have your key ready and quickly walk around the front of your car, facing traffic.
3. Get in and close the door. Don't stay in the street any longer than you must. Your presence there endangers other drivers as well as yourself.

BICYCLIST'S RESPONSIBILITY

Many of the difficulties bicyclists encounter in today's traffic could be reduced if everyone accepted the bicycle as a vehicle. Most states require bike riders to follow traffic laws. Drivers and bike riders use the same roadways except for expressways. Tragic conflicts are less likely to occur when each behaves in a manner that the other expects.

Causes of Bicycle-Car Collisions By far, the most common type of bicycle collision involves a motor vehicle. The bicyclist is at fault in about 75 percent of these collisions. Obviously, the tremendous difference in weight, speed, and visibility between car and bicycle places the bike rider at a major disadvantage in any conflict.

The following important factors contribute to bicycle collisions with motor vehicles:

- Inexperience and lack of skill among youthful cyclists.
- Disregard for the rules of the road.
- Unsafe or defiant attitudes by cyclists, especially by boys of junior high school age, toward the driver.
- Drivers' difficulty in seeing cyclists, even during daylight hours, but especially at night.
- Pavement hazards, such as oil slicks, loose gravel, ice, potholes, railroad tracks, water, and gratings.

Recommendations by safety groups for the protection of bicyclists include increased bicycle safety programs in elementary and junior high schools, increased police enforcement of bicycle riding violations, and greater motorist awareness of bike riders.

Safety Accessories for Bicyclists The small size and quiet movement of the bicycle make it less noticeable in traffic. Bicyclists can avoid many conflicts with motor vehicles by making themselves and their bikes more visible to other road users. Flags attached to the bicycle attract attention. So do reflectors on the front and back frame, on the wheels, and on the pedals. If riders wear light-colored clothing, their chances of being seen during day or night are improved. When riding at night, use bicycle lights.

Walk your bicycle across busy intersections.

Bicylists must ride in single file.

Vocabulary

bike flag,171

bike reflector,171

covering the brake,159

jaywalking,167

riding the brakes,159

stale green light,160

Summary

1. In the city, a driver encounters a great variety of road users, signs, signals, and pavement markings on congested streets that require numerous decisions and many controlled actions to avoid conflicts.
2. By slowing down when approaching complex situations, a driver has more time to react, can reduce stopping distances, and is able to steer the car less sharply.
3. A driver should look ahead one block or more. This makes it easier to check the traffic signal ahead and determine how to deal with it.
4. Cars parked at the curb present the threat of a door opening, a car pulling out, or a pedestrian darting out between the cars. Stay at least a car door's width away from parked cars.
5. Generally, the right lane is best in city traffic on two-way streets unless the driver is preparing to turn left or where left-turn lanes are provided. Proper position in a lane reduces possible conflicts with other road users.
6. One-way streets can be identified by signs on both sides of the street facing the driver, pavement markings, direction of moving and parked vehicles, and broken white lane lines.
7. Right turns from a one-way street are made from the right lane into the right lane; left turns are made from the left lane into the nearest left lane of traffic moving to the left.
8. Motorists should be especially alert for pedestrians and bicyclists when approaching crosswalks and intersections, turning corners, coming out of driveways and alleys, and approaching buses.
9. Proper seeing habits, car placement, communications, and speed control are techniques a driver can use to avoid pedestrians and cyclists.
10. When getting out of the car on the street side, a driver should check mirrors, look over left shoulder, get out, close the door, and move to the rear.
11. Bicyclists are involved in collisions with cars because of their lack of skill, their disregard for the rules of the road, their unsafe or defiant attitude toward motorists, their small size which makes it hard for motorists to see them, and pavement hazards.

Driving Situations

1. What clues should alert you to possible danger as you approach this line of parked cars?

2. You are approaching an intersection in the right lane just as the signal turns green, but the cars in the left lane do not move. What do you predict might be the reason? What should you do?

3. You observe a car behind the stopped bus as you approach. What should you predict might happen?

4. What is the bike rider doing wrong here? What can the driver do to protect the cyclist?

Chapter Review Questions

Basic Procedures for City Driving

1. In what three ways does a driver improve the chances for safety by slowing down when approaching complex driving situations? (158)
2. What possible hazards does a driver face when passing cars parked at the curb? (159)
3. Which lane is generally best to use when driving on a four-lane, two-way street? (160)
4. What are four precautions to foliow regarding car position in the lane in order to avoid conflicts in city traffic? (161)
5. What is meant by a stale green light? (160)
6. How should a driver approach a stale green light? (160)

Driving on One-Way Streets

7. How can a driver identify one-way streets? (164)
8. Which lane should a driver choose when driving on one-way streets? (165)
9. When turning left from a one-way street into a two-way street, from what lane should a driver begin the turn? Into what lane should the turn be completed? (165)
10. What special problems might a driver encounter on one-way streets? (165)

Protecting Pedestrians and Bicyclists

11. What age groups are involved in most pedestrian and bicyclist collisions with motor vehicles? (166)
12. What are three locations or conditions where drivers should be especially alert for pedestrians and bicyclists? (166-168)
13. What four techniques can a driver use to guard against conflicts with pedestrians and bicyclists? (168)
14. List the procedure for getting into a car on the street side. (170)
15. What are four important reasons why bicyclists are responsible for collisions with motor vehicles? (171)

Projects

1. Interview a representative of your police department to determine the number of motor-vehicle collisions (including pedestrians and bicyclists) in your city last year. Report to the class on the age groups involved and the major causes of the collisions.
2. Study a newspaper report of a pedestrian or bicyclist injury in your city. Visit the site of the collision and discuss the possible reasons for this collision.
3. Observe the actions of pedestrians and bicyclists at an elementary or junior high school just before or just after school. Report on the traffic violations and close calls that you saw. Discuss what the driver can do to prevent collisions in these circumstances.
4. Interview several elementary and junior high school teachers and principals regarding the pedestrian and bicycle safety programs in their schools. Get samples of materials used in those programs to show the class.

Chapter 10 · Test

(Write the correct answers on a separate sheet of paper.)

True-False

1. All pavement markings on properly marked one-way streets are white, broken lines. (164)
2. When you notice that the green light is about to change as you approach the intersection, you should speed up to get through before it turns red. (160)
3. In most bicycle fatalities, the bicyclist is at fault. (171)
4. Driving with the foot on the brake is a good way to avoid trouble in city traffic. (159)
5. One of the best things a bicyclist can do to avoid being hit by motor vehicles is to make the bicycle more visible in traffic. (171)
6. The main value of one-way streets is to provide more parking space on both sides of the street. (164)
7. The law in most states requires all motorists going in both directions on undivided two-way streets to stop when a school bus' red lights are flashing. (168)
8. A stale green light is one that was green when you first noticed it. (160)
9. In recent years, fatalities and injuries among adult bicyclists have been increasing. (166)
10. When road construction blocks a lane of traffic ahead, the driver in the opposite lane must yield the right-of-way. (163)

Answer the Question

11. What four decision-making skills help a driver avoid hitting pedestrians and bicyclists? (168)
12. On a four-lane, two-way city street, which generally is the best lane? (160)
13. From which lane must a left turn from a one-way street be made? (165)
14. When entering a car from the street side, from which end of the car should the driver approach? (170)
15. In addition to more time for decision-making, what advantages does a driver gain by slowing down when approaching complex traffic situations? (158)
16. In addition to signs and pavement markings, what other indication does a driver have that he or she is driving the wrong way on a one-way street? (164)
17. Under what conditions does a driver *not* have to stop when meeting a school bus with the red lights flashing? (168)
18. What three important clues warn a driver of danger from cars parked along the curb? (159)
19. Into which lane must a left turn into a one-way street be made? (164)
20. When you approach an intersection as the signal changes, what three factors determine whether you should stop or continue through? (160)

Chapter 11

Driving on the Open Highway

Objectives

1. Describe the correct actions to take in the presence of trucks, slow-moving vehicles, and animals on rural highways.
2. Describe a common cause of reduced visibility at uncontrolled rural intersections and the correct action to take.
3. Tell how hills and curves reduce visibility and how to determine a safe speed near hilltops and on blind curves.
4. Describe the basis for determining a safe speed on rural highways.
5. Tell what to look for when meeting vehicles and lines of vehicles on highways.
6. List five factors that a driver must consider in determining a safe path of travel on rural highways.
7. Describe how to learn to judge speed and distance of oncoming cars when considering a passing attempt.
8. List in order the steps for passing.
9. List four no-passing locations.
10. Describe the correct action to take when being passed.

Introduction

Wide open spaces make driving on rural highways look safer than driving in towns and cities. But the facts tell otherwise. Compare 30,200 rural deaths to 16,000 urban deaths, and the picture does not look the same. Over 60 percent of the nation's yearly traffic toll is the result of highway collisions. In some states, the figure runs over 80 percent.

Two reasons account for these high statistics:

- Higher speed.   In the country, higher speeds result in more severe injuries when crashes occur.
- Lack of emergency medical aid.   In cities, the injured can be rushed to a hospital in a matter of minutes. In the country, the same procedure could take hours. For this reason, an injury that occurs in the country is more likely to be fatal than the same injury that occurs in town.

What attempts are being made to correct this problem of increased injury and lower survival rates in rural crashes? While improvements have been made in emergency medical care, the most important task ahead is educating drivers in traffic safety.

This chapter will help you drive more safely on the highways by presenting various techniques for identifying and safely handling road and traffic hazards as well as making wise decisions when passing other vehicles.

Drivers must heed warning signs.

The sign warns of an intersection hidden by a hill.

Skid marks reveal drivers skidded to a stop from a high speed.

The Roads We Drive On

Most collisions are caused by a combination of factors. This is especially true of collisions on the highway. There are numerous places where several hazards can appear at one time. In addition, highway speeds can make a single factor more critical much sooner than at lower speeds generally found in the city.

By learning what to look for, a driver can spot hazards early and make proper adjustments before they build up to the danger point. Four major elements to remember in highway driving are:

1. Traffic controls.
2. Cars, trucks, slow-moving equipment, and animals.
3. Physical environment such as hills, curves, and intersections.
4. Your own vehicle in terms of speed, position, and timing.

TRAFFIC CONTROLS

As pointed out in Chapter 2, traffic controls help drivers respond safely to driving situations that are hard to see and evaluate. Missing a sign, signal, or pavement marking can be much more serious than just disobeying a traffic law. It can result in disaster.

The sign shown in the top picture warns of a dangerous curve. The yellow line indicates a no-passing zone.

In the middle picture, a warning sign and pavement marking warn of an intersection hidden by a hill.

The bottom picture shows skid marks that tell of last-second efforts to stop for the STOP sign.

OTHER USERS

In some parts of the country, you can drive for many miles and not see another vehicle. This could lull you into thinking the danger of a collision is not very great. However, nearly half of all rural fatalities result from collisions with another vehicle. These statistics indicate the need to watch for other vehicles and to predict that they may do unusual things in unusual places.

Trucks   Trucks take more room and time to turn corners than cars. They take longer to speed up. They slow down going uphill and speed up rapidly going downhill. If you want to pass a truck, pass the truck just as it starts downhill. If you wait until it is going very fast downhill, you would have to make a high-speed pass that might prove dangerous.

Slow-Moving Vehicles   From a distance, farm and road repair vehicles may appear to be moving at normal highway speeds. However, top speed for most of these vehicles is about 15 to 20 mph (24 to 32 km/h). Farm equipment is usually wide and may take up more than half of the roadway. A driver should slow down when nearing slow-moving vehicles and then pass with care.

Animals   Both wild and tame animals are unpredictable along roadways. You should slow down and move away from animals as you pass them because they can become frightened and jump into your path in an instant. Deer can become a major problem at night. A deer can leap quickly from a ditch into the path of a car before a driver can react.

Trucks creep uphill and speed rapidly downhill.

An orange triangle identifies a slow-moving vehicle.

A slow speed is required when animals appear in the driving environment.

The car at right is stopped but may enter the highway unexpectedly at any moment.

Slow down when approaching a blind curve, where your view is blocked.

INTERSECTIONS

Traffic at most country intersections is light compared to those in the city. However, collisions do occur there. STOP signs do not guarantee the safety of drivers on through highways. Some drivers are poor judges of speed and distance, so expect them to enter the highway ahead of you and to speed up slowly. Farm vehicles especially are not able to speed up quickly.

Crops and vegetation reduce the field of view and often hide the STOP signs on side roads that enter through highways. Farm and field driveways are also danger points. Be on the lookout for farm vehicles that might unexpectedly enter or leave the roadway.

CURVES

Curves on main highways are marked with signs as shown in the top picture on p. 178. The square "speed advisory" sign below the yellow warning sign gives the safe speed for ideal conditions only. Some drivers always feel they can take curves faster than the sign indicates. They may not be aware of the extra steering or braking effort that might be needed farther into the curve.

Always look across a curve as you enter it to judge its shape and size. At the same time *identify* oncoming cars and *predict* their speed and path. Then *decide* on your own speed and action, and *execute* that decision by setting the proper speed and placement of your car.

Braking Before a Curve Slow down *before* entering a curve. Braking can be safe in a curve only if you don't round the curve too fast. If a curve is taken too fast, both braking and steering control can be lost. The sharper the curve, the more slowly you have to go to get around it.

HILLS

To go up long steep hills, shift to a lower gear for extra power. To go down long steep hills, shift to a lower gear to control speed. Less braking will be required and thus keep the brakes from overheating. If brakes overheat and fail, shift to the lowest gear possible to slow the car down.

The steeper a hill, the shorter the sight distance near the top. As you near the top of a steep hill, reduce your speed in case an oncoming car tops the hill in your lane. There might also be a slow-moving vehicle or one that is stopped just beyond the crest of the hill. You must be prepared to stop as you top a hill. If stopping is impossible, try to swerve around the vehicle.

MOUNTAIN DRIVING

The following five rules are important for driving in the mountains:
1. Be sure that your car is in top condition.
2. If you have never driven in the mountains before, don't try to keep up with the natives who know the roads and are used to mountain driving.
3. Pull over and allow vehicles that have bunched up behind you to pass.
4. Keep your eyes on the road. Let the passengers look at the scenery.
5. Pass with extra care. Upgrades are frequently steeper than they appear to be. Altitude reduces engine performance.

Expect a sudden cross wind to hit your car as you enter and leave hilly areas.

Drive at a safe speed when driving through the mountains.

Be alert for roadside hazards.

Look out for cars leaving roadside stops.

High Altitude   At sunset, it gets dark early and quickly, as the sun seems to drop behind the mountains in which you are driving. Early morning fog, snow, and ice may appear at times.

Watch out for your engine overheating at high altitudes. Vapor lock, where the fuel line is blocked by an accumulation of vaporized bubbles, may cause uneven engine operation or stalling. If this happens, park along the road shoulder. Lift the hood and let the engine cool. Set your parking brake and put the car in PARK or REVERSE. For extra safety, block a wheel with a rock.

ROADSIDE HAZARDS

Some highways have many hazards that can kill. Yet most drivers are not always aware of roadside hazards. Over 3,500 people are killed each year in collisions involving fixed highway objects like trees, posts, and guard-rails.

Gas Stations or Roadside Stands   Remember that cars may enter and leave the highway at gas stations or roadside stands. A car in front of you may suddenly slow down to swing off the highway. Or a driver leaving a stand or station may pull out in front of you. Be on the alert.

YOUR OWN VEHICLE

The most important concern of highway drivers is to be sure that their vehicles are visible to other drivers. To be seen, turn on your headlights during times of reduced daytime visibility. A second step is to signal well in advance of turns and stops so that other drivers have ample time to react.

Speed   Many drivers overestimate how much time they gain by driving 5 or 10 mph faster. The chart below shows the times required to travel 10 miles. Notice how little time is saved by each 10-mph increase. Note how the time saved grows smaller with each increase in speed.

Speed (mph)	Minutes needed to go 10 miles	Minutes saved over last speed
40	15	
50	12	3
60	10	2
70	$8\frac{1}{2}$	$1\frac{1}{2}$
80	$7\frac{1}{2}$	1

For example, a 10-mph increase from 40 to 50 saves 3 minutes in 10 miles, but an increase from 60 to 70 saves only $1^1/_2$ minutes in 10 miles. In selecting a speed, drivers should weigh the actual time saved against the added danger and fuel consumption caused by the higher speed.

On most country trips, drivers will be unable to select one speed and stick to it. If they do, they could be taking unnecessary chances in the presence of hazards. Instead, a driver must look at all conditions on the roadway and select a safe speed for that particular moment or condition. Generally, the common speed of traffic is the safe speed.

Positioning and Placement   Positioning your car on the road is important to avoid traffic hazards. This can be done by moving away from hazards and allowing extra space between those hazards and your car. Increase your following distance to more than 3 seconds for an extra margin of safety under conditions of reduced visibility and traction, physical impairment, and distractions.

Where space is limited, let the other driver pass through first.

MEETING ON HIGHWAYS

Oncoming cars are only a few feet away when you meet them on undivided highways. Drivers should be especially alert when a swerve path is limited. If the shoulder is narrow or if the ditch is close, speed should be reduced.

Even on undivided four-lane roads, oncoming drivers are close to you and could easily be forced over the center line into your lane. It is usually safer to drive in the right lane.

Meeting Lines of Cars In almost every line of cars there will be drivers who are anxious to get ahead of the line. When they do so, they may fail to check for an oncoming car. To help them see you, turn on your headlights. Also, drive near, but not too close to, the edge of the pavement. Your car will be more visible there and protected against oncoming cars by more space.

Meeting at Hilltops At night, beams of light shining from beyond the hilltop will warn you of approaching cars. In daytime, a driver has no such clue. The closer you get to the top of a hill, the shorter the sight distance ahead will be.

When approaching a hilltop, be mentally ready for an oncoming car topping the hill in your lane. The split second gained by being properly placed could make the difference between a close call and a crash.

Meeting at Night Defensive drivers are aware that other drivers may have poor night vision. They also are aware that one in 50 drivers they meet at night is under the influence of alcohol or other drugs. When meeting at night, reduce speed, use low headlight beams, and be prepared to take evasive action.

Meeting Slow-Moving Vehicles Avoid meeting a slow-moving or standing vehicle while a car is coming up behind it. The driver could try to swerve around it into your path. If the oncoming driver should hit the slow-moving vehicle, the wreckage could be on your side of the road in an instant.

Reduce speed and keep to the right because the swerve path along this curve is small.

Safe Path of Travel

Collision-free driving is a matter of car control that results from planning ahead. In the planning phase of driving, consider traffic flow, line of sight, field of view, width of road, and traction. When any of these factors are reduced, car control becomes less certain and the possibility of a collision increases.

TRACTION

Traction on country highways can range from excellent on dry pavement to poor on rain-covered dirt roads. Mud tracked onto wet pavement from driveways or side roads can cause the unsuspecting driver to skid. Gravel can act like a floor covered with marbles when drivers try to turn or stop, as the middle picture shows. In order to maintain traction on gravel roads, a driver must reduce speed.

Experienced rural road drivers are constantly aware of the changing conditions of road surfaces and traction. These drivers are ready to adjust both speed and position when conditions require it.

WIDTH OF ROAD

The design and construction of some rural roads are better than others. The road shown in the bottom picture has many safety features. The shoulders are wide. Ditches are shallow, with gentle slopes. The end of the guardrail is buried to prevent major damage and injury to car occupants in the event of a crash.

Watch your speed on mud-tracked roads because you could skid easily.

Stopping and steering control can be lost without reduced speed on gravel roads.

Buried guardrails at the side of a highway are used for protection of road users.

The closer you get to the vehicle ahead, the less you can see ahead.

Dust cuts your visibility so that your view is blocked. Slow down and do not pass.

When your lane is blocked, yield to oncoming traffic.

FIELD OF VIEW

Not only must drivers look far ahead on highways, they must also look farther out to the sides. They must have a wide field of view to see hazards along the roadway and out to the sides at intersections. The narrower the field of view at intersections, the lower the speed must be. In the top picture, the driver is following the truck too closely, and as a result has very little view of the road shoulders ahead.

LINE OF SIGHT

The faster you go, the farther ahead you must be able to see. It would seem that in the country you should be able to see for miles, but that is not always so. Hills, curves, dust, and vegetation can reduce line of sight below a safe level. In the middle picture, an oncoming car is stirring up a cloud of dust on a gravel road. When following and meeting on dusty roads, reduce your speed until you are able to see clearly ahead.

TRAFFIC FLOW

After driving on a highway a few times, drivers may be tempted to let their guard down. They may feel that since nothing has happened, nothing will happen. Even though distances on highways are measured in miles, critical situations can be measured in a matter of seconds. Thinking ahead and being alert can pay off. Defensive drivers constantly look ahead with one thought in mind: *Will I have clear space to keep going?* If the answer is no, you do not have a safe path of travel.

Being Passed and Passing

Overtaking and passing on a two-lane highway is the most dangerous of all car maneuvers. A driver needs to learn all about safe passing before doing it successfully.

PASSING ON A TWO-LANE HIGHWAY

A driver must use good judgment when looking for a safe place to pass. Before deciding to pass, a driver must be able to answer "yes" to the following questions: Is it legal? Is it safe? Is it worthwhile?

RESPONSIBILITY IN PASSING

The law places the responsibility on the driver of the *passing* car. If the driver makes mistakes in passing, that driver is subject to arrest.

BEING PASSED

There is a possibility for error in any passing attempt. The safety of both drivers depends on cooperation.

A driver should remember three important ideas when being passed:

1. It is illegal to speed up when being passed. Continue at the same speed, or reduce your speed slightly.
2. Help other drivers to pass safely. Move to the right side of your lane to give the other driver more room and a better view ahead.
3. Show the passing driver the same courtesy and cooperation that you would expect from other drivers when you are passing.

Imagine yourself driving the yellow car in the pictures on this page. The passing driver misjudged the speed and distance of the oncoming car and is running out of space. In the left picture, the passing driver is speeding up. When this happens, apply your brakes so that the passing driver can get into your lane in front of you.

In the right picture, the passing driver is braking. In this case, the correct action is to speed up so that the passing driver can fall in behind you.

If the passing driver speeds up, brake to let that driver pass.

If the passing driver brakes, speed up to let that driver fall in behind you.

YOUR PASSING POTENTIAL

A typical passing maneuver requires about 10 to 12 seconds. Inexperienced drivers usually take longer. Passing times also vary from car to car, due to engine size, mechanical condition, and vehicle load.

IDENTIFY PASSING SITUATIONS

- Identify a clear safe distance ahead in the passing lane. This distance must be long enough to let you complete the pass easily. Can anything shorten it unexpectedly (such as a car from a side road ahead on the left)?
- If there is an oncoming car, be sure it is far enough away. Be sure it cannot reach a spot close to the far end of your safe-passing zone. Allow yourself a good margin of safety.
- Identify your end-of-pass gap where you will pull back into your own lane after you pass.
- Have a safe response ready for anything that might happen to make your pass difficult.

Traction   Check the traction of the road surface. When traction is poor, a longer distance is needed to pass safely. Under poor traction conditions, avoid accelerating quickly while steering. Accelerating will have to be done at a slower rate because of the danger of spinning the wheels or skidding.

10 STEPS FOR SUCCESSFUL PASSING

1. Check for safe, legal passing space ahead. Stay far enough behind the car to be passed so you can pick up speed quickly.
2. Check both mirrors.
3. Signal for a lane change to the left.
4. Recheck path ahead, sound horn, and/or flash headlights to warn driver ahead.
5. Check blind spot over left shoulder. Speed up. Ease out into passing lane. Try to attain 15-mph speed advantage.
6. Recheck conditions ahead. If space looks too short, brake and drop back.
7. Stay in left lane until both headlights of passed car can be seen in your inside mirror.
8. Give right-turn signal for returning to the right lane. Check inside mirror again and blind spot over right shoulder.
9. Return to the right lane.
10. Turn off signal. Check speedometer. Create space for car just passed.

First, stay back where you can see well. When clear, move into the left lane to pass which gives you more visibility. In third picture, you could pull back if anything threatened ahead. In last, return to right when passed car is in mirror.

WHEN NOT TO PASS

Some places where passing is illegal or unwise are clearly marked. However, many other places are unmarked. In the following situations passing would be dangerous:

- When there is a long line of cars ahead.
- When you intend to turn or stop very soon.
- When an oncoming car is too close.
- When the car ahead is going at or near the speed limit. Speed limits still apply when passing.
- When sight distance ahead is limited.

- When the maneuver would have to be completed in a no-passing zone such as a hill, curve, or intersection.

IDENTIFY NO-PASSING SITUATIONS

Most no-passing zones are marked by signs or by solid yellow lines in your lane. A solid yellow line or double solid yellow lines indicate no passing. All passing maneuvers must be completed before reaching the beginning of the solid yellow line on your side of the center line. Passing is illegal in the following situations:

Be prepared for drivers who take chances.

- **No passing going up a hill** Passing is not allowed for 700 to 1,000 feet from the top of a hill. You cannot see oncoming cars on the other side of the hill.

■ **No passing on blind curves**   On a blind curve you would not be able to see oncoming cars. Always stay in your own lane on any curve, out of the way of oncoming traffic.

■ **No passing at intersections or railroad crossings**   It is generally illegal to pass within 100 feet of an intersection or railroad crossing, where other vehicles or pedestrians may suddenly appear. Passing calls for increased speed; approaching an intersection calls for reduced speed.

■ **No passing near a bridge or abutment**   Do not pass within 100 feet of a bridge or abutment that blocks a driver's view. Also, a bridge or underpass may cut off a road shoulder. You or the car you passed might need to use the shoulder in case some emergency arose.

Never cross a solid line on your side of the road or double solid lines. Don't try to pass just before reaching a no-passing zone.

Vocabulary

abutment, 191   overtaking, 187
evasive action, 184 sight distance, 181

Summary

1. Trucks, slow-moving vehicles, and animals present problems that a driver must react to by adjusting speed and space.
2. Reduced visibility at some rural intersections due to high speed or crops and vegetation pose special problems that a driver can only resolve by greatly reduced speed and increased attention.
3. Curves and hills can reduce visibility. The less visibility a driver has, the lower the car's speed must be. Speed is determined by steepness of a hill and sharpness of a curve.
4. The correct speed on rural highways depends on conditions and adjusting speed to those conditions.
5. When meeting other vehicles on rural highways, safety depends on being seen, being aware of swerve path, and keeping to the right side of the road.
6. A safe path of travel can be determined by considering traction, width of the road, field of view, line of sight, and possible changes in the traffic flow.
7. A driver can learn to judge speed and distance of oncoming cars before passing by timing oncoming cars. The oncoming car should be far enough away in the distance before a passing attempt is considered.
8. A safe passing procedure includes selection of a safe passing location, consideration of oncoming vehicles, signaling to driver ahead and behind, proper lane change procedure, and adequate acceleration.
9. Passing should not be attempted going up a hill, on a blind curve, approaching an intersection or railroad crossing, or at other locations where visibility and space are reduced and where other vehicles might interfere with a safe maneuver.
10. The driver being passed must cooperate with the passing driver, moving over to the right side of the lane, and allowing the passing driver to complete the pass.

Driving Situations

1. You are driving on a paved road, planning to turn right onto a gravel road. What special problem in car control can you anticipate? What possible traffic hazards might develop?

2. You are approaching a blind curve where your view of the road ahead is blocked. What should you be alert for in this situation?

3. You are driving the yellow car on a highway. You and the oncoming truck are going to meet on the bridge. The wide truck takes up part of your lane. What should you do?

4. You are driving the yellow car, passing another car. As you draw even, the car being passed speeds up. What should you do?

Chapter Review Questions

The Roads We Drive On

1. What characteristics of trucks, slow-moving vehicles, and animals can make them a hazard on highways? (179)
2. What action should be taken when following trucks, approaching slow-moving vehicles, or animals on the highway? (179)
3. What can reduce visibility at rural intersections? What action should be taken under those conditions? (180)
4. Describe the relationship between speed and the sharpness of blind curves and the steepness of hills. (180)
5. Why should you slow down *before* entering a curve? (180)
6. How are speed choice and a safe path of travel related? (183)
7. What is the danger of meeting lines of cars on highways? What should you do? (184)

Safe Path of Travel

8. What are the five factors that must be considered in determining a safe path of travel on highways? (185)

Being Passed and Passing

9. What three questions must be answered before a driver decides to pass? (187)
10. List in correct order the steps required to pass safely. (188)
11. Name four no-passing situations. (190)
12. What should you do when you are being passed? (187)

Projects

1. Find out the number of passing accidents, injuries, and fatalities in your state last year. What percent of all accidents is caused by improper passing?
2. Next time you ride with someone who passes on a highway, count the number of seconds it takes for that driver to complete the passing maneuver.
3. Identify hazardous rural situations where danger might be reduced by means of signs or engineering improvements. Report results to county and state officials.
4. Check with tractor dealers and highway commission to cite actual speeds of farm and road equipment.
5. Set two objects 165 feet apart along a rural highway. With a stop watch, determine the percent of drivers who are covering that distance in less than 2 seconds and exceeding the 55 mph (88 km/h) speed limit. Report results to the class.
6. Write your state department of motor vehicles for a state-wide accident summary. Contact your local highway patrol office or sheriff's office for a summary of local rural accident statistics. Compare the two reports for causes of collisions, age groups involved, and proportion of fatalities to collisions.

Chapter 11 · Test

(Write the correct answers on a separate sheet of paper.)

True-False

1. The best time to pass a truck is about halfway down a hill. (179)
2. Farm crops and vegetation can reduce visibility to a dangerous level at rural intersections. (180)
3. The closer you get to the top of a hill, the farther you can see. (184)
4. The speed limit may not always be a safe speed on highways. (183)
5. Collision-free driving is mostly a matter of luck. (185)
6. Double solid yellow lines indicate no passing. (190)
7. Passing is legal at intersections on two-lane highways if speed is reduced. (191)
8. Most rural highways are free of hazards. (178)
9. You should reduce speed when driving past animals. (179)
10. You must slow down *before* entering a curve. (180)
11. If you are not used to mountain driving, try to keep up with a local driver. (181)
12. Turn on your headlights in daytime to help oncoming drivers see you when visibility is reduced. (184)
13. A solid yellow line in your lane means no passing. (190)
14. The law places the legal responsibility of passing with the passing driver. (187)
15. It is illegal to speed up when being passed. (187)

Answer the Question

16. What color lines indicate a no-passing zone? (190)
17. How many minutes can be saved on a 10-mile trip by driving 60 mph instead of 50 mph? (183)
18. What should you do when a driver passing you runs short of space in the other lane and brakes hard? (187)
19. What road factor determines your stopping ability in a safe path of travel? (185)
20. What is the best action to take when meeting or passing a slow-moving vehicle? (179)

Chapter 12

Driving on Expressways

Objectives

1. List five reasons why expressways have a lower collision rate than other roads.
2. Describe the importance of planning ahead in expressway driving, including the significance of reading signs.
3. Explain how to use the three basic parts of an expressway entrance area.
4. Describe the procedure for entering a crowded expressway.
5. Describe the importance of blending into traffic on an expressway.
6. Explain how the IPDE process is applied to expressway driving.
7. Explain why maximum and minimum expressway speed limits are important.
8. Explain why a space cushion and proper following distance is especially important in expressway driving.
9. Define "velocitation" and "highway hypnosis" and tell what can be done to combat them.
10. Describe the procedure to follow in case of a mechanical breakdown on an expressway.
11. Describe the correct procedure for leaving an expressway.

Introduction

Expressway driving has become one of the most common ways to travel. Interstate highways, freeways, and toll roads are all types of expressways. Controlled access and one-way traffic are characteristics that make expressways different from other roads.

Expressway driving can be more demanding because of higher driving speeds. For this reason, some new drivers are reluctant to use expressways. But once they learn the special skills needed to drive on them, drivers find expressways can be comfortable, convenient, and safe. The fatal collision rate on expressways is about half that of non-expressway roads.

Five main reasons why expressways have a lower collision rate are

1. Cross traffic is eliminated.
2. Expressways have a median or dividing strip or fence between opposing lanes of traffic.
3. Pedestrians, animals, and slow-moving vehicles are not permitted on most expressways.
4. Expressways are designed to help protect vehicles from hitting fixed objects.
5. Expressways are designed to help a driver anticipate conditions ahead.

This chapter will show how a driver can apply the IPDE process on expressways by:

- Identifying hazards well in advance.
- Predicting actions of other drivers.
- Deciding how to use extra distance to maintain an adequate "space cushion."
- Executing smooth driver responses to blend into traffic.

Preparing to Drive on Expressways

Before any expressway travel is undertaken, two steps must be taken. The driver must plan the trip carefully, and have the car checked.

DRIVER PREPAREDNESS

The driver should have a travel plan before getting onto an expressway. On short trips, the driver should know the name, route, or number for both the entrance and the exit to be used. On long trips, plans for food, rest, and fuel stops should also be made. Once on the expressway, a driver does not have time to think about trip planning details. Full attention must be given to driving. Planning ahead can also save time and prevent mistakes.

PREPARING THE CAR

A check of the vehicle should be made before a long trip. Long hours of expressway driving can put a strain on all parts of a car. Driving for long periods of time can build up heat, which is hard on the oil supply, fan belt, cooling system, and tires. If the car cannot perform well for extended periods at speeds above 45 mph (72 km/h), it should not be used for expressway travel.

More than half of all expressway emergency service calls are for gas, oil, or water. At higher speeds all vehicles use much more gasoline. To avoid unwanted trouble, a driver should check the gas gauge frequently and fill up by the time the gauge reads one-fourth full.

Before driving at expressway speeds for extended periods of time, you should inflate all tires to their maximum recommended pressure. This extra air will help keep tires from overheating. Low tire pressure and heat are the major causes of tire failure. Extra air will also improve the way the car handles.

Entering an Expressway

When approaching an expressway, a driver must be alert to find the proper entrance. Usually the entrance will be marked with a large rectangular green sign that indicates directions leading to the correct entrance lane.

It is necessary to know in which direction you wish to travel and a prominent city in that direction which may be marked on the sign. Once you enter an expressway in the wrong direction, it may be many miles before you can get off to head back.

Basically, all expressway entrances have three parts. Part one is the *entrance ramp.* This roadway is designed to give the driver time to ''size-up'' traffic and to get set for merging onto the expressway. Part two is the *acceleration lane.* This lane is long enough so that a driver can accelerate to the speed of traffic. Part three is the *merging area.* Here, the driver should enter at about the same speed as cars in the outside lane.

Expressway entrances are built so a driver can blend into the flow of traffic. A driver should accelerate to expressway speed when traffic permits.

PROCEDURE FOR ENTERING AN EXPRESSWAY

To enter an expressway, a driver should follow this procedure:

1. Make sure the ramp being used is an entrance. The driver who enters an exit ramp could meet high-speed traffic head-on. This mistake has been made so many times, usually by drinking drivers, that most states have put up signs saying, WRONG WAY, DO NOT ENTER.

2. Before driving onto an expressway entrance ramp, make sure the ramp is the correct one. If you should make a mistake by entering the wrong entrance ramp, drive on to the next exit and turn around. *Do not back up* on an entrance ramp.

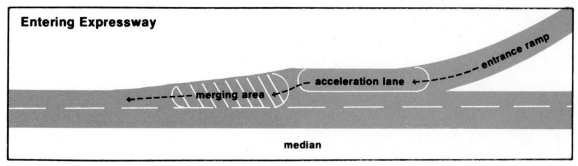

Entering Expressway

entrance ramp

acceleration lane ←

merging area ←

median

3. Once on the entrance ramp, be alert for vehicles in front, to the rear, and for traffic already on the expressway. Begin taking quick glances over your shoulder for a gap in traffic. The gap should be large enough so that a car can fit into it without crowding anyone. Before reaching the acceleration lane, turn on the correct turn signal and keep checking for a gap.

4. On the acceleration lane, accelerate enough to merge smoothly at the end of the acceleration lane. Accelerate and at the same time keep track of the gap in traffic through the rearview mirrors and with quick glances over the shoulder.

5. By the time you get to the end of the acceleration lane where the merge area begins, the gap in traffic should be near. If you have accelerated to the speed of approaching traffic, all you need do is make a simple lane change into the flow of traffic.

6. Once in traffic, cancel the turn signal and adjust to the speed of traffic. Establish a good following distance and maintain proper distance from vehicles to the sides and rear.

The driver of the red van keeps checking for a gap to enter. When a gap is available, the driver blends into the flow of traffic.

POSSIBLE ENTRANCE PROBLEMS

Heavy traffic, short entrance ramps and acceleration lanes, and mistakes by other drivers can cause merging problems.

In heavy traffic, gaps are more difficult to find. In tight situations, a driver must make an important decision early. If there is no gap, the driver must slow or stop before getting onto the acceleration lane. If the driver must slow or stop, traffic to the rear should be warned by flashing the brake lights. When the driver does spot a gap, rapid acceleration will be needed to enter the flow of traffic.

The vehicle ahead on the entrance ramp can also present a problem. When following a driver who does not seem sure about joining traffic, slow down and open up more space ahead. Give the other driver time to find a gap. Make sure the other driver is going to merge before you accelerate.

It is important to adjust to all traffic. This means being aware of others ahead, behind, and in the outside lane. Timed signal lights have been installed at some entrance ramps to help space out entering traffic. These lights go from red to green to red according to the condition of traffic on the expressway.

Car waiting until light turns green to enter the expressway.

Beware of sudden stops ahead. Entering acceleration lane, driver of car B sees A ahead waiting for a gap. A suddenly begins to move. The driver of car B looks back to see how through-traffic is doing, then steps on the gas hard. Suddenly, the driver of car A decides there is not enough room and stops. Car B, if not alert, can hit A.

Cruising on the Expressway

Once on an expressway, a driver must stay alert and adjust to the changing traffic scene. To do this, several driving skills are needed.

USING IPDE ON EXPRESSWAYS

Drivers use the same basic IPDE process that is used in other types of driving. However, some new abilities are needed.

Identify   Though expressways are engineered to give a driver good sight distance, receiving visual information may be more difficult in some situations. Multiple lanes increase the amount of information to be gathered. Large trucks can block a driver's view. Higher speeds will increase the distance a driver needs to look ahead in order to identify and predict possible trouble. At 55 mph (88 km/h) a driver needs to be looking about 1,000 feet (almost a fifth of a mile) down the road.

Predict   A predictable traffic flow is one of the safety features of an expressway. But drivers should always be on the lookout for the car that is stopped or even backing up. At a distance, a car that is backing up may even look as if it is still moving forward.

Whenever traffic slows ahead, a driver can predict some "near misses" will happen as other drivers try to avoid hazards. When this happens at high speed, all surrounding drivers have to brake suddenly or swerve. "Near misses" are the reasons a driver should stay away from groups of cars. By doing so, a driver can avoid having to make sudden moves.

Decide   Expressway speeds magnify a driver's indecision. Any change or last-second decision can put a driver's car unexpectedly in the way of high-speed traffic.

Interchanges are high-collision areas on expressways since many driver decisions are made there. The main thing a driver should remember is to think ahead and avoid last-second decisions. If an error is made and you miss an exit, drive to the next exit and get off.

Maintaining safe distances at increased speed is another problem. If a driver wants to go around a hazard, the decision must be made early. Drivers must remember that stopping distances are much longer at expressway speeds. At 55 mph it takes 211 feet, or over half a block, to stop under ideal conditions.

Execute   Avoid surprising other drivers by making sudden moves. Signal early, and have the car in the correct lane before executing any major maneuver.

SIGNS AND ROADWAY MARKINGS

Signs and roadway markings provide drivers with information they need. By reading these signs and markings and by thinking ahead, drivers can avoid sudden last-second decisions.

Expressway signs help avoid confusion. On many expressways, an exit area may look like the through-traffic lane. To avoid making this mistake, drivers who want to continue straight ahead should follow the signs for their specific routes.

Sometimes several overhead signs will be posted above the roadway at the same place.

At night it is especially important to watch for and obey expressway signs. Lower your speed and double the interval between you and the car ahead.

One sign may say EXIT here, another may tell of the NEXT EXIT, and another might say THROUGH-TRAFFIC. Drivers need to be alert for all expressway signs.

Most expressways have good roadway markings. At interchanges, no-driving zones may be marked off to channel the flow of traffic. On an open stretch of expressway, the edge of the roadway pavement may be marked with a white line on the right and a yellow line on the left. These lines help drivers position their vehicles. Lines at the edge of the roadway are especially helpful at night or in fog.

SPEED LIMITS

Posted speed limits on expressways are generally higher than on other roads. Since the energy crisis of 1973, maximum speeds have been limited to 55 mph (88 km/h) in all states. Under good conditions, most vehicles travel at the speed limit. Trucks may have a 5-mph lower speed limit and may be required to use only the right-hand lanes.

Because driving slowly is very dangerous where other cars are going fast, *minimum* speed limits are posted to help maintain a common speed. Legal speed is seldom below 40 mph (64 km/h) unless driving conditions are bad. Then, *everyone* must slow down.

DRIVE AT THE COMMON SPEED

Driving at the common speed (the speed used by most drivers) is part of blending with traffic. Differences in speed are often the cause of collisions. Driving too slowly can block the flow of traffic. A fast driver may crash into a slow driver or into the cars that jam up behind the slow one. Slow drivers also force others to change lanes, sometimes without warning. This action endangers everyone. A driver who wants to drive below the minimum expressway speed should travel on a different type of road.

Driving faster than most cars means the driver must pass more often. Needless passing sets up dangers and conflicts. To get the most good from the design of an expressway, drivers should travel at the common speed.

LEAVE ENOUGH FOLLOWING DISTANCE

One of the greatest causes of expressway crashes under all conditions is following too close. Rear-end collisions account for the largest percentage of expressway "through-lane" and exit-ramp crashes.

The only dependable protection a driver has is the space cushion ahead of the car. Apply the 2-second following distance rule. If a car cuts into the space ahead of a driver's car, re-establish a good following distance again by slowing down a little. Usually a driver can blend into traffic and adjust to an adequate following distance just by traveling 1 or 2 mph slower than other vehicles.

A following distance of more than 2 seconds is especially important in the following situations:

Overhead arrows tell which lanes to use. On a crowded expressway such as this, allow yourself plenty of space ahead.

- When following a big truck or bus which blocks your vision.
- When driving in bad weather.
- When driving in heavy traffic.
- When being tailgated.
- When driving a heavy vehicle or pulling a trailer.
- When operating a motorcycle.
- When exiting an expressway.

In these situations, a good following distance is the best way to prevent a collision.

DRIVE TO THE RIGHT

Most expressway driving is done in the right or center lane. By keeping to the right, a driver can help the flow of high-speed traffic. In general, a driver should expect traffic in the left lane to be moving about 5 mph faster. During rush-hour traffic when many cars are entering the expressway, a driver may want to avoid using the far right-hand lane.

LANE CHANGES

Lane changes are the most common expressway maneuver. They also are responsible for side-swipe collisions that occur.

Avoid changing lanes unless there is a need for a better position in traffic. Any change from the regular pattern of traffic can set up conflicts. Unnecessary weaving from one lane to another causes numerous crossing of paths that can lead to collisions.

Change lanes one at a time. Make it a habit to signal *every* lane change, regardless of whether other vehicles are present. But do not expect turn signals to clear the way. They only alert other drivers of the intent to move over. Check traffic in the rearview mirrors. Make a quick head check before moving for assurance that no one is in the blind spot to the right or left rear.

Avoid slowing down during the lane change procedure. Speed up a little when moving to the new lane to stay out of the way of any driver behind in that lane. When you have changed lanes, cancel the turn signal.

Expressway lane changing can be a little more complicated when there are three or more lanes moving in the same direction. Many times a problem occurs when two drivers head for the same space, or gap, at the same time. A quick head check should alert each driver of the problem.

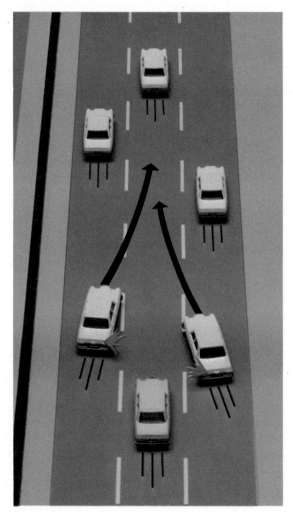

Make a head check for other drivers who may be heading for your gap.

PASSING

When passing another car on an expressway, all a driver needs to do is to follow the procedure for making a lane change to the left. Drive past the car, then repeat the procedure for making a lane change to the right when returning to the original lane.

In all expressway driving, two things should be automatic when making a lane change, passing another vehicle, or entering or exiting an expressway:

- Use turn signals.
- Check traffic to the rear and side with one or more quick glances over the shoulder.

There is one other thing to remember about lane changing and passing. Blending with traffic is just as important in passing as in getting on or off an expressway.

MINIMIZE, SEPARATE, AND COMPROMISE

How can drivers use basic decision-making skills over and above the regular skills needed for expressway driving? The secret is to apply the strategy of minimize, separate, and compromise whenever possible (see Chapter 5).

Drivers can use distance to minimize a hazard in situations where traffic is entering the expressway. If drivers are in the right-hand lane as a car begins to enter, a decision to change speed and/or position could be correct. They can minimize the threat of the entering car by slowing to open up a gap in front. Or a gap could be opened up behind the car by speeding up a bit. Or the drivers could change lanes to the left if the way were clear. The main thing to remember is to make a decision early enough to minimize the conflict so the other driver has a chance to blend with traffic.

Many times drivers can lower the risk in a situation by deciding to let hazards separate. Often on expressways, cars and trucks are bunched up while moving at high speeds. By slowing a little, drivers can usually allow cars and trucks to spread out, or separate. Then the drivers can move by and still have an "out" if something goes wrong.

Wolf Packs   Experienced drivers avoid groups or "wolf packs" of cars. By being a loner on the expressway, a driver reduces the chances of being involved in a conflict. With a little effort, most drivers can avoid driving into tight situations where difficult compromise decisions have to be made. A driver in the middle of a "wolf pack" is more likely to encounter trouble with a lane changer or speeder.

When forced to make a tough compromise decision on expressways, drivers should always try to use speed and distance to their advantage. If tailgated, a little extra distance to the front until the tailgater passes may be helpful. If forced into a tight situation with traffic on the left and right, small adjustments in lane positioning are necessary.

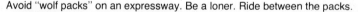

Avoid "wolf packs" on an expressway. Be a loner. Ride between the packs.

SPECIAL EXPRESSWAY PROBLEMS

Most expressway driving is easy on the driver because conditions are controlled. But there are a number of special problems a driver needs to be alert for so that trouble can be avoided.

To avoid fatigue, pull off the road and stop for a rest or refreshment.

Velocitation   Hours of driving may fool the driver into thinking the car is going slower than it really is. The driver who is "velocitized" may unconsciously go too fast. This condition can be especially hazardous if a driver is exiting an expressway. To avoid this condition, a driver should keep a close check on the speedometer and allow a little time to readjust to lower speeds.

Highway Hypnosis   Since expressways are designed to make driving easy, keeping alert may become a problem. Mile after mile at a steady speed with few hills, curves, or intersections can lull the driver into a passive state. Some drivers have actually gone to sleep at the wheel because of this. Other drivers may sit back in a sub-alert state and become a spectator instead of a driver.

At the first sign of drowsiness, a driver should do something different. Sitting up straighter, loosening a tight collar, opening a window, or changing a radio program can help. Stop at the next service or rest area for coffee and a short walk. If this rest stop does not help, find a safe place to sleep.

To help avoid highway hypnosis and fatigue before they become a problem, a driver can take these steps to stay alert:

- Avoid eating heavy meals.
- Wear comfortable clothes.
- Sing, or talk with passengers.
- Avoid driving long periods.
- Glance at the passing scenery once in a while.
- Keep shifting eyes down the road.
- Check rearview mirrors regularly.
- Maintain constant interest in traffic signs, signals, pavement markings, and the changing traffic conditions.

Toll Booths Toll booths can also create some special problems. Last-second lane changes and quick stops are common occurrences before reaching toll booths. Rough "rumble strip" pavement has been put in the approach lanes to many toll booths to help drivers avoid collisions.

When approaching a toll area, watch for signs that tell where automatic change collecting machines are. Drivers need exact change for these machines. If exact change is not available, the driver must head as early as possible for a booth with a toll collector.

Disabled Car Meeting a car stopped on the expressway is one of the most dangerous experiences a driver can have. The instant a disabled car is identified, the driver should start checking to see if a lane change can be made. If not, the driver should slow and warn others to the rear by flashing brake lights. If a complete stop must be made before getting around the trouble spot, stop well in advance. When you can safely pass, it will be easier to accelerate into the next lane.

At the first hint of trouble in your own car, signal and get off the road to the right, if possible. Once off the road, have all passengers get out of the car and stand away from the road and car. Turn on the four-way emergency flasher lights. At night, the dome light may help draw attention to the car. As soon as possible, raise the hood, tie a white cloth to the antenna or door handle, and set out emergency flares, if available. If flares are used, they should be set at least 500 feet (170 paces) behind the disabled car to warn others that the car is there. The more advance notice others have, the less chance there will be for trouble.

Exiting an Expressway

Leaving an expressway can be a smooth operation if the driver knows in advance what exit to take. Signs indicate which lane to move into. Most expressway exits provide an extra lane, called a *deceleration lane,* in which to pull out of the flow of traffic and slow down without blocking vehicles behind. An exit ramp then helps a driver get ready to join traffic off the expressway.

SIMPLE EXPRESSWAY EXITING

The following steps are taken in exiting from an expressway:

1. About one half mile before the exit, signal and move into the lane that leads to the deceleration lane. At the exit area, move into the deceleration lane. Don't slow down until the car is out of the traffic flow.
2. As soon as the car is in the deceleration lane, cancel the turn signal and begin to brake. Slow down gradually to keep a space cushion to the front and rear.
3. When you see the exit-ramp speed sign, adjust to that speed.

   When entering traffic, be on guard against the feeling of security developed while driving on the expressway. Two-way traffic, pedestrians, intersections, and the need for lower speeds must be anticipated.

COMPLEX EXPRESSWAY EXITING

Exiting can be more difficult as a result of other drivers' mistakes, poor road design, and heavy traffic.

High-Speed Exiting   Exiting an expressway at too high a speed is one of the most common causes of expressway collisions. Every driver should reduce speed as soon as the exit speed sign is identified.

Last-Second Decisions   Deciding to exit at the last second is another serious driver error. By making an unexpected move for an exit, a driver can cause a dangerous situation to develop.

Backing   A third serious driver error is backing up on an expressway or in an exit area. This action is prohibited because of the high risk involved. Nevertheless, every driver should be alert for the possibility of a driver actually backing up from an exit ramp.

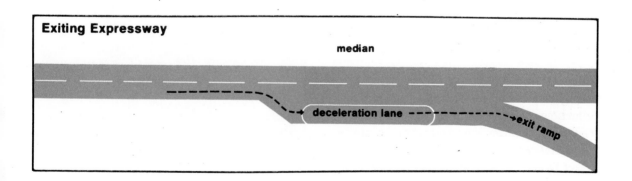

Exiting Expressway

median

deceleration lane

exit ramp

If same lane is used for acceleration and deceleration lanes, watch for crossing traffic.

Crossing Paths On some expressways, the same lane is used for an entrance and an exit. This means one driver will want to accelerate to enter the expressway while another will want to decelerate to leave the expressway at the same time in the same lane. To avoid trouble in this type of situation, both drivers need to watch out for each other. It is often better to allow an entering driver to go first to avoid a conflict.

Ramp Overflow Extra heavy traffic is another cause of expressway exit collisions. Sometimes a driver faces a situation where traffic is backed up from an exit ramp into the expressway. In such a situation, the driver has two choices. One, the driver can go past the exit and use the next exit. Two,

if the exit must be used, the driver should start slowing early. The minute a driver sees trouble ahead, the brakes should be pumped lightly to flash brake lights in order to warn traffic behind. Rear traffic should be checked to see if it is slowing. If not, the driver should try to pass the jammed exit area smoothly and drive to the next exit. Adding extra miles to a trip is a small price when compared to being involved in a multiple rear-end crash.

HOW TO STAY ALIVE ON EXPRESSWAYS

In order to drive expertly on an expressway, the following are some helpful hints.

Cooperate with Other Drivers   While the mileage death rate on expressways is about half that of other streets and highways, collisions that do occur are often more serious because of higher speeds. A greater following distance and large space cushions are very important for safety. Equally important is a willingness to cooperate with other drivers. This may be difficult when someone cuts you off or occupies the space cushion ahead of your car. The urge to challenge another driver for space is often greater than some can resist. But the satisfactions gained by competitive behavior cannot compare with the risks involved. The sense of responsibility that marks the mature driver does not permit use of the expressway (or any other road) to contest his or her "rights."

Concentrate on the Driving Task   Because of the more serious dangers of collisions at higher speeds, survival on expressways demands continued concentration on the driving task. Traffic conflicts develop more rapidly at higher speeds, especially in multilane operation. Only by strict attention to the changing scene can these conflicts be avoided.

Build Your Experience Gradually   When you first drive alone on an expressway, select a time when traffic is light. Then practice key maneuvers. Take enough of these trips in light traffic to get used to solo expressway driving before you drive in heavier traffic.

In driving, as in sports, skills and good judgment develop with successful experi-

When the road is empty, the 55-mph speed limit may be fine, but . . .

. . . when you see traffic like this around you, reduce speed.

ence. The complex functions of the driving task increase in difficulty at higher speeds. So limit your exposure at first to sections of the expressway where traffic is light. Stay out of rush-hour traffic and avoid driving during the late hours when many drivers are tired or under the influence of alcohol.

Vocabulary

acceleration lane, 199
common speed, 204
deceleration lane, 211
emergency flare, 210

entrance ramp, 199
highway hypnosis, 208
merge area, 199
rumble strips, 209

through-lane, 202
velocitation, 208
wolf pack, 207

Summary

1. Five reasons explain why expressways have a lower collision rate than other roads.
2. Before driving on an expressway, a driver should plan the trip carefully, know what signs to look for, and have the car checked.
3. The entrance area to an expressway includes the entrance ramp, which gives a driver time to "size-up" other traffic; the acceleration lane, which is used to speed up to the flow of expressway traffic; and the merge area, where a driver actually blends into the flow of traffic.
4. When entering a crowded expressway, a driver should look for a gap in traffic. If there is no gap, the driver should wait on the entrance ramp until there is a gap.
5. By blending into traffic, a driver can avoid conflicts resulting from differences in speed and position with other vehicles.
6. A driver identifies potential conflicts by looking well ahead, to the sides, and rear when driving on an expressway. Predictions must be made well in advance so that effective decisions can be made ahead of time. All driver actions must be executed smoothly.
7. Maximum and minimum expressway speed limits are set so that traffic will flow smoothly without large differences in speed.
8. Maintaining a space cushion, especially to the front, is important on expressways because of high speed and multilane traffic. Keep a 2-second or 3-second following distance between your vehicle and the vehicle ahead.
9. "Velocitation" and "highway hypnosis" are two feelings a driver may experience after long hours of expressway driving. To prevent velocitation, or the feeling of going slower than one really is, a driver should keep checking the speedometer. To combat highway hypnosis, a lulled condition that can put a driver to sleep, a driver needs to take steps to keep mentally alert before and while driving for long hours on an expressway.
10. If a driver has a mechanical breakdown on an expressway, passengers should be moved away from the car, and steps must be taken to warn other drivers.
11. When leaving an expressway, a driver should get into position ahead of time, signal, and then use the deceleration lane and ramp for slowing.

Driving Situations

1. Three drivers on this ramp have different problems. What should the driver of the last car be doing? What should concern the driver of the middle car? What should the driver of the van have identified?

2. The yellow car in the center lane is closing on the car ahead. If drivers don't adjust, a tight situation could develop. To avoid trouble, what should the driver of the yellow car do?

3. In this slowdown situation, what should the driver already have identified? Predicted? Decided? Executed?

4. In this situation, the driver of the yellow car wants to exit the expressway. The same lane is used for entering and exiting. To avoid trouble, what should the driver of this car do?

Chapter Review Questions

Preparing to Drive on Expressways
1. What steps must a driver take before driving on an expressway? (198)
2. Why could it be dangerous to drive on an expressway without a trip plan? (198)

Entering an Expressway
3. How should a driver check for a "gap" in expressway traffic? (200)
4. What steps should a driver follow if there is no "gap" to merge into? (200)
5. How can following another car too closely onto an expressway cause trouble? (201)

Cruising on the Expressway
6. At expressway speeds, how far down the road must a driver look? (202)
7. What are five expressway situations or conditions in which a following distance of more than 2 seconds should be used? (204)
8. What are the steps a driver must take when making a lane change on an expressway? (205)
9. What should a driver do to avoid feeling "velocitized"? (208)
10. Why should a driver try to avoid driving in "wolf packs"? (207)

Exiting an Expressway
11. What steps should a driver follow when exiting an expressway? (211)
12. After long hours of driving, what should a driver be alert for after leaving an expressway? (211)
13. Leaving an expressway at too high a speed is a common cause of collisions. To prevent this, what should a driver do? (211)
14. Many expressways use the same lane for entering and exiting traffic. What should be done if a driver wants to exit while another driver is entering? (212)
15. What action should a driver take who wants to leave an expressway at an exit that is blocked with backed-up traffic? (212)

Projects

1. When riding with different drivers, keep a record to show how many of them used over-the-shoulder checks when merging onto an expressway and when making lane changes on the expressway.
2. As a passenger, practice measuring a 2-second and 3-second following distance on an expressway by picking fixed reference points and counting off seconds of time.
3. When riding in a car, keep track of about 30 cars on the expressway that make lane changes and see how many drivers used turn signals when making the lane change.
4. Stand in a place where an expressway entrance can be seen and watch to see how drivers handle tight merging situations in heavy traffic.

Chapter 12 ▪ Test

(Write the correct answers on a separate sheet of paper.)

True-False

1. Having a trip plan enables drivers to pay full attention to the driving task. (198)
2. Most expressway emergency service calls are for drivers who have had a serious mechanical break-down. (198)
3. Most expressway driving should be done in the center or right-hand lanes. (205)
4. When entering an expressway, a driver should make quick checks for a "gap" in traffic while on the entrance ramp. (200)
5. When following another car onto the entrance ramp, it is a good idea for both to merge into the same expressway gap. (200)
6. When driving on an expressway, a driver should look only about half a city block ahead. (202)
7. Backing is permitted only on expressway exit ramps. (211)
8. Most drivers can experience "highway hypnosis" after long hours of expressway driving. (208)
9. A 2-second following distance on expressways is long enough for almost all expressway conditions. (204)
10. Emergency flares should be placed at least 500 feet (170 paces) behind a car that is disabled on an expressway. (210)

Answer the Question

11. What is one of the most common causes of expressway collisions? (204)
12. To avoid conflict with other traffic, where should a driver reduce speed when exiting an expressway? (211)
13. How does being "velocitized" make a driver feel? (208)
14. Most expressways have minimum speed limits. How do minimum speed limits help the flow of traffic? (204)
15. How can a driver warn other drivers to the rear on an expressway of an emergency situation? (200)
16. Most expressways have lines painted at the edge of the roadway. How do these lines help drivers? (203)
17. How can driving at the common speed help a driver? (204)
18. Which side of an expressway should a driver who has a disabled car try to pull onto for repairs? (210)
19. Avoiding "wolf packs" is a good expressway driving habit. How can avoiding them help a driver? (207)
20. What else beside signaling should a driver do before making any move to the left or right on an expressway? (205)

Chapter 13

Driving in Adverse Conditions

Objectives

1. Explain how a driver can see ahead clearly when driving under adverse conditions.
2. Explain the techniques for successful night driving.
3. Explain "overdriving the headlights" and the basic hazards involved.
4. Compare the use of low-beam headlights in conditions of rain, fog, and twilight.
5. Compare road surface conditions during the first minutes of rain with conditions after it has rained a while.
6. Describe how car control may be lost when hydroplaning occurs, the dangers involved, and the defensive actions to take.
7. Explain the procedures for recovering from a power skid, a braking skid, and a cornering skid.
8. List special equipment used for driving on snow and ice and how they are used.
9. Describe how to drive on snow without skidding.
10. Describe the special difficulties caused by a strong cross wind.

Introduction

The driving task becomes more difficult when visibility is reduced or when the road surface is covered with snow, ice, or rain. Unfortunately, reduced visibility and traction problems often occur at the same time.

In good driving conditions, the car responds to the controls in the same manner time after time. When a change occurs on the road surface, the car responds differently or fails to respond at all. The driver must adjust to changing conditions.

Seeing properly becomes difficult in fog, rain, or snow. Windows steam up or frost may form on the windshield in adverse weather conditions. Drivers must operate the windshield wipers and washers, and the defroster before problems develop. This equipment must be kept in good working condition so that drivers will have optimum visibility at all times.

Driving when visibility is reduced requires extra seeing ability. Driving when road surfaces are slick also takes special skills. It is necessary for a driver to recognize the adverse condition, reduce speed to prevent problems from developing, and adjust to changing situations that do occur in adverse weather.

The special abilities and driving techniques needed to accomplish this task are discussed in this chapter.

Reduced Visibility

Visibility problems are created by many weather conditions in addition to loss of light at twilight and at night. Since most driver information is received through the eyes, the *identify* part of IDPE is more difficult to carry out when visibility is reduced.

VISIBILITY THROUGH CAR WINDOWS

Weather changes can reduce visibility through the car's windows as well as limit the range of headlights. The windshield and windows will often steam up on the inside during bad weather or during a temperature change in good weather. Steamed-up windows can be cleared by using the defrosters, by opening windows, and by turning on the air conditioner.

Accumulations of snow, frost, or ice on the windows that limit visibility must be removed before driving. A driver who is willing to drive with only small peepholes to see through cannot get the big picture and apply the IPDE functions properly.

At dusk you need to take extra care to see potential danger.

TWILIGHT

Light fades gradually as the day ends. There is not as much light as in daytime; yet it may not seem dark enough for headlights. The time and amount of available light are also affected by the weather. Light fades earlier when the weather is not clear.

By turning on low-beam lights long before lights are needed, a driver can make the car more visible to other drivers. However, be aware that some other drivers may not have turned on their headlights. Pedestrians and cyclists are also more difficult to see.

It is important to use headlights rather than parking lights, which are intended to be used only when the car has been parked.

DARKNESS

At night, a driver must substitute headlights for daylight. It is a poor substitute. Headlights are designed to light the way ahead of the car. Although there may be other forms of illumination, such as street lights and the lights of other cars, the total light reduction is great. Side vision is especially limited. Drivers must learn to perform the driving task within the severe limits imposed by darkness. Darkness calls for reduced speed.

Use of Headlights   High-beam headlights light the road farther ahead of the car than low-beam lights. Use high beams on highways when no other car is coming toward you or traveling within 300 feet ahead of you. Switch to low beam whenever you meet an oncoming car or when following a car to prevent blinding the other driver.

When driving in towns and cities, use low beams. Generally, this is required by law. Driving safely in a city without using high beam is possible because of the lower speed limit, the added illumination of street lights, and the lights of other cars.

In business districts, the blinking and flashing of the different colors and intensities of lights sometimes make identifying traffic clues difficult.

Low-beam headlights are also needed in adverse weather conditions, when visibility is poor. Since headlights are near the road surface, they get dirtier than the windshield. The dirt severely reduces their efficiency. Clean headlight lenses and a clean windshield are important for driver visibility.

Lights are even more distracting than usual on a night when pavements are wet.

Overdriving Headlights   Overdriving headlights means *driving at speeds that make stopping distance longer than the distance lighted by headlights.* You must be able to stop within the distance lighted by the range of your headlights. At higher speeds on dark roads, stopping distances are often longer than sight distances. By the time a driver can see a problem ahead, it may already be too late to stop to avoid a crash.

When low beams are used, drivers must slow down. Reduced visibility caused by bad weather requires slowing even more.

Drivers must also remember that headlight range does not change if the road surface becomes slick.

Meeting Cars   One purpose of low-beam lights is to direct the bright intensity of the lights downward to avoid blinding the oncoming driver. In case the lights of the oncoming car are not dimmed, a driver can adjust by glancing toward the right edge of the road. Then by glancing ahead, below the bright lights, a driver can determine that the oncoming car is maintaining lane position. Avoid looking directly at bright headlights. Reduce speed when facing the glare from oncoming headlights.

Remember, too, that headlight beams shine straight ahead. They do not follow the road around a curve. Headlights are not as effective on a curve at night as on a straight road.

222

SUN GLARE

Bright sun, early in the morning or late in the afternoon, creates a glare problem for the driver who is driving toward the sun. Glare can be reduced by wearing sunglasses and using the sun visor. Drivers must realize that if the sun is behind them, oncoming drivers have the glare problem. They may not see your signals or you because of the glare.

FOG

Fog reflects light, whether it be daylight or headlights. Visibility is reduced in any degree of fog, light or dense. Drivers must be careful even in light fog because it often has thick spots. In areas near large bodies of water, fog is usually a dark, pea-soup variety. In inland areas, fog can be fleecy white. It sometimes occurs in layers that fill the valleys and leave the hills clear. Occasionally, the hilltops will be covered while the valleys are clear. Drivers must guard against entering a foggy area at a speed that was safe only in a clear area.

In any fog, day or night, drivers must use low-beam headlights. With high beams on, the light is reflected back toward the driver by the fog and may not penetrate to the road surface at all. Low beam directs the most intense light downward and is more likely to bore through the fog to the road surface. In any fog, speed must be reduced.

When driving in fog, drivers must be able to do the entire IPDE process in the greatly restricted, ever-changing sight distance available. An added space cushion is necessary because of the second-by-second changes in conditions. Street lights and the lights of other cars will help, but the changing intensity of fog makes it extremely difficult to judge distances accurately.

Reduce speed in fog.

RAIN

A heavy rain reduces visibility markedly. If the wind is blowing, the situation is worsened. The driver must turn on the windshield wipers and also the defroster if the windshield begins to steam up. Rain on the other windows interferes with and distorts vision. Other cars are difficult to see, particularly if their headlights are not on. It is especially difficult to identify cars to the rear and in the blind-spot areas. Drivers have to check by looking through rain-spattered windows.

Drivers must use low-beam headlights in order to see and to be seen, day or night. Speed must be reduced enough to adjust to the difficulty of seeing and being seen, and to the wet road surface.

SNOW

Wind-driven snow also limits visibility. Drivers must use low-beam headlights, day or night, to see and be seen. Speed must also be reduced. Often, snow covers the lane markings and creates another visibility problem. The difficulty can be lessened if, while the first snow is falling, drivers continue to center the cars in their lanes. The tendency, however, is for drivers to move away from the edge of the roadway as it disappears under the snow, to be sure of not driving off the pavement. This, in effect, narrows the road space. Snow creates an added problem of poor traction.

OTHER ROADWAY USERS

Snow and rain create special problems for cyclists and pedestrians. Both are uncomfortable, have visual limitations, and are anxious to get where they are going. They may take chances they would not otherwise take. Pedestrians may use umbrellas in such a way

that they cannot see the cars. Some rain clothing is dark in color and difficult for a driver to identify.

Reduced Traction

Many situations where visibility is bad are made more difficult by poor traction. A traction problem occurs during a rain or a snowfall and remains after visibility is clear again. Drivers must be aware of a car's capabilities and limitations, and must apply special skills in order to manage reduced traction situations successfully.

WET SURFACES

The reduced traction situation that affects more drivers than any other is driving on wet pavements during and after a rain.

When Rain Starts Pavements are most slippery when it first starts to rain. Road dust and oil drippings mix with rainwater to form a "greasy" mixture on the road surface. This condition remains until enough rain has fallen to wash the road clear. This may be done in a few minutes, or it may take quite a long time, depending on how hard it rains. Even then, clear water mixed with dust or oil is a film on the road surface which continues to reduce traction. Reduce speed when driving under these conditions.

Hydroplaning If the rain is heavy, the front tires tend to ride up on top of the water which keeps piling up in front of the front tires. This process is called *hydroplaning*. Much of the road-gripping tread of the front tires is not gripping the road at all. The car cannot be steered quickly or accurately; braking efficiency is also impaired. The car tends to travel in a straight line when the driver tries to turn. Just when the loss of control happens depends on the amount of water on the pavement, speed of the car, tire pressure, and depth of the tire tread. Hydroplaning may begin when there are patches of standing water on the pavement. With badly worn tires a few pounds low in pressure, hydroplaning can begin at speeds as low as 30 mph (48 km/h). Even with good tires properly inflated, hydroplaning may occur at 50 mph (80 km/h). It can also occur in slush when snow begins to thaw.

Hydroplaning makes tires ride on the water. Some stopping and steering control are lost.

Wipes   Tire wipes are the tracks left on wet pavement by the car in front. Wipes stay drier than the rest of the pavement for at least a half block or longer. Drivers who can drive in wipes will have a drier surface and better traction.

Deep Water   Unless it cannot be avoided, good drivers do not drive through deep water. Water can be deep enough to stall a car. If possible, determine in advance the depth of the water by checking parked cars, fence posts, hydrants, and other objects of known height. Check what other drivers are doing.

The trip through deep water must be made at a slow, steady speed. Water tends to pile up in front of the car; it must have time to part and not pile up too high. Applying the brakes gently and steadily with the left foot may prevent the brakes from getting wet. Check the brakes after leaving the water to see if the car will slow and stop evenly. If brakes on one side of the car are wet, the car will pull to the other side when brakes are applied. To dry the brakes, depress the brake pedal gently for a few seconds with the left foot while accelerating with the right foot.

Friction will generate the heat needed to dry the brakes. Do this in an area free of traffic and at low speed.

Remember that some roads are normally a little higher in the center. The water will not be quite so deep there. Also, the shoulders, off the edge of the pavement, will be soft and muddy.

Cars should not meet in deep water. One car should go entirely through before another starts through from the other direction.

SNOW

Cars perform differently under various snow conditions. Drivers need to know the driving problems that result from the various types of snow:

- New fallen snow, powdery in texture.
- New fallen snow, heavy snowball type.
- Snow packed by traffic into a flat sheet, much like ice.
- Crusted snow, caused by slight thawing followed by refreezing.
- Slushy snow.

In crusted snow and in heavy snowball snow, the car will not skid sideways as easily as in packed snow, but it may be more difficult to get the car moving. The car may be

put into motion more easily in powdery snow, and it may not be quite as likely to skid. Slushy snow has a bulk caused by water being held in position and may cause hydroplaning. Snow packed down by traffic is much like ice; skids of any kind happen easily. Refer to the skid chart below.

Snow Driving Techniques   Safe driving on icy and snowy roads demands greater skill and effort. A car is designed basically to perform on dry surfaces. It will perform well in many adverse winter conditions if it is driven with care and at greatly reduced speeds. Sometimes special equipment, such as snow tires, good for soft snow, or tire chains, good for traction, may be necessary for safe performance.

The key word in driving on snow or ice is *gently.* The problem is maintaining traction between tires and road. A layer of snow or ice between the tires and the road reduces the grip.

Putting a car in motion has to be done gently, with minimal application of power. The limited traction between tires and snow must not be lost.

Without special equipment, a car on snow or ice cannot be started and moved across an intersection quickly. Because of this, the driver must allow more time for the move.

Steering also needs to be done gently. The driver must plan ahead and execute the steering move without sudden actions that would cause the car to skid. If the wheels do not

Skids

Kind	Cause	Car Actions	How to Prevent Skids	How to Recover from Skids
Braking Skid	Braking too hard.	Can hear tires slide. No steering control. Car slides straight ahead; or side slip toward curb.	Brake early, smoothly and gently. Pump brakes (disc brakes will lock if road condition is too slick).	Promptly release brakes and steer; then reapply brakes gently.
Power Skid (from standstill or at low cruising speed)	Too much acceleration.	Engine races; car sits or creeps. Rear end slides toward curb. If cruising, car does not pick up speed much.	Gentle acceleration.	Release accelerator promptly. Steer to straighten car. Accelerate gently to regain and maintain traction.
Cornering Skid	Speed too high into a turn. Rear wheels will slide on dips in road or on a crowned road.	Back slides left during right cornering, right on left cornering; front wheels still have traction.	Reduce speed before the turn. Reduce speed for dips and crowned road.	Steer car in the direction you want to go. Do not brake.
Fast-Idle Skid	Choke causes engine of automatic-shift car to run fast when first started. With no acceleration, car travels too fast.	Car will run 15 to 20 mph on its own with no gas being fed; braking can cause a skid.	Shift to NEUTRAL for a stop. Quick kick of gas pedal in NEUTRAL may stop fast idle.	Shift to NEUTRAL as skid starts (or before). Brake gently to a stop.

roll, the car cannot be steered. With rolling traction, the car will respond to steering much more effectively than to braking. The car can be steered as needed in many situations when it cannot be braked in time to avoid a crash.

Stopping is the most crucial action when driving under poor traction conditions. A good safety precaution is to decelerate and brake so that the stop can be made *before* the desired stopping point.

Rocking the Car When a car is stuck in deep snow, you may free it by "rocking" it out. To do this, move the car forward in DRIVE with gentle acceleration. At the instant the car stops moving forward, shift to REVERSE and gently accelerate until it stops. When rocking an automatic-shift car, stop *completely* before changing gears. Continue this back-and-forth motion. The weight and momentum of the car will clear a longer track with each motion, and the car can be driven out of the snow. The accelerator is used lightly during the in-gear intervals, and is released during the gear changing. The front wheels must be kept straight so that the car will stay in the same tracks.

Pumping the Brakes The best way to stop a car on snow or ice (or any slick surface) is to brake gently in plenty of time. Applying the brakes hard will lock the wheels and cause a skid. When the front wheels stop rolling, steering control is lost.

Pumping the brakes is a useful technique when braking and steering are necessary. The driver alternately applies and releases the brakes. Some braking is accomplished, and in between braking, some steering can be done.

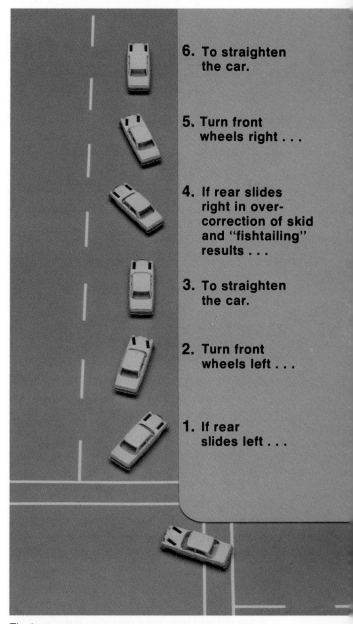

6. **To straighten the car.**

5. **Turn front wheels right . . .**

4. **If rear slides right in over-correction of skid and "fishtailing" results . . .**

3. **To straighten the car.**

2. **Turn front wheels left . . .**

1. **If rear slides left . . .**

The best way to remember how to steer when a skid occurs is "steer in the direction you want to go." Do not brake—the front wheels must keep rolling to maintain steering control.

Added traction may be obtained with the use of tire chains for winter driving.

ICE

If it rains while the temperature is falling rapidly, a special traction problem may develop. Freezing can begin without any visible change in the road surface. Ice usually forms first on bridges. The cold air around and underneath a bridge lowers the roadway temperature there more quickly than elsewhere.

The pavement surface can be checked, in an area clear of traffic, by a sudden bit of acceleration. If a small power skid occurs, ice is forming. Immediately correct the skid by releasing the accelerator; then gently reaccelerate. Once ice starts to form, expect the roadway to get icy quickly. Sometimes the windshield and windows will also get icy. Anticipate this and prevent it by using the defroster and heater.

Parking Brake   When a car is parked after being driven in a freezing rain, the parking brake should not be set. It may freeze, perhaps so solidly that the car cannot be moved.

Temperature   Ice causes loss of traction. When the temperature rises to or above freezing, an icy road becomes wet and even more slippery. In 32° weather, ice is slicker than at lower temperatures.

Snow-Covered Ice   After ice freezes in low places, at corners, or near edges of roadway, snow will sometimes cover the ice as well as areas that have no ice. This situation can be quite hazardous. Drivers tend to judge the traction by the snow, which they can see, and not be aware of the even more limited traction on the ice beneath.

WIND

A strong wind makes car control more difficult, particularly if it is a cross wind. Good drivers slow down in order to maintain control. They must be aware of wind gusts that occur when driving past a large truck or out from under a bridge. A head wind requires additional acceleration, and makes steering more difficult. A tail wind will build speed and will require earlier deceleration and more braking to stop. Wind may also cause a visibility problem by blowing dust or snow around in the air. Some areas have sandstorms that hamper visibility.

Different types of vehicles handle differently in high wind. Lightweight vehicles, as well as vans and trucks with large cargo bodies, may be more difficult to manage than heavier vehicles. Cars pulling trailers have a special problem; in a cross wind, trailers may sway or weave if they do not have special equipment to prevent it. Car-top carriers make any car harder to manage.

OTHER REDUCED-TRACTION SURFACES

Gravel roads have loose gravel that acts somewhat like marbles under the tires and can cause skids. Usually the more heavily traveled tire paths are packed, and the loose material can be avoided. The situation may be present whether the road is wet or dry.

Near construction areas, mud or dirt may be dropped on the pavement by vehicles leaving the construction area. If it rains, an extremely slick condition results. Dirt and sand left behind when flooded roads have dried can also reduce traction.

Wet leaves on the road surface act much like mud mentioned above. Skids can result.

DRY ROADS

Skids can occur on dry pavement if enough power or enough braking occurs to overcome the traction between tires and road. Part of the driving task is to recognize the skid po-

tential of every road surface used, the presence of rough spots, loose material on the road, as well as situations caused by the weather.

TIRE CONTACT WITH THE ROAD

All driving decisions must be based upon the working relationship between four patches of rubber and the road surface. On roads covered by ice and snow, or any time traction is reduced, safety margins need more room. However, in good conditions, good traction works in all normal driving situations and requires no special attention.

In adverse weather, maneuvers require more time and space for all drivers to perform the IPDE process successfully. Therefore, it is necessary to reduce speed when driving in any kind of adverse weather conditions, and to increase following distances to 3 or 4 seconds.

A defensive driver will be watching the child playing near the street as well as the parked car ahead.

Vocabulary

hydroplaning, 224
low-beam, 220
overdriving headlights, 221
"pumping," 227
"rocking," 227

skids: braking, 226
    cornering, 226
    power, 226
snow tire, 226
sun glare, 222
tire chains, 226
tire wipes, 225

Summary

1. In adverse weather conditions, keep windshield and headlights clean. Use defroster and open windows enough to clear steamed windows. Clear frost, sleet, or snow from all windows before driving.
2. At night, it is important to know the limitation of headlight vision. Glare is also a problem. IPDE functions require reduced speed at night.
3. Do not overdrive the headlights; a driver must be able to stop the car within the distance lighted by the headlights, no matter how short it is.
4. Use low-beam headlights in rain and fog to direct the strongest light beam to the pavement for better visibility. Use low-beam headlights in twilight to make the car visible.
5. The slickest rain surface happens in the first few minutes, when dust and oil drippings combine with water. Later, the rain washes the pavement clean.
6. Hydroplaning occurs when the front tires ride up on top of surface water. The resulting loss of friction causes loss of steering control. Slow down when there is water on the road surface.
7. Reduce power when a power skid starts, then accelerate gently. In a braking skid, release the brakes; brake again, more gently. In a cornering skid, do not brake; steer to keep the car going straight in the direction you want to go.
8. Snow tires are good for driving in soft snow. Chains give the best traction but must be removed when snow or ice melts.
9. When driving on snow-covered roads, start gently, steer gently, brake gently, and stop gently.
10. Cross winds cause handling problems, especially for lightweight vehicles, vans and trucks, and cars pulling a trailer.

Driving Situations

1. What are the driver's visibility and traction problems in this picture?

2. What driver actions should be happening in this situation?

3. What mistake is the driver making by not cleaning off all the snow from the windshield in bad weather?

4. The headlight area indicates the area of a driver's vision at night. Comment on speed, potential hazard, stopping distance, and the concept of "overdriving your headlights."

Chapter Review Questions

Reduced Visibility

1. What two road conditions often occur in bad weather at the same time that call for a speed adjustment? (219)
2. Why should drivers use low-beam headlights in rain and fog? (222-223)
3. What factors require drivers to reduce speed when driving at night? (220)
4. How does rain affect normal safety habits of pedestrians and bicyclists? (223)
5. What does "overdriving the headlights" mean? (221)

Reduced Traction

6. When is the most slippery time during a rain? Why is this so? (224)
7. What is meant by hydroplaning? Under what conditions may hydroplaning occur? (224)
8. What are the four types of skids and how are they caused? (226)
9. What special driving problem may develop during a rain when the temperature falls? Where is this problem most likely to occur? (228)
10. What driver actions are needed when driving on snow-covered roads? (226-227)

Projects

1. Get an accident summary from your local or state police showing the total number of accidents for each month of the year and each hour of the day. Is there any relationship between darkness and the number of accidents? Between adverse weather and the number of accidents?
2. Use a wagon or a similar vehicle on which the front wheels can be steered to give a class demonstration of what happens when a car skids and what you have to do to "regain control."
3. In winter, walk around a block when it snows and record rear tire statistics: snow tires, chains, special equipment or no special equipment that can be observed on cars. Report the information to the class.
4. What percentage of drivers maintain the equipment that protects them in adverse weather? Talk to a service station operator about this to determine which equipment is mostly kept up. Report your findings to the class.

Chapter 13 ▪ Test

(Write the correct answers on a separate sheet of paper.)

True-False

1. Headlights are more effective for a driver on a straight road than on a curved road. (221)
2. One purpose of headlights is to help other drivers see your car. (221)
3. Pedestrians are more likely to observe safety practices in a rainstorm. (223)
4. When driving in fog, day or night, drivers should use the emergency flashers. (222)
5. The most slippery time in a rain is right after the hardest downpour. (224)
6. Temporary vision difficulty due to glare can occur during the day and at night. (221, 222)
7. Hydroplaning can take place only when there is water or slush on the road surface. (224)
8. A driver should use the lowest forward gear and accelerate heavily for sufficient power to put a car in motion on ice. (226)
9. "Rocking" can be used to get a car out of deep snow. (227)
10. In a braking skid, all steering control is lost. (226)
11. Pumping the brakes is an effective way to control a power skid. (226)
12. Icy road conditions are most likely to develop first on bridges. (228)
13. If the rear of a car skids to the right, the driver should correct by steering to the right. (227)

Answer the Question

14. In fog, what beam headlights should drivers use?   (222)
15. What two things are drivers affected by in adverse weather conditions?   (219)
16. In which adverse visibility condition should the driver use high beam?   (220)
17. What traction equipment should be used for winter driving?   (226)
18. What is the most important rule to remember when driving in any kind of adverse weather conditions? (229)
19. What three kinds of vehicles are most likely to encounter handling problems in a strong wind? (228)
20. In addition to rain, snow and ice, what other three road conditions reduce traction?   (229)

Chapter 14

Handling Emergencies

Objectives

1. List some actions to take if the brakes or the steering system should fail.
2. List emergency actions a driver can take if forward vision becomes blocked.
3. Describe the actions to take if a tire has a blowout.
4. Describe the actions to take if the accelerator sticks.
5. Describe the actions to take if the car catches fire.
6. Explain how to start a car with a stalled engine.
7. Explain some actions to take if the car stalls on railroad tracks.
8. Describe what to do if the car runs off the road.
9. List some actions a driver may take to avoid a head-on crash.
10. Explain the actions a driver can take to avoid a side-impact collision.
11. Describe what a driver can do to minimize the effects of a collision.

Introduction

Emergency situations develop suddenly. Drivers may have only a fraction of a second to make the correct move. Some drivers freeze at the wheel because they don't know what to do. In these tight situations, special driving skills are needed.

Most emergency situations result from two causes: First, the driver's car may have a mechanical breakdown, such as a tire blowout. Drivers can eliminate most car failures with proper preventive maintenance.

The second cause is driver mistakes. They cause more emergency situations than mechanical breakdowns. The person who makes a wrong move at the last second can put other drivers into emergency situations.

Even under the best conditions, drivers must be alert to avoid involvement in a collision. Their chances of survival are improved if they know how to handle emergency situations. Equally important is the practice of keeping a space cushion around their car at all times and making sure doors are locked and seat belts are securely fastened to help maintain car control if an evasive maneuver is necessary.

Brake Failure Procedures

1

2

3

4

Equipment Failure

Whenever a person drives a car, there is always a chance of car trouble. Signs or warning symptoms usually occur before real trouble develops. The driver should repair these parts to prevent serious problems from developing. (The maintenance of cars is covered in Chapter 18.) However, equipment can sometimes fail without warning, and that failure can put the surprised driver into an emergency situation.

BRAKE FAILURE

A simple situation like stopping for a traffic light can turn into an emergency if the car's brakes fail. Should this happen, a driver should immediately follow this procedure:

1. Pump the brake pedal as fast and hard as you can. This may activate the brakes enough to slow or stop car. In a power brake failure, brakes will last about 3 pumps. Use both feet on brake pedal.
2. Shift the car to a lower gear to use the braking power of the engine.
3. Apply the parking brake. To make sure you remain in control, hold the parking-brake release lever in the "off" position so the parking brake can be released if the car starts to skid.
4. If none of these steps slow the car fast enough, reduce speed by rubbing the tires along the curb or against a dense hedge.

Overheated and wet brakes can cause the brakes to fail. To prevent brake fading, caused by overheated brakes, a driver should not ride the brakes all the way down a long, steep hill. Instead of constant braking, the driver should use SECOND or LOW gear to slow the car. The steps to take if brakes are wet appear in Chapter 13.

If the hood should fly up, look through the opening between the hood and the body of the car.

STEERING FAILURE

Steering system failures can become serious problems if the driver does not know what to do. A driver can take several types of emergency actions if steering failure occurs.

- If the power-assist part of the steering system fails, the driver can still steer by exerting more effort to turn the steering wheel.
- If one front wheel collapses because of a steering system breakdown, you should shift to a lower gear and apply the parking brake. Be sure to hold the parking-brake release lever in the "off" position.
- If you lose all steering capability, use the foot brake to slow the car as quickly as possible.

LOSS OF FORWARD VISION

At night if the headlights start to flicker or go out, a driver should take the following action:

1. The driver should try to slow down while following from memory the image of the road just before the headlights went out.
2. At the same time, the driver should hit the dimmer switch several times. If the lights do not come on, use the turn signals, parking lights, or emergency flashers for added light. These lights may work since they are on a different circuit.
3. When the car has slowed down, the driver can pull off the road to a safe spot.

Sometimes, a driver's forward vision is blocked by frost on the windshield. The driver should clear the windshield before driving. Antifreeze in washer fluid will help keep the windshield clean. To prevent fogging, warm air should be circulated through the defroster.

If a driver's windshield is blocked by dirt or mud splashed from a passing car, the driver should turn on the windshield washers and wipers while slowing down.

If the hood flies up, a driver's vision through the windshield can be blocked. In this situation, a driver should try the following procedures to regain visibility quickly:

1. Bend down and look through the crack between the back of the hood and the engine compartment. If vision ahead is completely blocked, look out the window on the left side.
2. Pump the brakes to flash brakelights and slow the car.
3. Pull off the road to a safe spot.

Make sure the hood is securely latched every time it is closed.

TIRE FAILURE

A tire blowout is one type of emergency that can usually be prevented. Most tire failures occur when 10 percent or less of the tread remains.

If a tire does blow out, a driver should take these actions:

- Maintain as much steering control as possible. *Do not hit the brakes!* Don't try to save the tire by slowing down quickly. Don't give up trying to steer out of the problem.
- If the right front tire blows out, the car will pull to the right. Let up on the accelerator and continue steering to the left. Light braking may be used after the car has slowed. A blown left front tire requires steering to the right. When the car is under complete control at a slow speed, drive off the road so the tire can be safely changed.
- If a rear tire blows out, the car may tend to *fishtail,* that is, move from side to side. The emergency action for a blown rear tire is much like correcting for a series of small skids. Maintain lane position by releasing the accelerator and making small steering corrections as necessary toward the side of the blowout. If the tire blows in a curve, the driver may have to leave the road when correcting the skid. This is better than losing complete control if the car skids sideways off the road. Once the car is under control, drive to a safe spot out of the way of traffic before changing the tire.

A sudden rear tire blowout must be handled as a skid.

Changing a Tire   Before changing a tire, check the instructions, which can be found in the owner's manual, inside the trunk lid, or in the spare tire compartment. There are different types of jack and wrench combinations for changing tires.

These basic steps should be followed when changing a tire:

1. Park the car on a level spot away from traffic. Set the gear selector in PARK or in REVERSE for a stickshift car.
2. Set the parking brake and block the wheel diagonally opposite the flat with a brick or a rock.
3. Get all passengers out of the car.
4. Take out the spare tire before jacking up the car.
5. Jack the car part way up. Flat tire is still touching the ground.
6. Remove hubcap and loosen each lug nut.
7. Continue to jack the car until the flat tire clears the ground. Don't get under or so close to the car that it could fall on an arm or leg. Bumper jacks can be unstable.
8. Remove lug nuts and place them in the hubcap; then remove the flat tire.
9. Mount the new tire and replace and tighten lug nuts.
10. Lower the car.
11. Replace hubcap.
12. Put the tire-changing equipment and flat tire in trunk. Remove blocks from under tire.

Changing a tire must be done quickly and safely. Try to keep yourself, your passengers, and equipment away from traffic.

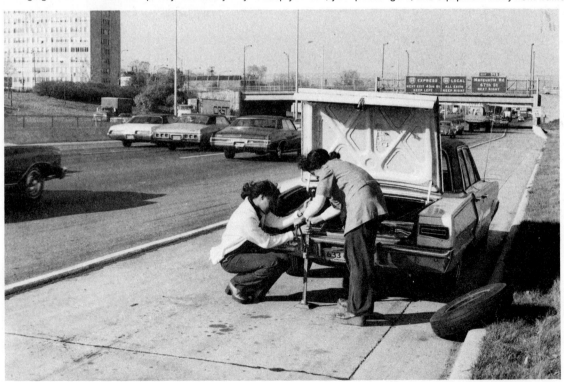

STUCK ACCELERATOR

Frozen slush underneath the floor of the car or a broken spring can cause the accelerator pedal to stick in the open position. If this happens while the car is moving, the driver should do three things:

1. Turn off the ignition switch.
2. Shift to NEUTRAL or just press in the clutch in a stickshift car.
3. Steer to a safe spot off the road. If the car has power steering, extra effort will be needed to steer the car.

After the car has come to a safe stop, the driver can free the accelerator. The car should then be checked to make sure the problem does not occur again.

CAR CATCHES FIRE

Putting out a car fire can be dangerous. A driver should carry a portable fire extinguisher for all types of fires. If your car is on fire, stop in a safe place (not in a gas station) and turn off the engine. Then, call the fire department as quickly as possible. Other steps you can take are

1. Open the hood carefully because the fire may flare up. The metal hood may be hot, so protect your hands.
2. If you have no way to put out the fire, leave the hood closed. If you do not have a fire extinguisher, get a blanket, dirt, or sand to try to smother the fire. Once the hood is up, the fire will burn hotter as it gets more air.
3. If the fire continues to burn after you attempt to put it out, get at least 100 feet from the car so you and your passengers will not be injured if the gas tank explodes.

ENGINE FAILURE

Usually the driver has very little warning when an engine stops due to an ignition or fuel system failure while the car is moving. This is less likely to occur if the car receives regular preventive maintenance service. If this occurs, look for a safe place to get the car off the road. The alert driver may be able to keep going long enough to get out of traffic by following these steps:

- If the engine sputters while the car is traveling at any speed, shift to a lower gear, even in an automatic-shift car, and then pump the accelerator. This action may keep the engine running for a short enough period to get you off the road.
- If the engine stops completely, shift to NEUTRAL. Then, by pumping the accelerator and turning the ignition switch on, the driver may start the engine again for a brief period.
- If the car's motion stops while the car is still on the road, a driver may be able to move a stickshift car a short distance by shifting to FIRST or REVERSE and turning the ignition switch on. The driver of an automatic-shift car does not have this option.

If the starter works, but the engine does not want to start because it is flooded, do not pump the accelerator. Pumping will only make the situation worse. Instead, follow this procedure for starting a flooded engine:

1. Depress the accelerator to the floor and hold it there to let in more air.
2. Turn the ignition switch on while still keeping your foot on the accelerator.
3. With about 10 to 20 seconds of steady turning, the engine should start. If it does not, wait five minutes and try again.
4. When the engine starts, release the accelerator gradually to allow excess gasoline to clear out of the engine. Do not race the engine.

Driver's Errors

By far, the greatest number of emergencies are the result of a driver's error. The driver may run off the road, or may be going too fast for conditions, which might cause a skid or rollover. Other emergencies are caused by other errors, such as improper lane changing, which may threaten a side impact, or an approaching driver over the center line, which may cause a head-on crash.

OFF-ROAD RECOVERY

If two or even four wheels drop off the edge of the road, returning to the road can be easy if the shoulder is paved and in good condi-

tion. But in a large number of fatal one-car crashes, the driver went off the right side of a road with a poor shoulder and then rolled all the way across and off the left side of the road. Head-on crashes may result from a car making an off-road recovery and then crossing the center line. To reduce the risk of these kinds of crashes, a driver needs to know how to make an off-road recovery.

If two wheels drop off a road, a driver should take the following actions:

1. Hold the steering wheel firmly. If the two outside wheels are riding on uneven ground, the car will want to pull to the right. Keep the car going straight.

2. Slow to 5 or 10 mph (8 or 16 km/h) by letting up on the accelerator. At this point, decide if it is best to stop while the tires are off the road or to attempt a moving recovery.

3. If you decide to make a moving recovery, check traffic and then signal.

4. Position the car so it *straddles* the edge of the road. In this position, the right wheels should be about two feet away from the edge of the road.

5. Pick a spot where there is no oncoming traffic and the shoulder and road are almost level.

6. Start the recovery by quickly steering sharply left toward the pavement.

7. When the front tire hits the pavement, steer sharply to the right. This last countersteer will keep the car in the lane.

8. Cancel the turn signal if it is still on and adjust to traffic.

If the driver leaves the road to the right at high speed in an area with an obstruction immediately ahead, this same procedure must be applied without taking time to slow down, to signal, or to make a head check. The driver must make the steering movements very quickly and be careful not to cross the center line of the road.

If you have to push your car off a railroad track, keep looking for trains.

CAR STALLED ON RAILROAD TRACKS

A stalled car on railroad tracks is one emergency an alert driver can prevent.

If the car actually stalls on the tracks, the driver should

1. Make sure everyone gets out of the car.
2. Have someone keep watching for an approaching train.
3. Try to restart the engine.
4. With a stickshift car, put the manual shift lever in FIRST or REVERSE. Let the clutch out, and turn the ignition.
5. If all steps fail, shift to NEUTRAL and try to push the car off the tracks by hand or with another car.
6. If the car is still on the tracks and a train is approaching, everyone should move down the side of the tracks toward the direction the train is coming. If the car is hit, it will scatter in the direction the train is going.

This driver, who escaped, lost control of the car that plunged into the swimming pool.

CAR IN WATER

Wearing seat belts is especially important if the car plunges into a lake or river. Without seat belts, a driver might be knocked out or dazed from being thrown against the inside of the car and might have little chance of survival.

If the car enters the water with all windows up and unbroken, the car will float for a few minutes. The driver in this situation should

1. Release seat belts and get near the window, which is farthest out of the water. Many times, the front of the car will sink first. If this happens, the driver should use the rear windows for escape.
2. When possible, open or knock out the window and get out of the car. If the car has power windows that do not work and if the windows cannot be broken, try to open the door and leave quickly. Once the door is open, the car will sink fast.

If the car has sunk, the driver should take the following actions:

1. Since air will remain trapped inside the car for a little while, try to get a full breath or two while locating a window or door that is facing up.
2. When the air inside the car is almost gone, open the door or window and leave the car.

ROLLOVER

If the car rolls over, the driver and passengers face serious injury if they are thrown out of the car. This chance can be greatly reduced by locking the doors and wearing seat belts.

If a driver is inside a car that has rolled over, the following actions should be taken:

1. To avoid falling, the driver should be careful when releasing the seat belts.
2. Leave the car as quickly as possible.

THREAT OF HEAD-ON COLLISION

A head-on collision has the highest fatality rate of any collision. If you find yourself threatened with a head-on crash and have some time, you should

1. Slow down as much as possible.
2. Start moving to the right and onto the shoulder. Don't go left.
3. Flash headlights and blow horn to alert the oncoming driver in case that driver fell asleep at the wheel.

If your lane is blocked at the last second, you should make a quick lane change to the left or right in the shortest possible distance:

1. Decide which direction provides the best escape route.
2. Grip the steering wheel firmly.
3. Turn the wheel sharply in the direction the car needs to go.
4. In the same motion, quickly countersteer in the opposite direction to stabilize the car. Straighten the wheel and continue to steer for the desired path.

THREAT OF REAR-END COLLISION

In some ways, a driver is very defenseless when the car is standing still. If you are stopped at an intersection and see another car approaching fast from the rear, you can take three actions:

1. If there is time, see if the way is clear to pull ahead. Just by pulling ahead a little, you can avoid much damage.
2. At the same time, flash your brakelights. If a crash cannot be avoided, release the brake just before being hit. Thus, the car

will move a little and reduce the force of the impact. Immediately after impact, you should hit the brake to keep from rolling into the intersection or into another car.
3. As quickly as possible, get everyone out and away from the car in case the gas tank has ruptured and a fire starts.

Be alert for a driver crossing head-on into your lane.

THREAT OF SIDE IMPACT

Improper expressway lane changing and merging, cars coming out of alleys, and drivers trying to run yellow lights are only a few situations that lead to side-impact collisions. To avoid a side-impact collision, a driver can take two actions:

Be alert for a driver suddenly emerging from a side road into your path.

1. Try to brake quickly or accelerate out of trouble, whichever seems most likely to prevent or minimize the conflict.
2. Change lanes quickly to the right or left to open up more room. But remember to make a quick head check and, if possible, blow the horn while starting to move so you will avoid the risk of another conflict in the other lane.

MINIMIZING THE EFFECTS OF A COLLISION

In any collision situation, panic is always a threat. In any situation where a collision is about to occur, a driver should

1. Try to steer for something "soft" that would cause the least damage or injury. Instead of hitting a car or a telephone pole, the driver should try to run into a hedge or into an open field.
2. Above all, don't give up. Each action that lowers speed will help the driver maintain control of the car and work out of the situation.
3. Alert passengers to protect themselves by bending forward and bracing on the dash or on the back of the front seat.

To develop accident-avoidance skills, all drivers should mentally practice what they would do in various collision situations. Any time you have a close call, take time to think the situation through. Practice is the key to developing good driving skills.

Vocabulary

countersteer, 243
fading brakes, 236

fishtail, 238
straddle, 243

Summary

1. If the brakes fail, a driver should pump the brake pedal, shift to a lower gear, use the parking brake, and, if necessary, rub tires against the curb. If one wheel collapses, the driver should shift to a lower gear and apply the parking brake.

2. A driver can maintain forward vision when the headlights fail by using other lights, such as turn signals or parking lights. If the hood blocks forward vision, the driver should look under the hood.

3. If a tire blows out, the driver should slow down by removing the foot from the accelerator and steer to a safe spot out of traffic.

4. If the accelerator sticks, the driver should turn off the ignition switch, shift to NEUTRAL, and steer to a safe place.

5. If a car catches fire and a fire department is not near, a driver can try to smother the fire. If this does not work, everyone should get out of car and stand at least 100 feet from it in case the gas tank explodes.

6. If the engine stalls, the driver should look for a safe place to stop, shift to NEUTRAL, and turn on the ignition switch while pumping the accelerator.

7. If a car stalls on railroad tracks, the driver should get everyone out of the car while looking to see if a train is coming from the other direction. If there is no train coming, the driver should try to restart the engine. If all actions fail, the car may be pushed off the tracks.

8. If two wheels go off the pavement, the driver should firmly grip the wheel, straddle the edge of the pavement, try to slow the car before returning, turn the wheel sharply toward the pavement, and then quickly countersteer as the car returns to the pavement.

9. To avoid a head-on collision, slow down, move right, and flash headlights.

10. To avoid side-impact collisions, brake or accelerate or make a quick lane change.

11. To minimize the effects of a collision, a driver should try to maintain control. If a collision cannot be avoided, the driver should aim for something soft that would cause the least injury or damage.

Driving Situations

1. What actions should the driver take to avoid hitting the car in this head-on situation?

2. The car is moving at 45 mph (72 km/h). What actions should the driver take to avoid a serious off-road collision?

3. The driver has just exited from an expressway, and the left front tire blows. What actions should the driver take?

4. The driver cannot possibly stop in time to avoid hitting the bicycle rider. What should the driver do?

Chapter Review Questions

Equipment Failure

1. What should a driver do when the brakes fail? (236)
2. What should a driver do if the right front tire blows out? (238)
3. What steps should a driver take to change a tire? (239)
4. If the accelerator sticks, what should a driver do? (240)
5. If the hood flies up, what is the first thing a driver should do? (237)
6. What are the steps to take if your car catches fire? (240)

Driver's Errors

7. What actions should a driver take to make an off-road recovery? (242–243)
8. What actions should a driver take if trapped on the railroad tracks with a stalled engine? (244)
9. If the car rolls over, what should the driver do? (245)
10. How can a driver get out of a car that has fallen into a lake? (245)
11. If a driver has some warning of a head-on collision, what should the driver do? (246)
12. If a car comes across the center line at the last second, what emergency maneuver can the driver use to avoid a head-on collision? (246)
13. What can the driver of a stopped car do just before being hit from the rear by another car if there is not much room ahead? (246)
14. What actions can a driver take to avoid a side-impact collision? (247)
15. What can a driver do to minimize the impact or reduce the risk of a collision? (247)

Projects

1. Raise the hood of a car in a parking lot and see how much of the road ahead the driver can see under the hood. Then decide how you would handle this emergency.
2. Check five adult drivers to see which of the following emergency items they carry: fire extinguisher, blanket, or blocks for a tire change.

Chapter 14 · Test

(Write the correct answers on a separate sheet of paper.)

True-False

1. If the brakes fail, the first thing a driver should do is pump the brake pedal. (236)
2. If a left rear tire blows out, the first thing a driver should do is hit the brakes. (238)
3. If a left front tire blows out, the driver will have to steer more to the left. (238)
4. If the accelerator sticks, the driver should bend over and try to free the pedal before stopping. (240)
5. If the headlights go out while driving at night, a driver should use the dimmer switch. (237)
6. If a driver is trapped on railroad tracks with a stalled engine, the first action the driver should take is to push the car off the tracks. (244)
7. If the right wheels of a car drop off the edge of the road where there is no obstacle ahead, the driver should slow to 10 mph before returning to the road. (243)
8. If the windshield is covered with mud, the driver should bend over and look through the clear spots. (237)
9. If the car goes into a lake, the driver should climb out the nearest window. (245)
10. When changing a tire, the driver should be sure to block the wheel diagonally opposite the flat tire. (239)

Answer the Question

11. If the car catches fire, what are the first steps a driver should take? (240)
12. What are the first actions a driver should take when the engine sputters while the car is moving? (241)
13. In a head-on collision situation, which direction should you move? (246)
14. What steps should the driver take if the accelerator sticks in the open position? (240)
15. If the driver sees a car coming up fast from the rear, what is the best action to take? (246)
16. What besides acceleration can be used to avoid a side-impact collision? (247)
17. If a collision is about to happen, what type of object should the driver head toward? (247)
18. What action should the driver take if his or her car is off the road and an obstacle is suddenly seen ahead? (243)
19. What causes most emergency situations? (235)
20. How can seat belts help in accidents involving rollovers? (245)

True-False

1. Driving in city traffic requires the driver to make more decisions than other driving environments. (157)
2. The "point of no return" means the position in which the driver can no longer change lanes. (160)
3. Pedestrians in marked crosswalks can depend on drivers to yield the right-of-way. (167)
4. The proper time to slow down is before you enter a curve. (180)
5. High altitude increases engine performance. (181)
6. When traveling long distances on highways, select a safe speed for conditions. (183)
7. Because of higher speeds, collision fatality rates on expressways are generally higher than on other roads. (197)
8. Inflate tires to maximum recommended pressure prior to driving on expressways for a long period of time. (198)
9. On expressways, you should travel at the common speed of traffic. (204)
10. "Overdriving headlights" is a condition in which dirty headlight lenses reduce visibility ahead at night. (221)
11. The pavement is generally most slippery when it first starts to rain. (224)
12. If brakes on the left side of the car are wet, the car will pull to the left when brakes are applied. (225)
13. If the hood flies up, the first thing the driver should do is to stop as quickly as possible. (237)
14. Most tire failures occur anytime regardless of the depth of the tire tread. (238)
15. If a car stalled on the railroad tracks is about to be hit by a train, the occupants of the car should run in the direction from which the train is coming. (244)

Answer the Question

16. Upon what factors does the proper lane choice on a one-way street depend? (165)
17. Why are "rumble strips" placed in the pavement at the approaches to a toll booth? (209)
18. What purpose do headlights serve at twilight? (220)
19. In the event of a tire blowout, what should a driver *not* do? (238)
20. What are two reasons most traffic fatalities occur on rural roads? (177)

Chapter 15

Qualifying Physically

Objectives

1. Tell how central and peripheral vision work through eye fixations and how they relate to a driver's visual needs.
2. List five kinds of visual abilities a driver must have and how each applies to the driving situation.
3. Tell what effect fatigue has on a driver's performance and how to combat it.
4. Explain how a driver's temporary illness and physical disability can impair the ability to drive safely. Tell how a driver can compensate for these problems.
5. List at least one way a driver can correct or compensate for impairments in visual acuity, peripheral vision, depth perception, color vision, glare recovery, and hearing.
6. Describe possible effects of medicines and drugs on a driver. Tell what precautions should be taken when using medication.
7. Explain how carbon monoxide might get into a car. Describe symptoms to recognize and tell what action to take.
8. Identify some permanent physical disabilities. Tell how people can compensate for them and how their driving records compare with those who have no physical handicaps.

Introduction

A driver's physical fitness is vital to safe driving. A driver must see well, think clearly, make correct decisions, and react quickly. Anything that affects vision, dulls thinking, or slows reactions reduces ability to drive safely.

A good driver allows for the fact that a person's physical and mental condition changes from day to day. When tired, ill, or upset, a person must limit driving or handle it with extra care. This is each driver's personal responsibility.

Many people are aware that they may have some physical condition, whether temporary or permanent, that could reduce their driving ability. An understanding of the condition and its possible effects enables them to make necessary corrections. For example, a person may need glasses to improve vision; a hearing aid may help a person who is hard-of-hearing to hear horns of other vehicles.

Where a condition cannot be corrected, the driver may be able to do something to make up or *compensate* for the limitation. A one-armed driver uses special devices on the steering wheel to help in steering. The deaf driver learns to make more effective use of the eyes to compensate for not being able to hear.

By correcting or compensating for physical defects, disabled persons have been able to maintain driving records as good or better than those who have no physical defects.

Objects recognizable but blurred.

Area of central vision, objects in sharp focus.

Objects recognizable but blurred.

Your Eyes and Your Driving

Good vision is important to driving. Probably 90 percent of the decisions made while driving are based on what the driver sees.

A driver must see quickly, clearly, and accurately, at points near, far, or widely separated. Seeing too late makes decisions come too late. Not seeing correctly can produce wrong decisions.

When driving, you must first see what is happening and send the information to the brain. Then the brain must *identify* this information and use it to *predict* what will happen next. Guided by this prediction, you *decide* what to do. Anything that makes it harder to see will also make it slower to *identify, predict, decide,* and *execute.*

Many young adults have never had their vision checked by a qualified eye specialist, such as an ophthalmologist or optometrist. About 20 percent of teen-agers have some eye problem. In most instances where a problem is discovered, it can be corrected by properly fitted glasses.

If eyes work properly, the brain receives information on which it can make correct decisions. You look with your eyes, but you see or perceive with your brain. More than that, the brain can *foresee* a situation you cannot

see. For example, if a truck or bus is beside your car, you don't pull ahead of it as it slowly starts up because you can't see beyond it. You foresee that someone might dash in front of it into your path.

HOW DO THE EYES WORK?

Eyes move rapidly, making an average of 3 to 5 stops or *fixations* per second. During these fixations, the eyes look at only one thing or event and send messages to the brain. No meaningful messages are sent while the eyes are moving.

There are two different kinds of vision. *Central vision* is a narrow cone of vision used to concentrate on things. The other is *fringe* or *peripheral vision.* This is the upper, lower, and side parts of eyesight. Fringe vision is used to find those things that a person wants to direct the central vision toward. For instance, if we see a rapid movement at the right (peripheral vision), we then look more closely (central vision) to see exactly what is there. Our peripheral vision warns us of possible danger from the sides and gives us information. It does this without having to direct our main attention to each separate object.

VISION INCLUDES VARIOUS SEEING ABILITIES

A variety of seeing abilities are needed for safe driving. Drivers must be able to see clearly at a distance, to judge distances accurately, and to see well at night.

Visual Acuity *This means being able to see an object sharply and distinctly, both near and far.* In today's traffic, a driver must be able to read a sign far down the road as well as the instrument panel only inches away. Licensing tests in all motor vehicle departments in the United States check distance visual acuity.

A rating of 20/20 is normal for distance visual acuity. This means that a person can read letters about 3/8 of an inch high on a Snellen chart at a distance of 20 feet. With a rating of 20/40, a person must be as close as 20 feet to see what someone with 20/20 vision can see at 40 feet.

A minimum visual acuity of 20/40 is recommended for driver licensing. But 12 states still issue licenses to drivers with 20/50 to 20/70 acuity, with or without glasses.

Field of Vision (Peripheral Vision) *This is the ability to see objects at either side while looking straight ahead.* Most people can see about 90 degrees to each side—a full half circle.

Drivers with a normal field of vision can see a car coming from a side street. They notice a pedestrian who comes out from behind a parked car. A reduced field of vision is dangerous to safe driving. A very narrow field of vision, called *tunnel vision,* is rare, but cases are sometimes found. A driver who stares at an object becomes less aware of objects in the field of vision.

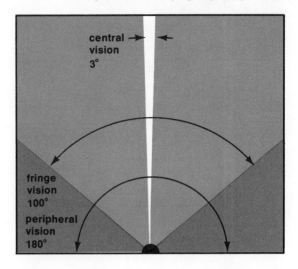

Here's what to do with visual acuity and field of vision defects:
- Consult an eye specialist.
- Drive at moderate speeds.
- Move the eyes and turn the head slightly to see things at the sides as you watch the road ahead.

Depth Perception *This is the ability to judge the distance between yourself and other things, especially when both are moving.* Depth perception (also called distance judgment) tells a driver how far away the car ahead is and how rapidly that distance is opening or closing.

Here's what to do for poor depth perception:
- Stay farther back from the car ahead.
- Wait for greater clear distance ahead when you prepare to pass another car.
- Use known distances, such as parked cars, city blocks, and distances between telephone poles to judge distances.
- Use extra care in judging distances at night since darkness hides many of the guides used in daytime.

Night Vision At night you drive in a tunnel of light, surrounded by darkness. Night vision is made up of several different, though related, kinds of vision.

- **Night Visual Acuity** *This is the ability to see clearly with very little light.* Reduction in the amount of light affects different people differently. Some who can see clearly in the daytime may have poor night visual acuity.

- **Glare Resistance** *This is the ability to see in spite of glare at night.* The bright lights of an approaching car at night are more blinding to some people than to others. The *pupil* of the eye protects the eye by getting smaller when exposed to a bright light. When the light is removed, the pupils open up. The speed of closing and opening is different for different people.

- **Glare Recovery** *This is the ability to see after being blinded by a strong light.* It usually takes 5 to 10 seconds for the pupils to fully open again. But it can take longer if the eyes must adjust to complete darkness. This is a long time for a driver not to be able to see after an approaching car with bright lights has passed.

Some precautions to take when driving at night are:

- Slow down at sundown. Even the best eyes see less well with less light.

- Avoid looking directly at headlights of oncoming cars. Use quick glances to check approaching traffic and your own position.

- Slow down and look beyond the lights or to the right of them. Use your side vision to keep track of the approaching car.

- Protect your eyes by wearing sunglasses in the daytime—*never at night.*

- Be sure your windshield is clean.

- Keep interior car lights turned off.

Color Vision *This is the ability to tell one color from another.* Nearly 8 percent of the American people have some defect in color vision. But of all drivers with poor color vision, less than 1 percent are unable to tell the red from the green traffic light.

Color blindness is a trait inherited much more often by men than women. There is no known "cure" or correction for this defect. Color-blind drivers can usually tell which traffic signal is on by the intensity of the light. So most of them are not handicapped in their driving. Anyone with poor color vision can compensate in these ways:

- Know what the *shapes* of traffic signs mean.
- Remember the top traffic light is red.
- Watch other drivers at signal lights, but also check *all* traffic before following someone else's example.
- Read warning signs that accompany flashing signals. When in doubt, signal and stop.

FACTORS THAT AFFECT VISIBILITY

Traffic dangers may be hidden behind anything that obstructs a driver's view. Some view-blockers are fixed parts of the car, but others can and should be removed.

On the Car Corner posts, supports for the roof, and rearview mirror create "blind spots" in the car that prevent a driver from seeing something on or near the road. Objects hanging from the rearview mirror or lying on the rear window ledge add to the trouble. Dirt on the windshield interferes with vision far more at night than during the day. So does dirt on the headlights, which reduces the intensity of the headlight beam. A driver can see beyond these blind spots by moving the eyes and head.

Car Speed Speed is one of the most important factors that affect a driver's vision. Side vision decreases as speed increases. At any speed over 50 mph, a driver's clear field of vision is narrowed. The term *speed smear* describes the driver's view, distorted by speed. This has an effect like tunnel vision. The eyes tend to focus further ahead where the road appears stationary. Thus the driver becomes less and less aware of what is happening at the sides.

As speed increases, the need for accurate vision also increases. Yet the driver actually sees less quickly and less clearly, and the field of vision is narrowed. Seeing distance is said to decrease about 20 feet with each 10-mph increase in speed.

In addition to these effects on eyes and brain, speed and monotony may cause *highway hypnosis* (see Chapter 12). In this dazed condition, a driver may not respond soon enough to a dangerous situation.

Here's what to do for reduced visibility:

- Slow down enough to be sure you can see well.
- Keep moving the eyes to make up for any loss of side vision.

Physical Condition of the Driver

Many factors affect one's fitness for driving. While a driver does not require the physical condition of an Olympic champion, a study of traffic collisions proves that many drivers are physically unable to perform effectively behind the wheel.

FATIGUE

The most common condition that lowers driving fitness is fatigue. Fatigue may come from lack of sleep, from excessive physical exercise, or from mental and emotional stress. Eyestrain from long hours of driving during daytime or night also contribute to fatigue.

Fatigue dulls the mind and slows down nerve and muscular responses. This lengthens decision-making time. Whether in athletics or driving, fatigue reduces one's ability to think and act quickly and accurately.

Fatigue may also cause drowsiness. During the first three years after the Pennsylvania Turnpike was opened, nearly half the fatal crashes were caused by drivers who fell asleep at the wheel.

Combating Fatigue   Rest is the only safe remedy for fatigue. "Pep pills" of any kind can be very dangerous (see Chapter 17).

Here's what to do to avoid fatigue:

- Avoid driving long distances without a break. Stop often for coffee or a soft drink. Pull off the road and get out for some exercise. Breathe deeply and move around. Stop in a safe place and take a nap if you feel drowsy.
- Keep your eyes moving over the road. Do not stare straight ahead.
- Keep the windows open wider than usual.
- If other drivers are with you, change drivers often.
- Don't try to "stretch" a driving day.

ILLNESS AND PHYSICAL CONDITION

Any illness or physical disability may impair one's driving. This may result from reduced strength and endurance, limited range of movement, or distraction due to pain.

Drivers with temporary disabilities often do not compensate as well as drivers with permanent disabilities of a similar nature.

Temporary Illness   A simple head cold or allergy may cause the eyes to water and may make it difficult to see well for driving. Other temporary illness may bring about fatigue more quickly and reduce alertness.

Temporary Physical Disabilities   Bone, joint, and muscle disorders, such as a sprained ankle, aching muscles, or a broken bone, may cause pain and limit a driver's movement. This can cut down driving efficiency, especially in an emergency. When bothered by pain, stiffness, and soreness, let someone else drive.

Here's what to do if you are ill or physically impaired and must drive:
- Drive more slowly and choose quiet roads.
- If you have a sudden attack of illness, pain, nausea, dizziness, coughing, or sneezing, pull over to a safe place and stop.
- Have someone else drive, or call a taxi, rather than risk a crash.

Medicines and Drugs   Some medicines and drugs that seem harmless can have serious side effects on driving performance. Many common remedies sold in drugstores, as well as medicines prescribed by physicians, may cause drowsiness, dizziness, and reduced alertness.

Here's what to do about medicines and drugs:
- Find out from your doctor or pharmacist what the possible side effects of prescribed medicines may be.
- Do not drive when you must take medicines or drugs that may lower driving ability.
- Never take more than the recommended dosage.

- If you must drive, be extra alert and drive only a short distance on quiet roads.

Temporary Loss of Hearing   The temporary or partial loss of hearing may be more of a handicap in driving than permanent deafness. Driving with car windows closed and with radio and air conditioner or heater on may keep a driver from hearing the sound of horns or the sirens of emergency vehicles.

CARBON MONOXIDE

Carbon monoxide is a deadly gas found in the exhaust of all gasoline engines. While it has no smell, color, or taste, it is possible to tell when it is getting into a car because it is mixed with other exhaust gases that do smell. But the smell cannot tell you how concentrated it may be. Smaller amounts of this gas can cause drowsiness, headaches, nausea, dizziness, muscular weakness, confusion, and mental dullness.

No one knows the exact level at which carbon monoxide concentration will always lower driving ability. Studies have shown dangerous amounts in all kinds of cars. It usually impairs driving ability before it makes a person ill.

The danger of carbon monoxide is greater in slow-moving, heavy traffic. Exhaust gas of the car ahead may be drawn into the car through the front vent. Driving with the trunk lid up or with the tailgate of a station wagon down may suck exhaust fumes into the car.

Here's what to do about carbon monoxide:
- Never run a car's engine in a closed garage.
- Never keep the engine running, windows closed, and heater on.
- Drive with a window at least slightly open, except with air conditioner on.

- Keep engine and exhaust system in top condition.
- Be alert for symptoms of carbon monoxide poisoning. If there are any, get out into open air right away and breathe deeply.

SMOKING

Although the relationship between smoking and collision involvement is not clear, a Columbia University study showed that smokers have more car crashes than nonsmokers.

Smoking one cigarette has been found to raise the amount of carbon monoxide in the blood to a level of 5 to 10 percent. A level of just 3 percent affects vision (especially night vision) and heart function. So it is best not to smoke while driving. Smoking may distract a driver's attention as a cigarette is being lit, held, or put out.

FITNESS FOR IPDE

Each driver must consider whether he or she is fit to perform the driving task. This requires an awareness of those conditons which can reduce that level of fitness.

Fit to Identify   If fatigue or even a slight illness affects the eyes, vision is impaired. Not only will important clues be missed, but even if they are seen they may not be interpreted in a meaningful way.

Fit to Predict   Predicting the ways in which a traffic scene is likely to change requires a good store of knowledge. It also requires alertness to every clue in the scene. Because fatigue and illness take the edge off one's alertness, they lower ability to drive safely.

Fit to Decide and to Execute   Making sound decisions is the very heart of the driving task. Sound decisions are less likely when the driver doesn't feel well. They also take longer and driver actions are generally slower and less precise. In an emergency this can determine whether or not a driver can avoid a crash.

If you get over-tired or ill, recognize your responsibility to drive as little as possible. Shift any long driving plans to another day. You'll enjoy the drive more and do a better job of it.

The Physically Disabled Driver

As a result of illness, accidents, or battlefield combat, increasing numbers of men and women are partially or almost completely disabled physically. Disabilities may vary from relatively minor handicaps for driving, such as deafness or loss of an arm or leg, to paralysis of both arms and both legs or severe muscular conditions. Other disabilities may result from chronic illness.

LOSS OF HEARING

A person who is deaf or who has a hearing defect may not hear important sounds like police whistles, sirens of fire engines, or the horns of drivers who wish to pass.

However, deafness is not a major problem in driving. Most deaf drivers can overcome this defect by use of a hearing aid or compensate for it by using the eyes more. As a rule, driving records of the deaf and hard-of-hearing are among the best.

PHYSICAL DISABILITIES

State departments of motor vehicles require permanently disabled persons to put special

devices on their cars for proper control. In this country, many disabled veterans drive with special equipment purchased for them by the government. Their driving record is as good as the record of drivers who have no physical disabilities.

CHRONIC ILLNESS

Many people are subject to chronic illness—one that lasts over a period of years. In some kinds of chronic illness, sudden attacks may cause a person to faint or lose muscular control.

Some states permit people with a chronic illness to drive if they are under the constant care of a physician and are taking prescribed medicines. In these states, people who are subject to heart or epileptic attacks must obtain the approval of their doctors and permission of the state department of motor vehicles. This may also apply to people who have to take sedatives, tranquilizing drugs, or other medicines that could have serious side effects on their ability to drive safely.

Vocabulary

carbon monoxide, 261
central vision, 256
color vision, 259
compensate, 255
depth perception, 257

fixation, 256
fringe vision, 256
glare recovery, 258
glare resistance, 258
night visual acuity, 258

peripheral vision, 256
speed smear, 259
tunnel vision, 257
visual acuity, 257

Summary

1. Messages are sent to the brain by the eyes only during each stop or fixation. Fringe or peripheral vision picks out objects to the sides, above, or below the line of sight. The eyes then focus the narrow cone of central vision on the object that requires attention.

2. Visual acuity enables a driver to see an object sharply and distinctly; field of vision—to gain information from all parts of the traffic scene; depth perception—to judge distances; night vision—to see under conditions of dim light, to see in spite of glare at night, and to recover from the glare of oncoming headlights.

3. Fatigue dulls the mind, slows muscular response, and lengthens decision-time. Rest is the best remedy. Avoid driving for long periods. Keep eyes moving and windows open.

4. Temporary illness affects vision, brings on fatigue, and reduces alertness. Physical disabilities limit movement and slow muscular action. When ill or temporarily disabled, avoid driving or drive slower on lightly traveled routes.

5. For impairments of visual acuity, wear corrective glasses; peripheral vision—move eyes continuously; depth perception—leave more following distance and wait for greater clear distance when passing; color vision—know shapes of traffic signs, watch other drivers at signals, read warning signs on flashing signals; night vision—slow down, look beyond oncoming headlights, wear sunglasses during the day, keep windshields clean, interior car lights off; hearing—wear hearing aid, keep radio volume low, window open.

6. Some medicines and drugs can cause drowsiness, dizziness, and reduced alertness. Find out possible side effects from physician or pharmacist. Take only the recommended dosage and wait until after driving to take medicine.

7. Carbon monoxide can get into a car from a poorly operating engine and from a faulty exhaust system, from air vents in heavy traffic, and from an open tailgate or trunk lid of a moving car. It is also present in cigarette smoke. Don't run the engine in a closed garage; keep car window partly open at all times; keep engine and exhaust system in good repair. Carbon monoxide can cause headaches, nausea, drowsiness, dizziness, muscular weakness—then unconsciousness and death. Get the victim into the open air fast.

8. Hearing disability may be corrected with a hearing aid or compensated for by more active use of the eyes when driving. Persons who have lost the use of arms or legs, or have other muscular disabilities, may drive with special controls. Persons with chronic illness must be under a physician's care and be licensed. The driving record of permanently disabled drivers is as good or better than that of drivers without physical disabilities.

Driving Situations

1. A young athlete, just injured playing football, has his arm in a sling. What special problems in car control would he probably have if he attempted to drive home? What would be a safer alternative?

2. You are driving at night on a 2-lane, 2-way road at 45 mph. An oncoming car has the "brights" on. You flick the dimmer switch on and off; the other driver does not dim the lights. What should you do?

3. Deafness is not a major problem in driving. Most deaf drivers can overcome the defect by wearing a hearing aid. In what other way might this driver compensate for his hearing defect?

4. Some medicines and drugs may cause reduced alertness. How would they affect this driver's ability to react to a car suddenly pulling away from the curb?

Chapter Review Questions

Your Eyes and Your Driving

1. How do fringe or peripheral vision and central vision work together to provide necessary information for a driver? (256)
2. What is a person's field of vision? What effect would a narrow field of vision have on driving and how might a driver compensate for it? (257)
3. What is depth perception? How can a person compensate for poor depth perception? (257)
4. How can a driver compensate for defects in color vision? (259)
5. Why is each kind of night vision important in driving? Name four ways a driver can minimize problems in night vision. (258)
6. Name three parts of a car that create "blind spots" for a driver. How can a driver overcome these problems? (259)
7. What is meant by "speed smear"? How can a driver overcome this problem? (259)

Physical Condition of the Driver

8. What four things can a driver do to avoid driving problems if drowsy at the wheel? (260)
9. How can temporary physical disabilities affect a driver's performance? (261)
10. Why is a temporary or partial loss of hearing dangerous for a driver? (261)
11. List situations in which carbon monoxide could be dangerous in a car. (261)

The Physically Disabled Driver

12. How can a person with poor hearing overcome this disability when driving? (263)
13. How does the driving record of physically disabled drivers compare with that of other drivers? Why do you think this is so? (263)

Projects

1. Interview members of your police department regarding the accident and violation record of older drivers in your community. How do they compare with younger drivers?
2. Interview members of your police department regarding the accident and violation record of physically disabled drivers in your community. How do they compare with drivers who have no physical disabilities?
3. Discuss the problem of physically disabled and chronically ill drivers with a physician. Report to the class on conditions and illnesses which may disqualify a person from driving.
4. Interview a representative of the state department of motor vehicles regarding legal restrictions on licensing of physically disabled and chronically ill persons and report to the class.
5. Interview an adult driver with a major physical disability about his or her driving experience. Examine the driving controls in his or her car and report to the class.

Chapter 15 · Test

(Write the correct answers on a separate sheet of paper.)

True-False

1. To see as much as possible in traffic, a driver should focus the eyes on each object in the line of sight. (256)
2. A person with 20/20 vision is considered to have normal vision. (257)
3. Depth perception tells a driver how close the car ahead is. (257)
4. When blinded by the glare of an oncoming car's headlights, a driver should turn on his or her own high-beam headlights to improve visibility for both drivers. (258)
5. Sunglasses can effectively help a driver overcome the glare of an oncoming car's high-beam head-lights. (258)
6. Speed smear describes impaired vision from moving the eyes too quickly. (259)
7. A driver with defective color vision generally has no difficulty compensating for this disability. (259)
8. The most common condition that lowers fitness to drive is fatigue. (260)
9. Carbon monoxide from a car's engine can be detected by its smell. (261)
10. Drivers who have lost an arm or leg are generally able to compensate for their physical disability better than those who have temporarily lost the use of arm or leg. (263)
11. The deaf driver is more likely to be handicapped in driving than a driver whose hearing is limited by closed windows and a loud radio. (263)

Answer the Question

12. What are stops between eye movements called? (256)
13. Learning the meaning of the shapes of traffic signs is most likely to aid a driver with what type of defective vision? (259)
14. Good eye movement is most likely to aid a driver with what type of defective vision? (256)
15. What three parts of a car create blind spots? (259)
16. Why is carbon monoxide extremely dangerous? (261)
17. What common condition lowers a driver's fitness? (260)
18. What is one effective way a driver can combat fatigue? (260)
19. What three side effects of medicines and drugs might reduce ability to drive safely? (261)
20. How can smoking hinder safe driving? (262)

Chapter 16

Emotions Affect Driving

Objectives

1. Explain how emotions can affect IPDE.
2. List three physical changes that take place when a person is gripped by strong emotion.
3. Name the emotion that most often interferes with driving, and list three other emotions that can affect driving.
4. Explain how emotions can affect a driver's decision about how much risk to take.
5. Explain how a driver can reduce risks in driving.
6. List five techniques to use to control or avoid the effects of emotion while driving.
7. List three methods by which passengers can aid the driver to accomplish the driving task successfully.
8. List the characteristics of drivers who drive for many years without collisions or violations.

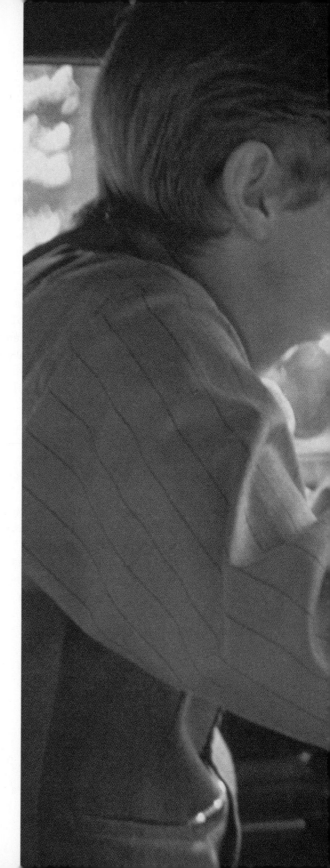

Introduction

Safe driving requires the driver to perform almost without error. Human beings, however, do make mistakes. Some of these mistakes result because drivers allow emotions to block out their reasoning ability. Part of the job of learning to drive well is learning to understand and make adjustments for human emotions that can affect driving.

Some people use the car as an extension of their own personalities. If they have an aggressive personality, they act aggressively with their car. People who are angry often drive as if they are angry, and this emotion can lead them to make serious mistakes.

The good driver has learned to cope with these emotions and to use the IPDE process to perform the driving task safely and effectively. This chapter will enable you to learn procedures that can help you control your emotions and keep them from impairing your driving ability.

The Nature of Emotions

Emotions are one of the special qualities of humans that make life interesting and enjoyable. Different people feel different degrees of emotions. However, they can become a problem for drivers when emotions affect driving performance.

EMOTION AND IPDE

Reasoning, which is needed for the IPDE process, is unlike emotion. Strong emotion tends to block out or limit a person's ability to reason out the solution to a problem. Faulty driving decisions can result. How much an emotion interferes with the driving task depends on how strongly a person is gripped by the emotion and what preparations the person has made to counter its effects.

More than one emotion can have an effect within a short period of time. For instance, a student might, on the same day, do extremely well on one exam, do badly on another, and have a misunderstanding with a friend. Just thinking about one or the other can quickly change the way a driver performs in traffic.

PHYSICAL EFFECTS OF EMOTIONS

Emotions can vary in intensity. They cause internal changes in some body functions. In a strong emotion, such as anger, the rate of the heartbeat increases; breathing is faster; and digestion slows down. The body prepares for combat. If the emotion is fear, the preparation is for flight. Some lesser emotions, such as boredom or disappointment, can slow down the ability to think clearly.

Continuous emotional stress is physically and mentally tiring. A driver, who becomes angry often, tires more quickly than a calm driver. The driver tires because of changes in heartbeat and other body functions caused by anger.

Many people have to drive when they are already tired, especially at the end of a workday. When people are tired, their ability to reason clearly is lost, and they tend to lose emotional control more easily.

ANGER WHILE DRIVING

Often in normal driving, a situation will occur in which other drivers interfere with the driver's intended speed or path of travel. Other drivers slow down in front, cross without having enough time, and take many other frustrating actions. All of them are performing their own driving plans, but to the driver it may sometimes seem as if everyone is trying to put the driver into an accident.

Because other drivers make such mistakes, anger is the emotion that probably occurs most often while driving. It can range all the way from mild irritation to furious rage.

Don't act like a child behind the wheel. Put common sense and cooperation into your driving.

A strong emotion, such as anger, tends to concentrate a driver's attention on one person in the traffic situation. It may very well be an object that is no longer important, such as a jaywalker who has now reached the curb, but is still the cause of the anger.

Anger can also carry over from some event that happened before the person started driving. The driver thus finds it difficult to focus attention on the total driving task.

Since anger sets up the body for combat, it impairs the performance of smooth braking and accelerating. The angry driver is not only likely to see less but is likely to stop suddenly or to accelerate too fast into unexpected places. These actions can create hazards for other road users.

OTHER EMOTIONS AND DRIVING

Although anger is a chief offender in driving, other emotions can also block the IPDE process.

Anxiety occurs often in driving. It can appear when a driver is forced to drive in an unfamiliar, difficult environment. When a new driver is in heavy traffic on an expressway for the first time or in downtown rush-hour traffic, anxiety can become a problem.

Anxiety differs from anger because drivers recognize anxiety and try to avoid it. Angry drivers can have more difficulty calming themselves. Anxious drivers can realize when they are in trouble and try their best to successfully complete their trip. However, they may make some panic decisions because they have difficulty identifying potential hazards and predicting the actions of other road users.

Excitement and happiness are emotions that can also prevent wise decisions necessary for safe driving. The safe driving performance of a happy, excited driver can be as impaired as that of an angry driver. People who have had a big success, such as a win over a rival team in a close game, become excited and happy. If they are too excited, their driving ability may be just as impaired by emotions as the sad, angry losers of the game.

Pouring your animal-like anger through the gas pedal hinders your driving competence.

Be considerate to all on the road, especially to over-cautious drivers.

Risks

Most children have teetered on board fences and experienced the enjoyable sensation of maintaining balance while facing danger bravely. Many young bicyclists ride with no hands and enjoy the thrill of risking a fall. Except for bruises and an occasional broken bone, the price of failure is not high.

Risk-taking in a car is different. Deliberately taking chances in a car, with its great capability for destruction, is unthinkable. The potential loss is too great and the possible penalties are too serious. An immature driver who takes risks is using the car as a toy and the street as a playground.

When young people reach the driver's license age, they are at a maturity crossroads.

Young people do not necessarily become instant adults when they become drivers. However, when they drive, they must perform the driving task with maturity.

REDUCING DRIVING RISKS

By its very nature, driving involves risk. Using the same streets and highways with all other road users can make driving risky. All road users have emotions to control and all make occasional human errors.

In Chapter 1, you learned that driving is a social task because so many road users need to cooperate. A willingness to share the road and to compensate for the mistakes of others reduces the risk for everyone using the highway transportation system.

Taking risks by running through an intersection on a yellow light is asking for trouble.

Now mature judgment and performance are a must. In choosing a legal driving age, a state must determine when most young people are mature enough to fulfill their responsibility.

Accepting some risk in normal driving is not an emotional act. A driver's decision to accept risk or not should be based on sound judgment of the available information and prior driving experience and not on the person's emotional condition. That decision should provide for the best possible chance for a safe and efficient trip at the least risk. A person who decides not to drive after having several drinks shows maturity.

The amount of risk in any traffic situation rises as emotion threatens to replace good judgment. A desire to get home or anxiety at being late may lead a driver to decide to accept more risk. Such a driver may try to pass when the margin of safety is small or go through a yellow light rather than stopping.

Drivers use different risk levels in certain situations. The amount of risk a driver will take rushing someone to the hospital may be higher than returning to visit the same person there a week later. Even the rush trip to the hospital must be carefully performed. If the driver takes so many risks that everyone ends up in the hospital, the purpose for the trip is defeated.

Sometimes drivers develop the habit of taking a certain risk over and over again. If the driver is successful each time, the driver loses the awareness that risk is still there. People who drive the same route every day tend not only to start at the same time but also expect to arrive at the same time, regardless of changing conditions. This can lead a driver to take an unthinking risk, which is just as dangerous as if the risk-taking had been done deliberately. Occasionally, someone is hit by a train at a railroad crossing that he or she has crossed regularly for years. The driver has crossed many times just ahead of the train and is not afraid of being hit.

Don't be a foolish driver and attempt to beat a train at any time.

Emotional Control

Within limits, people can learn to control their emotions. For instance, a person who enjoys music remains quiet during a selection. The emotional enjoyment builds up and bursts into applause only after the selection has ended. A driver can and must learn the same kind of control in order to perform at a safe level at all times.

While growing up, most people learn to control and direct their emotions. The automobile presents opportunities for continued progress toward emotional maturity. For many people it is a means of satisfying certain personal needs and goals. A car can represent independence and the achievement of personal worth and self-esteem.

The car itself is a special environment. For the first time, perhaps, a young person is alone, safely isolated in the driver compartment, protected from the comments, criticisms, and presence of other people. Driving thus can be a tremendously satisfying as well as an emotion-producing experience.

Some people's emotional shortcomings and characteristics carry over into driving. Even though a person has learned to control emotions in most daily situations, driving often causes emotional traits to surface again. Traffic conditions may lead to tensions and frustrations. The car tends to become an extension of one's personality. The need for emotional control is greatest where the loss of control could be most dangerous. So it is extremely important that the new driver quickly learns emotional control behind the wheel.

Sometimes occasions will arise to make drivers angry. Try to choose areas free of frustrating situations.

TECHNIQUES FOR COPING WITH EMOTION

The following techniques can help a driver learn to cope with emotions while driving. In order to make these techniques work when they are needed, a driver must think about and practice using them in other situations as well.

- Drive in an organized, orderly fashion. Use correct procedures for all maneuvers even when no one else is near. Humans are creatures of habit. A driver who habitually applies IPDE is less likely to make a mistake. This will help reduce the number and stress level of difficult traffic situations.

- Choose routes free of frustrating situations, such as traffic jams and extensive road repairs. Do not choose routes that overtax your abilities and invite emotional upset.

If you must wait long in certain situations, be patient and try to keep your emotions in check.

Your passengers are happier if you don't turn to look at them as you talk to them.

- Anticipate an emotion-producing traffic problem and mentally prepare to face it. A driver might say: "I have to drive home during rush hour. I know I may be frustrated by delays. There will be other tired people in a hurry, some of whom will be thoughtless and careless. I will not let them upset me. I will not lose my temper even if other careless drivers take unfair advantage of me."
- If you are already tired, make a special effort to keep emotions under control because people can become more emotionally upset when they are tired.
- Analyze the events that occurred when you lost your temper. What went wrong? What **identify** tasks did you omit? What necessary **predict** tasks did you forget or do incorrectly?

- If you are angry or feel some other strong emotion before you enter the car, make a self-check: "OK, I am angry, but to drive well I must cool down. I must not allow my anger to interfere with my driving or with my applying the IPDE process."
- Analyze the mistakes you make and the near misses you have to determine how to prevent others. Be analytical and decide whether emotions may have interfered.
- Decide what the penalties of becoming emotional during a trip may be. Realize that the people in the car are friends and relatives whom you least want to see hurt.
- Know yourself and be honest about the emotional characteristics of your personality.
- Don't drive if you are unable to control your emotions.

TECHNIQUES FOR PASSENGERS

Passengers have an obligation to help drivers perform safely. They can also show emotional maturity by using the following techniques to help the driver:

- Passengers should never do anything to interfere with the driver and make the trip more dangerous. They should not distract the driver with conversation, questions, or other activity when the driver must make important decisions.

- If a street name or an address needs to be found, passengers should do the searching and allow the driver to pay full attention to driving.

- If someone needs to read the map, a passenger should do it.

- If the car is approaching a toll booth, the passenger should handle the change.

- On a long trip or at night, someone should talk to the driver to help maintain alertness.

- Passengers should discourage the driver from reckless behavior. They should be mature enough not to dare a driver into trying a high-risk maneuver that offers little possibility of success.

- Passengers may occasionally have to make more serious decisions. If the driver's reasoning ability is clearly impaired by anger, alcohol, or any other reason, mature passengers may decide to risk a friendship by refusing to let the driver drive or by refusing to ride in the car.

Your passenger can help you be a safe and defensive driver by helping to keep you alert on a long trip.

GOAL OF EMOTIONAL CONTROL

Following these driver and passenger techniques will lead to the goal of safe driving. Safe driving is a task that can be helped by the desire to do well.

In addition to car capabilities and limitations, the driver also has capabilities and limitations. For safe driving, the driver needs an understanding of self, a knowledge of physical limitations, and an awareness of emotional make-up. The good driver operates well within these human limits.

Safety experts have studied people who have driven for years without a collision or a violation to determine how they accomplished such records. The characteristics reported were very similar. They drove carefully using the IPDE process all the time and completely controlling their emotions.

Perhaps the best indication of their competence is the lack of passenger reaction at the end of the trip. If they do not remember anything special about the trip, if nothing unusual happened, and if nothing seemed about to happen, the driving was undoubtedly competent and controlled.

An expert driver does not use the car to show off and usually drives it with quiet control.

Vocabulary

coping, 274

emotion, 269

risk-taking, 272

stress, 270

Summary

1. Emotions can interfere with and block out the normal IPDE process and can result in faulty driving decisions.
2. Emotions cause changes in heartbeat, breathing rate, and digestive process.
3. Anger is the most common emotion shown by drivers. All emotions, such as fear, anxiety, excitement, and joy, tend to interfere with driving.
4. Emotions can lead a driver to deliberately take risks with a car. This action is immature because the potential dangers are too great compared to the benefits.
5. By performing the driving task without emotional control, a driver can reduce the risks involved in driving.
6. A driver can learn to cope with emotions by using some of the following techniques: drive in an organized fashion, choose routes free of frustrating situations, anticipate emotion-producing traffic and prepare to face it, and make special efforts to keep emotions under control when tired.
7. Passengers can aid the driver by not distracting the driver, discouraging reckless behavior, and not allowing a friend to drive when person is impaired.
8. Drivers who drive for many years without collisions or violations have a desire to drive safely, recognize their own capabilities and limitations, and apply IPDE with controlled emotions.

Driving Situations

1. What emotions do you think each person is feeling? What might be happening?

2. You are stopped at a red light when another driver pulls alongside and challenges you to a drag race. The street seems deserted. How do you respond?

3. How is each passenger affecting the driving task? What should each passenger be doing?

4. The driver of the last car in this situation wants to go straight through the intersection. What emotion might the driver be feeling? What must the driver's action be?

Chapter Review Questions

The Nature of Emotions

1. How does the reasoning ability of a driver overcome by emotion differ from the same person's ability when calm? (270)
2. What emotions are most likely to occur as a result of delays in traffic and actions of other drivers? (270-271)
3. What bodily changes occur during a strong emotion? (270)
4. Why does anger interfere with a person's ability to concentrate on the whole driving task? (271)
5. Describe the possible driving difficulties of a person who becomes angry enough to slam doors. (271)

Risks

6. Give three examples of immature risk-taking by children. (272)
7. What risks are present in any driving? (272)
8. Name three things drivers can do to lessen normal driving risks. (273)

Emotional Control

9. How can people control their emotions? (274-275)
10. How can a passenger help a driver with problems of emotional control? (276)
11. What are the usual driving characteristics of people who have driven for many years without a collision or violation? (277)
12. Why is learning to control their emotions important for drivers? (274)

Projects

1. Pick an intersection or busy section of road. List risks you see drivers take. Show photos or slides of the area to the class.
2. Choose three friends or acquaintances who do not yet drive. Analyze their emotional tendencies and predict how their emotions will influence their driving.
3. Ask three professional drivers, such as bus drivers, police officers, or cab drivers, about examples of bad driving resulting from emotion. List the situations and determine the action that person should have taken to control the emotion.
4. Think of a young driver who has already had two or more collisions. List the emotional characteristics of that driver when not driving.

Chapter 16 · Test

(Write the correct answers on a separate sheet of paper.)

True-False

1. Most traffic situations require emotional control for successful driving performance. (274)
2. When a person becomes angry, the heartbeat slows down. (270)
3. A person who is angry tends to drive angrily. (270)
4. To succeed in traffic, a driver must be aggressive; otherwise all other drivers will arrive first. (270)
5. Passengers are most likely to remember the events of a trip with a competent driver. (277)
6. Anger is the only emotion that detracts from good driving. (271)
7. Emotions can cause an ordinarily safe driver to be temporarily unsafe. (270)
8. To drive safely, a driver must separate emotions from driving. (274)
9. Anger improves a driver's attention and IPDE reasoning. (270)
10. Using IPDE in traffic does not involve risk. (272)
11. The risk level rises as a driver becomes emotional. (273)
12. The driving task should be a thinking task, rather than an emotional experience. (270)
13. A person can be undergoing some emotional stress and still control physical actions if prepared to do so. (275)
14. Wanting to drive safely is the first step toward driving safely. (277)
15. Passengers have the obligation not to distract the driver. (276)

Answer the Question

16. What are five of the possible techniques a driver can use to control emotions? (274-275)
17. What are the reasons a new driver might feel secure in the driver compartment? (274)
18. What actions can passengers take to assist the driver to maintain emotional control? (276)
19. What kind of passenger reaction is the goal of a mature driver? (277)
20. What three physical changes occur as a person becomes angry? (270)

Chapter 17

Alcohol, Drugs, and Driving

Objectives

1. Describe how alcohol affects a person's ability to perform each IPDE step of the driving task.
2. Describe how to minimize and cope with the effects of alcohol.
3. Explain why alcohol presents special problems for young drivers.
4. List five common misconceptions about alcohol and give reasons why they are not true.
5. Explain the legal levels of intoxication and how these levels are determined by traffic police.
6. Explain what is meant by the "implied consent law."
7. Describe the steps being taken by state and federal governments to remove drinking drivers from the road.
8. Describe the role of common remedies and medicines in causing traffic crashes.
9. Name two non-prescription medicines which may impair driving ability.
10. Explain how taking non-prescription medicines can reduce driving ability.
11. Give two examples of dangerous drugs and describe how each one may impair driving performance.

Introduction

Attitudes concerning the use of alcoholic drinks vary widely in our society, depending on a person's cultural and religious experience. Although most people who drink can do so without harmful effects, some people do not or cannot drink with moderation. Their drinking leads to various social problems. One of those problems is the drinking driver.

Here are some plain facts about alcohol and driving:

- Recent studies have shown that among drivers under 20 years old who were killed in motor-vehicle crashes, nearly one-half had alcohol in their blood.
- Among crashes that occur after midnight, 60 to 70 percent involve heavy drinkers.
- For an experienced driver weighing 160 pounds, the chances of causing a crash *doubles* after drinking about 4 bottles of beer in a two-hour period.
- For a young driver in the first few years of driving, even one or two beers will *triple* the chances of a collision.
- With a blood-alcohol level (amount of alcohol in the blood) of 0.10 percent, a driver is 6 or 7 times more likely to cause a crash than a non-drinking driver. And at 0.15 percent, it increases 25 times.

How Alcohol Affects Driving Performance

Alcohol greatly affects the IPDE process. A driver who has been drinking will be less able to identify hazards quickly and to predict accurately what others will do. This frequently leads to impaired judgment and poor decisions. When the driver executes a decision, coordination may not be sufficient for the driver to avoid trouble.

EFFECTS ON THE BODY

The effect of alcohol on the body depends on a number of factors:

- the amount a person drinks.
- the strength of the drink.
- the length of time over which a given amount is drunk.
- the amount and kind of food in the stomach.
- the weight of the person.

Alcohol enters the bloodstream quickly through the walls of the stomach and small intestine. It does not have to be digested like other foods. As a result, it quickly reaches the brain where it has its greatest effect.

Food in the stomach slows down the rate of absorption of alcohol into the bloodstream. Therefore, the blood-alcohol level is not as likely to go as high as it would on an empty stomach.

Effects on the Brain Alcohol affects the brain in much the same way as a shortage of oxygen. The parts of the brain first affected are the parts that control judgment and reasoning. The drinker feels as if the process of thinking and reacting are sharper than usual. On the contrary, they are slower. The drinker loses the inhibitions that provide restraints needed for good driving.

Reaction Time and Coordination As more alcohol enters the bloodstream, the brain centers that control muscular movement and body control are slowed down. It takes longer for a driver to recognize danger. Once it is recognized, it takes the brain longer to process the information. Messages to different parts of the body may even be confused. The driver may oversteer or not brake hard enough. Movements are clumsy. That is why so many impaired drivers are involved in collisions.

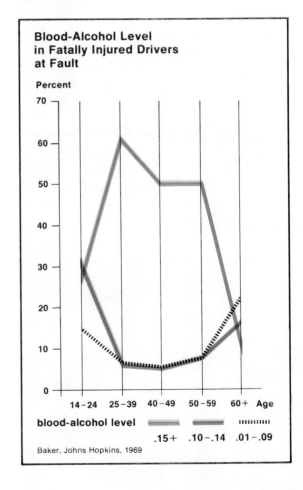

Blood-Alcohol Level in Fatally Injured Drivers at Fault

Percent

blood-alcohol level: .15+ / .10–.14 / .01–.09

Baker, Johns Hopkins, 1969

Pedestrian as seen by a driver at night.

Pedestrian as seen by a drunk driver at night.

Effects on Vision   In addition to impaired judgment and reasoning, vision is also affected by alcohol. After a drink or two, more light is needed to see dimly lighted objects. If you could barely see a pedestrian on a dark night, you might not see the pedestrian at all after a few drinks.

Alcohol affects the reflex action of the eyes. At night, this can be critical. As headlights of oncoming vehicles come closer, the pupils of the eyes normally become smaller to cut out the excess light. As the headlights pass, the pupils become larger to gather in all available light. After a few drinks, these reflexes are impaired. As the bright lights approach, the pupils do not contract properly. When the lights pass, pupils do not open properly. As a result, the driver is temporarily blinded.

Blurred vision is another impairment caused by alcohol. The eyes normally pick up two separate images of an object. The brain then coordinates them so that just one image is identified. After a few drinks, vision becomes blurred. The driver may see two

center lines on the highway or an oncoming car may appear to be on both sides of the road at the same time.

Alcohol also impairs depth perception. This is important in judging the distance and speed of oncoming vehicles, the space from vehicles ahead, and the distance from signs and signals. Many rear-end collisions involved a driver who had too much to drink.

CONTROLLING THE EFFECTS OF ALCOHOL

Control Intake   Here are some ways a person who drinks can control intake of alcohol to protect his or her fitness as a driver:

1. Drink water or soft drinks. Few people will notice the difference.
2. Leave part of the drink in the glass. An empty glass invites a refill.
3. Set an unwanted drink down and walk away from it.
4. Watch drinks being mixed. Guard against excess liquor in drinks.
5. Space drinks about one hour apart.
6. Eat some food before or while drinking to slow the absorption of alcohol.

286

Control Impairment   Once alcohol enters the bloodstream, only time can reduce the blood-alcohol level and the impairment.

How long must a person who has been drinking wait before he or she is fit to drive? Length of time varies from one person to another. It depends on one's weight, physical condition, the amount drunk, the "strength" of drinks, and the amount of food in the stomach. Young people are usually affected at lower blood-alcohol levels than are older, more experienced, drinkers. For young people, the effect may begin after one drink.

The waiting period depends mostly on how much was drunk and the time period within which it was drunk. The average person "burns" alcohol at the rate of about one drink per hour. Even waiting an hour after the last drink might not be long enough if a person has been drinking heavily or is not used to drinking.

The chart shows the number of drinks needed to reach different blood-alcohol levels. A line from a person's weight through the number of ounces of 80 proof liquor consumed in an hour points to the blood-alcohol levels. These are *average* blood-alcohol levels. A new, young driver who is a beginner at both drinking and driving should allow a greater margin.

Feeling "high" may be psychological, and not based just on the number of drinks. Many people get "high" with very little to drink. For some young drivers, any amount of alcohol in the body may impair driving.

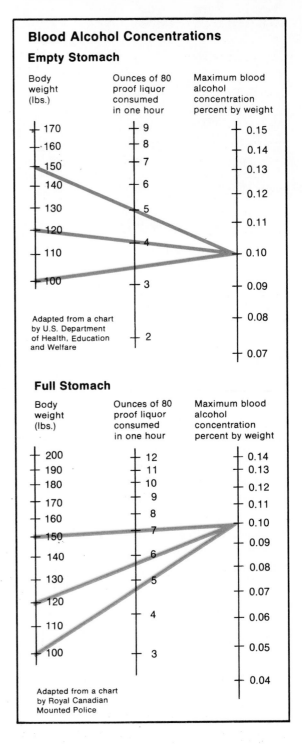

Reduce Passenger Risk   Do not drive with someone who is impaired, but if you must, here are some things to do:

1. Get the driver to let someone else drive.
2. Lock the door of the car to provide greater protection in case of a crash.
3. Fasten seat belt and shoulder harness and adjust the head restraint.
4. Assist the driver by pointing out signs, traffic signals, and possible hazards.
5. Enlist group opinion in favor of more moderate driving.
6. If it is obvious that the driver's control is seriously impaired, get out of the car at the first safe opportunity.

Each drink contains approximately the same amount of alcohol.

MISCONCEPTIONS ABOUT ALCOHOL

Many people have mistaken ideas about alcohol. For example:

- *I can "burn off" alcohol by strenuous activity.* You can slow your body's absorption of alcohol by eating before or while you drink. But you cannot get rid of alcohol faster by doing strenuous activities. Only time will reduce the effects of alcohol.

- *I've built up a tolerance.* Some people *appear* to build up a tolerance because an experienced drinker has learned to control some of the more obvious signs of impairment. The same amount of alcohol in the bloodstream of an experienced and an inexperienced drinker of the same weight should give them about the same blood-alcohol level. By the time they reach a blood-alcohol level of 0.10 percent, they would both be too impaired to drive safely.

- *I can "sober up" by drinking black coffee and taking a cold shower.* Even the stimulation of black coffee and a cold shower cannot overcome the effects of alcohol.

Nor do tomato juice, egg whites, or other drinks have any value in reducing impairment. Only time will reduce the effects of alcohol.

- *I can drive safely after a few drinks.* Some people may have driven on occasions while impaired. They may believe they can continue to do so without special precautions, but the odds are against them. To improve their chances they must consciously remember to concentrate on their driving, keep their eyes moving, and avoid any distractions. This means turning off the radio and not talking to passengers.

- *I'm OK. I'm only drinking beer.* A 12-ounce bottle or can of beer contains as much alcohol as an average highball or cocktail. A 160 pound person who drinks three beers or more in a three-hour period will begin to build up the alcohol level in the blood. Although the food substance in beer tends to slow the absorption of alcohol, the carbonation (bubbles) in beer speeds up the passage of alcohol into the blood.

Alcohol and the Law

In most states, persons convicted of driving while intoxicated (first offense) may be imprisoned for at least 5 to 10 days or fined a minimum of $100, or both. In either case, the driver's license may also be suspended. The judge may order a medical examination and further treatment if the person is a problem drinker. Such persons usually pay very high insurance rates for several years after getting their licenses back.

LEGAL LEVELS OF INTOXICATION

Most states have set the legal evidence of intoxication at a blood-alcohol level of 0.10 percent. According to the chart on p. 286, a 150 pound person who consumed about 5 ounces of 80 proof beverage on an empty stomach in one hour would be legally intoxicated. However, drivers may be charged with driving while impaired with blood-alcohol levels of 0.05 to 0.10 percent if there is other sufficient evidence.

Remember, 0.10 percent is the level at which *everyone* is legally under the influence of alcohol. Many people are impaired at

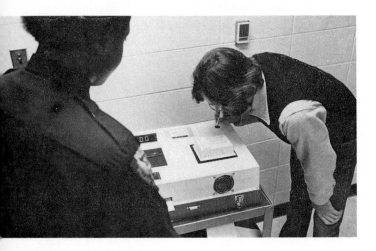

levels well below that. In fact, for some persons, it begins with the first drink.

Chemical Tests for Intoxication A blood-alcohol level of 0.10 percent means that there is one part of alcohol for each 1,000 parts of blood in the body. The amount of alcohol in the blood is determined by analysis of various body fluids like blood, urine, and saliva. The simplest, most economical and most widely used method is a breath test.

Many people believe that the odor on one's breath is what determines how high the test reading will be. This is not true. The instrument records only the amount of alcohol in the breath. The alcohol in a drink is almost odorless. The instrument also provides a safeguard for drivers who may be ill or injured, but who appear to be drunk.

Implied Consent Law All states have an implied consent law. This means that at the time they accept a license, drivers give their consent to have their breath tested if they are arrested on suspicion of driving "under the influence." The driver's license can be suspended, generally for six months, if the test is refused. However, this law gives police the right to test drivers *only after they are arrested and charged with driving while intoxicated.*

Police often hesitate to arrest drivers unless they are quite sure that driving ability has been impaired. As a result, several states now have laws requiring drivers who have been in collisions to take the blood-alcohol test *before* being charged. Drivers refusing to take the test may be arrested and their licenses suspended. Under this law, police can perform the breath test within minutes right at the scene of the crash.

HEAVY DRINKERS

The more a person drinks, the more likely he or she will be involved in a crash, and the more likely to have *started* the crash. Furthermore, the crashes in which alcohol plays a part tend to be much more serious than those in which alcohol is not involved. An estimated 90 percent of all one-car crashes that occur after midnight involve drinking.

Among drivers tested for alcohol after being killed in crashes for which they were at fault, 43 percent had blood-alcohol levels of 0.10 percent or higher. But only about one percent of all drivers on the road who were not involved in collisions had levels in that range.

Plans to Control Drunken Driving   Since heavy drinkers cause so many crashes, state and federal authorities have devised programs to reduce this problem. Such programs include efforts to:

- Identify the heavy drinking drivers.
- Work with medical authorities and state license bureaus to develop a plan for suspending or restricting their licenses.
- Provide them with counseling courses, medical treatment, and other programs.
- Provide them, through community efforts, with transportation for necessary trips.

IT'S YOUR DECISION

At the start of your whole lifetime of driving, you can resolve whether to be part of the drinking-driving problem or to contribute to its solution. Regardless of your decision to drink or not to drink, you can support legislation to help get drinking drivers off the road. You can support efforts of local police and courts and other agencies to arrest, convict, and treat motorists who drink and drive. If you drink, you can resolve to be a responsible drinker and to leave the driving to those who are fit for the task.

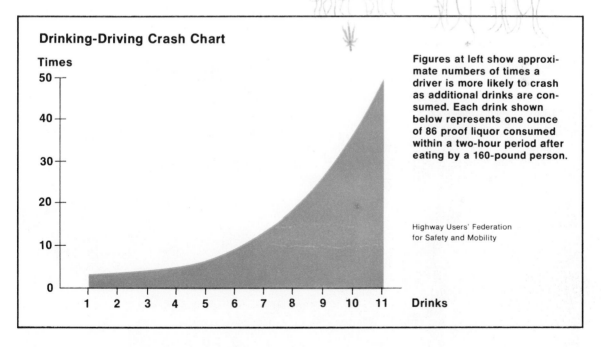

Drinking-Driving Crash Chart

Times

Drinks

Figures at left show approximate numbers of times a driver is more likely to crash as additional drinks are consumed. Each drink shown below represents one ounce of 86 proof liquor consumed within a two-hour period after eating by a 160-pound person.

Highway Users' Federation for Safety and Mobility

Drugs and Driving

Almost any drug can reduce one's driving ability. But it's not just the illegal drugs that cause the problem. More traffic crashes result from medicines and non-prescription remedies bought at a drugstore than from illegal drugs. Because these remedies are widely advertised and on display in stores, few people consider them a problem. Yet many syrups, drops, sprays, pills, and tablets taken for headaches, hay fever, colds, allergies, or nervous conditions may cause drowsiness and dizziness. These side effects are all the more dangerous because they are unexpected. They affect driver alertness without warning.

Other common side effects include slowed reaction time, irritability, faulty judgment, blurred vision, and impaired depth perception. All of these effects reduce ability to drive safely.

Ask a pharmacist about a drug's side effects.

The side effects of these common drugs, as well as others to be discussed, are multiplied when taken before or after an alcoholic drink. Sometimes, when two different drugs are taken together, their side effects are also multiplied. Read the label before taking any drug or medicine. Note any warning about drowsiness or dizziness that could impair driving ability.

TRANQUILIZERS AND ANTIHISTAMINES
Tranquilizers are used to relieve tension and anxiety, to treat high blood pressure, and to calm the nerves. They depress the central nervous system, thus reducing alertness and clear thinking. In larger doses they can cause drowsiness, dizziness, and blurred vision.

Drugs and medicines sold for the relief of colds, hay fever, and allergies usually contain antihistamines. These also depress the central nervous system. Even small doses may cause drowsiness and reduced attention in some people.

STIMULANT DRUGS

Amphetamines, such as Benzedrine and Dexedrine, and cocaine are stimulant drugs. Amphetamines, also called "pep pills," "speed," "lid proppers," and "wakeups," stimulate the nervous system. When taken, these drugs give a feeling of energy and alertness. They "wake up" the body with boundless energy. People who take them never seem to feel tired. Only when the drug wears off and all available energy is used up, does the body begin to feel the effects of a letdown. This can be dangerous, especially when a person begins to feel extremely tired. A tired driver is not alert at the wheel, and this can be hazardous for drivers, their passengers, and everyone else on the road.

SEDATIVE DRUGS

Barbiturates, sometimes called "blue devils," "yellow jackets," "blue heavens," and "goof balls," are sedative drugs. Barbiturates, generally found in sleeping pills, slow down the nervous system. They reduce tension and anxiety and tend to cause drowsiness. Because of this, they are properly called *depressants* or "downers." Body processes and reactions are slowed down when these drugs are taken. If a driver takes them, they can slow down his or her ability to function properly behind the wheel. If a driver cannot concentrate or react quickly in traffic, accidents may result.

Amphetamines and barbiturates should be taken only under a doctor's supervision. Before taking any kind of drugs, however, ask your doctor about their effects.

HALLUCINOGENIC DRUGS

Marijuana and LSD are hallucinogenic drugs. Hallucinogenic drugs distort vision and perception, as well as alter the other senses.

Marijuana, sometimes called "grass," "pot," or "reefer," is a mild hallucinogen. The effects of marijuana are not completely known. As with all drugs, marijuana affects different people in different ways. There is no medical evidence as to how marijuana affects people or to what degree their driving is impaired by its use. The effects of the use of marijuana continues to be controversial.

LSD, also called "acid," is a strong hallucinogen. This mind-altering drug may hamper a person's coordination and judgment and thus may present problems for a user whether he or she is driving or not. Reactions are always unpredictable. Though different people react differently to this drug, a person who uses LSD one time without ill effects may experience a "bad trip" another time.

NARCOTIC DRUGS

Narcotics depress the nervous system. Among the narcotic drugs are heroin, morphine, codeine, and methadone. Though they are dangerous drugs, some have medical uses. These drugs are given to relieve anxiety and pain. It is dangerous and illegal to take narcotics without medical supervision.

Continued use of a narcotic can lead to addiction. Because the body can develop a tolerance to the drug, more and more of the narcotic is needed each time to get the same effect. The more the drug is taken, the more dangerous the drug becomes. An overdose can cause death.

No drug is harmless. Any drug taken contrary to medical direction or without medical supervision is very risky. Such abuse of drugs holds potential dangers, the effects of which are hard to predict for certain people under certain circumstances.

amphetamine, 291	hallucinogen, 291	narcotic, 291
antihistamine, 290	impairment, 286	sedative, 291
barbiturate, 291	implied consent law, 288	stimulant, 291
blood-alcohol level, 284	inhibition, 284	tranquilizer, 290

Summary

1. Alcohol causes slowed reaction time and faulty coordination, which affect a driver's ability to respond to the IPDE process correctly and quickly in an emergency.
2. Controlling the amount and manner of drinking can somewhat limit the effects of alcohol.
3. Young drivers who are inexperienced at both drinking and driving are impaired at lower blood-alcohol levels than are experienced drinker-drivers.
4. Five common misconceptions about alcohol are: I can "burn off" alcohol by strenuous activity; I've built up a tolerance; I can "sober up" by drinking black coffee and taking a cold shower; I can drive safely after a few drinks; I'm OK. I'm only drinking beer.
5. Most states have set the minimum legal limit for intoxication at 0.10 percent blood-alcohol level as determined by chemical tests for intoxication.
6. Under the implied consent law, drivers agree in advance to take a chemical test for intoxication if arrested on suspicion of driving "under the influence."
7. State and federal governments have developed programs to identify heavy drinker-drivers, suspend or restrict their licenses, provide counseling and medical treatment, and provide transportation for essential trips for those in the program.
8. Common remedies and medicines cause many collisions because they are so widely used and people don't realize their dangerous side effects.
9. Antihistamines and tranquilizers are two common drugs that can impair driving ability.
10. Non-prescription medicines can reduce alertness and clear thinking. They can also cause drowsiness, dizziness, and blurred vision.
11. Amphetamines stimulate the nervous system. After the first effects wear off, the body's energy reserves are used up, followed by a dangerous let-down. Barbiturates slow down the nervous system. They cause drowsiness and slow reactions.

Driving Situations

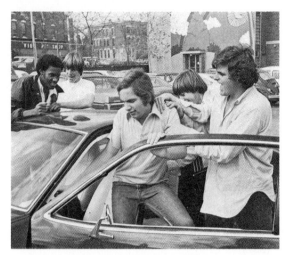

1. You just left a party with some friends, one of whom had been drinking a lot. He expects to drive you and several others home. How will you deal with this situation?

2. A driver, stopped by police on suspicion of driving while intoxicated, was asked to take a breath test. If you were that driver and had been drinking earlier, how would you respond to the request?

3. A teen-ager, who had just finished a six-pack of beer with a friend, is driving home at night. How might alcohol affect his driving when he tries to pass another car?

4. A group of friends spent the day in a park, eating and drinking beer. Assuming everyone had a license and was a skillful driver, what is the best way to decide who should drive home?

Chapter Review Questions

How Alcohol Affects Driving Performance

1. If a young driver who is inexperienced at drinking and at driving has one or two beers in an hour, what happens to his or her chances of being involved in a crash? (283)
2. Why is the decision process of the driving task more difficult for a driver who has been drinking? (284)
3. What five factors determine the effects of alcohol in the body? (284)
4. Why does alcohol have an effect on the body so quickly? (284)
5. How does alcohol affect one's ability to recover from the glare of headlights? (285)
6. In what six ways can a person protect his or her fitness as a driver when at a party where alcohol is served? (285)
7. Why do drivers under the age of 20 years have collisions at lower blood-alcohol levels than older drivers? (286)
8. What is the only way to get rid of alcohol in the bloodstream? (286)
9. In what six ways can a passenger reduce the risk of a collision and possible injury when riding with a driver who may be somewhat impaired by alcohol? (287)
10. How effective are coffee and food in reducing the effects of alcohol? (287)

Alcohol and the Law

11. What is meant by "implied consent law?" (288)
12. What are state and federal governments doing to reduce the drinking-driving problem? (289)

Drugs and Driving

13. Why do legal drugs and medicines have a greater effect on driving performance than illegal drugs? (290)
14. What are the effects when drugs and alcohol are taken together? (290)
15. Give two examples of dangerous drugs and their effects on driving. (291)

Projects

1. Obtain information from local or state police regarding the number of drivers convicted in one year of driving under the influence of alcohol or drugs in your state.
2. Interview representatives of your police, public health, and mental health departments and other public or private agencies concerned with the problem of drinking-drivers. Report to the class what is being done in your community on this problem.
3. How do police in your community determine whether a driver is under the influence of alcohol or drugs? Follow a typical case from the time the driver is stopped to the time the license is returned to the driver. In what ways is the procedure different for handling juvenile (under 18 years) drivers?
4. Attend a session of your municipal or traffic court to observe a drunk-driving trial and make a report to the class on the outcome.

Chapter 17 · Test

(Write the correct answers on a separate sheet of paper.)

True-False

1. A person weighing 100 pounds will reach a blood-alcohol level of 0.10 percent after drinking less alcohol than a 200 pound person. (286)
2. Alcohol is absorbed into the bloodstream quickly because it doesn't have to be digested like other food. (284)
3. Young drivers are usually involved in collisions at lower blood-alcohol levels than older drivers. (286)
4. The effects of alcohol can be overcome by drinking black coffee and taking a cold shower. (287)
5. The effects of alcohol can be limited by spacing drinks about one hour apart. (285)
6. In most states the minimum legal blood-alcohol level for intoxication has been set at 0.10 percent. (288)
7. The odor of an alcoholic beverage determines the reading on the breath test. (288)
8. Most persons do not begin to show the effects of alcohol until their blood-alcohol level reaches 0.10 percent. (288)
9. If a driver refuses to be tested when stopped by the police on suspicion of driving while intoxicated, the license can be suspended for up to six months. (288)
10. A 12-ounce bottle of beer contains about as much alcohol as a cocktail. (287)
11. A driver with a blood-alcohol level of over 0.10 percent may be found not guilty of driving while intoxicated if that driver can convince the court he or she is an experienced drinker. (288)
12. State and federal government programs to remove heavy drinkers from the road usually depend on long term jail sentences to correct the problem. (289)
13. Common drugs and medicines cause more crashes than illegal drugs, such as pep pills and narcotics. (290)
14. Barbiturates generally have the same effect on a person as amphetamines. (291)
15. Drugs and medicines bought in drugstores for the relief of colds and allergies are not likely to affect driving performance unless taken in large doses. (290)

Answer the Question

16. What function of the brain is first impaired by alcohol? (284)
17. What is the only thing that can reduce the effects of alcohol? (287)
18. What is the best evidence to present in court to prove a driver was under the influence of alcohol? (288)
19. When alcohol and drugs are taken together, what is the effect? (290) *multiplies*
20. What are three side effects of common drugs and medicines which may impair driving ability? (290)

Chapter 18

Owning and Maintaining a Car

Objectives

1. Describe ways to find a competent mechanic to repair and maintain a car.
2. Explain the meaning and importance of preventive maintenance for car owners.
3. List the preventive maintenance measures a driver can take before starting the engine, after the engine is running, while driving, after stopping at a gas stop, and while having the car lubricated.
4. Identify the major elements and describe the warning signs which indicate the need for repair, replacement, or maintenance to keep the following systems running:
    a. Power train
    b. Ignition and electrical
    c. Cooling
    d. Fuel and exhaust
    e. Lubrication
    f. Steering and suspension
    g. Braking
5. Describe three types of tires, how to maintain them, and rules for replacing them.
6. Explain how a driver can calculate the miles per gallon of gas for a car. What economy measures for good gas mileage and reduced wear on car parts can a car owner and driver take?

Introduction

Before each flight in a commercial airplane, the airline makes a careful preflight check to be sure that the plane is in good mechanical condition. Many people who fly with confidence might fail to keep their own cars in good condition and are not even aware that their cars need repairs. Yet, they would expect their friends and members of their families to ride in those cars.

In a broad sense, defensive driving is often defined as preventing crashes before they develop. Since keeping a car in good repair helps prevent crashes, understanding a car well enough to maintain it is an important part of the driving task.

Just how much must a driver know about the mechanics of an automobile? Car engines are complicated and require specialized knowledge and tools for proper repair. The average driver does not invest the time and money to learn how to fix an automobile. But every driver should know enough to spot the signs of trouble and see that repairs are made right away. Understanding how a car runs is the basis for keeping it running well. A car that runs well costs less to operate and is less likely to be involved in a collision resulting from mechanical breakdowns.

Car Maintenance

Finding a competent and dependable mechanic is important to a driver for proper maintenance and for prevention of car problems before they become critical.

SELECTING A GOOD MECHANIC

Your life and that of many others may depend on the mechanic's judgment and skill. Look for a qualified mechanic *before* your car breaks down. Friends, neighbors, and auto shop teachers may recommend a good mechanic.

Some states now require qualified mechanics to pass written and practical examinations. These mechanics wear special patches on their uniforms certifying their skill in various automotive systems, such as electrical systems or automatic transmissions.

Their places of business will display proper certificates, which could serve as a basis for selecting a mechanic for your car.

Usually, new-car dealers must meet certain standards for repair facilities and mechanics' abilities as set by the car manufacturer. In the absence of other information, a new-car dealer may be your best choice for keeping your car in good condition.

CAR CLINICS

Automobile diagnostic centers, known as car clinics, put a car through electronic and mechanical tests to find out what is wrong with it. The car owner is told whether any systems or parts fail to function at acceptable standards. Such clinics may reveal car defects *before* they cause trouble. This test can save the car owner money in the long run.

Tune-ups must be done as recommended in the owner's manual.

Maintenance Schedule

Services (Refer to owner's manual for details.)	Mileage for Servicing					
	7,500	15,000	22,500	30,000	37,500	45,000
Fluid levels check; chassis lubrication	■	■	■	■	■	■
Engine oil change	■	■	■	■	■	■
Oil filter change	■		■		■	
Tire rotation	■		■		■	
Cooling system check		■				■
Wheel bearing repack				■		
Auto. trans. fluid and filter change				■		
Tire and wheel inspection	■	■	■	■	■	■
Exhaust system check	■	■	■	■	■	■
Suspension and steering check	■	■	■	■	■	■
Brakes and power steering check	■	■	■	■	■	■
Engine idle speed adjustment	■		■		■	
Fuel filter replacement		■		■		■
Spark plug replacement		■		■		■
Air cleaner element replacement				■		

PREVENTIVE MAINTENANCE

Preventive maintenance is the care a car should get to stop trouble before it starts. This means not only day-to-day care, but periodic attention at a service station or garage at the times listed in the owner's manual.

The schedule for having certain maintenance jobs done is extremely important. A new car's warranty may not be good unless items covered by the warranty are done at the scheduled times.

Before Starting the Engine   Before starting the engine, clean the windshield, headlights, and taillights if they are dirty. Remove any glass or other objects on the pavement in the way of your car that might damage the tires. Note whether any of the tires seem softer than the others. A tire that loses air may go flat without warning. It is easier and less expensive to change a tire at home or at the corner service station than on an expressway or deserted highway.

For better visibility to the rear, clear books and packages off the rear window ledge. If it looks like rain, check the windshield wipers and washers. If you plan to drive after dark, check the headlights and all other lights. Also check the horn.

After Starting the Engine   With the ignition on, all gauges and warning lights should come on. If one does not, have it fixed. With the engine running, check your instruments and gauges. Alternator and oil-pressure lights should be off. The gas gauge should show at least half a tank of fuel. As you prepare to drive, press on the foot brake prior to shifting. Note the "feel" of the brake pedal. It should be firm, not spongy or soft.

While Driving   Listen for unusual noises that may warn of trouble. Notice any differences in steering, braking, or accelerating, and in the ride or handling of the car. A hard, bumpy ride may point to the need for new shock absorbers. Check the gauges frequently while driving. A warning light indicates trouble.

At a Gas Stop   While filling your gas tank at a service station, turn off your engine. Clean the windshield and outside mirror; check the battery, oil level, fan belt, radiator hoses, and hose connections. Also check tire pressure.

At a Service Station for Lubrication   When your car is being lubricated (greased) and the oil changed, have the mechanic:
- Check differential, generator, starter, distributor, and the anti-smog device.
- Check tires for cuts, nails, excessive or uneven wear, and proper inflation.
- Check water level of the battery and see that the terminals are clean.
- Check air filter; clean or replace.
- Check brake master cylinder for proper level of brake fluid. If the fluid is low, check for a leak in the wheel brake cylinders.
- Check the parking brake for tension.
- Check windshield wipers and washer. In winter, be sure there is antifreeze in the washer container to prevent freezing.
- Check radiator coolant level, fan belt, radiator hoses, and hose connections.
- Check automatic transmission fluid level and add fluid if needed.
- Check exhaust system (muffler and tailpipe) for leaks.
- Lubricate door locks and hinges.
- Oil linkages in the accelerator assembly.

Cylinders and Pistons

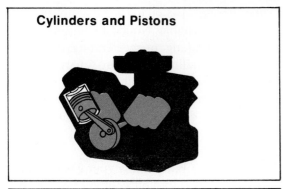

Spark Plug Firing

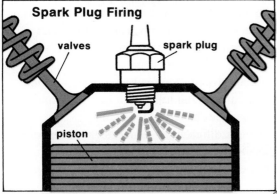

valves · spark plug · piston

Cylinder Sends Power to Rear Wheels

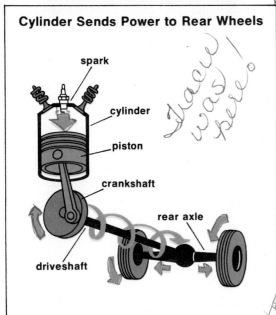

spark · cylinder · piston · crankshaft · rear axle · driveshaft

THE ENGINE AND THE POWER TRAIN

How It Runs Explosions of an air-gas mixture in the combustion chambers or **cylinders** of the engine produce power by forcing **pistons** downward. The **crankshaft** changes the up-and-down of the pistons into a rotary motion which is transmitted to the rear wheels (in most cars) by a power train. The major parts of the power train include the **clutch** and **transmission, driveshaft, differential,** and **rear axle.**

The **transmission** enables the driver to use the power of the engine to move the car at various speeds and directions. In a stickshift car, the driver shifts gears by first pressing down on the clutch pedal. This disconnects the engine from the transmission so that another gear can be selected. In an automatic transmission, the driver selects the gear position and the shifting is done automatically without a clutch.

The **driveshaft** is a long metal shaft, which is turned by the transmission and carries the power to the differential.

The **differential,** located midway between the rear wheels, changes the direction of power from the turning driveshaft to the **rear axle,** which then turns the rear wheels. The differential has gears that allow one rear wheel to turn faster than the other when a car is turning a corner.

Keeping It Running When the **engine** is first started, do not race it. Wait until the engine has warmed up. This will allow all parts to receive proper lubrication and work at full efficiency before the engine is speeded up.

To maintain good performance, tune up the engine about once a year, depending on the number of miles driven and the way the car is driven. As part of a tune-up, **spark plugs**

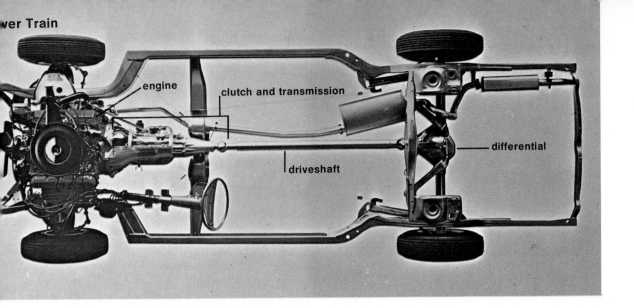

engine

clutch and transmission

differential

driveshaft

are cleaned and gapped or replaced. **Distributor points** and **condenser** (not found on newer cars) and **air cleaner** may also be replaced.

With the engine running, check the **automatic transmission** fluid by using the transmission dipstick at least once a month. Do not let the fluid level get low. Repairs on an automatic transmission are among the most expensive. If a car does not seem to shift smoothly when you accelerate or seems to take hold suddenly, the automatic transmission may be low on fluid.

Operating Cautions for Automatic Transmission

- Accelerating the engine with brakes applied and transmission in REVERSE, DRIVE, or LOW can damage the transmission.
- Use brakes to hold the car on an upgrade for prolonged periods instead of speeding up the engine with transmission in gear.
- Prolonged idling while in DRIVE, especially when the car is idling fast, may damage the transmission.
- Downshift to LOW only at very slow speeds.
- Always bring the car to a complete stop before shifting to PARK or REVERSE.
- Never work under the hood with the engine running and the transmission in any position other than PARK.*

*From "Pontiac Owner's Manual for 1976." Reprinted courtesy of Pontiac Motor Division, General Motors Corporation.

THE IGNITION AND THE ELECTRICAL SYSTEMS

How It Runs   Turning the **ignition key** sends an electric current from the **battery** to turn the **starter motor.** At the same time, electricity from the battery also goes to each **spark plug** at the proper instant to explode the air-gas mixture in the cylinders. Once the engine is running, the **alternator,** connected by a belt to the engine, generates electrical current. It also puts power back into the battery.

Keeping It Running   Since the battery is used in starting the car, it is important to keep the battery in good condition. Add distilled water if the level is low. Keep the **terminals** free of corrosion and the **cables** tight. Some batteries are sealed when manufactured and do not require the addition of water.

If the alternator warning light stays on while the engine is running, the alternator is not generating electricity. The car is thus using up the battery's power, and there may not be enough power left in the battery to keep the engine running. Have the problem corrected promptly.

In cold weather, the engine is harder to start because the battery is cold and has less power. If the starter doesn't turn the engine over quickly, get your car to a garage and have the battery charged or, if necessary, replaced. By doing this at once, you will avoid having the battery fail when you are far from a garage or service station.

Fuses and Circuit Breakers   **Fuses** and **circuit breakers** are safety devices. Fuses will burn out if there is a short or an overload in the electrical system. Check the owner's manual or ask your mechanic to show you where fuses are located and how to replace one. Circuit breakers will allow lights to come on automatically after an overload.

Lights   The bulbs of headlights, taillights, and turn signal lights sometimes burn out. Check them from time to time by watching their reflection on a wall or garage door. Have the aim of the headlight beams tested at tune-up times.

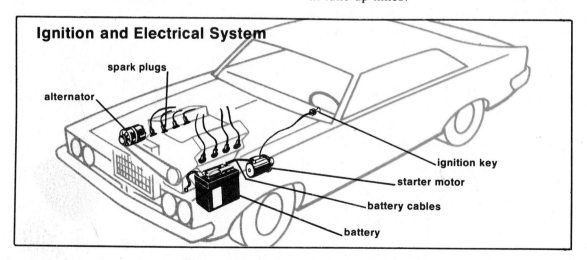

Ignition and Electrical System

spark plugs

alternator

ignition key

starter motor

battery cables

battery

STARTING A CAR WITH A DEAD BATTERY

If you turn on the ignition switch and the starter does not make a sound, you probably have a dead battery. You can start the car by using jumper cables. The following procedure should be used with jumper cables:

1. Position the cars so that the jumper cables can easily reach between the two cars.
2. Turn off the engines and place the shift in NEUTRAL or PARK.
3. Make sure the batteries are the same voltage, either 6 or 12.
4. Connect the positive terminal of the live battery to the positive terminal of the dead battery. The negative terminals should then be connected. *Caution:* If cables are crossed, the alternators of both cars will be damaged.
5. Follow the instructions in your owner's manual for the correct way to attach the clips to the battery.
6. Be careful not to cause sparks, which could ignite any hydrogen present. Do not attempt to start a car with a frozen battery because it may explode. Look in the cell caps. If ice can be seen or fluid cannot be seen, do not attempt to jump the battery.
7. Start the car with the good battery first and then turn the ignition switch on in the other car.
8. When the other car has started, disconnect the negative terminals first, then the positive ones.

PUSH-STARTING A STICKSHIFT CAR

Sometimes a stickshift car with a dead battery can be pushed to start it. Remember that this can be dangerous because the car being pushed blocks the view of the driver pushing it. In some states, pushing a car is illegal.

Make sure the bumpers of the two cars are the same height, or one may slip under the other and become locked. The following procedure can be used to push-start a stickshift car:

1. Turn on the ignition.
2. Press the clutch pedal down and keep it down.
3. Move the stickshift lever to SECOND gear.
4. Signal the other driver to start pushing.
5. When your car has reached a speed of 15 mph (24 km/h), slowly let up on the clutch. At the same time, press down on the accelerator, and your engine should start. Wave off the other car.

TOWING

In many instances of equipment failure, if you are unable to start the car yourself, you will have to call a mechanic to repair the car. The mechanic may bring a tow truck and haul your car to the garage.

Before the mechanic attaches the tow-truck lift to your car, release the parking brake, shift to NEUTRAL, and turn the ignition switch off. The towing lift should be attached to the structural parts of the car, not to the bumper or the brackets.

The tow truck must pull an automatic-shift car from the rear rather than the front because if the rear wheels are on the ground, the transmission can be damaged. If the front wheels of the car are on the ground, be sure the steering mechanism is tied securely to keep the car in line behind the tow truck. The tow truck may attach to either end of a stickshift car.

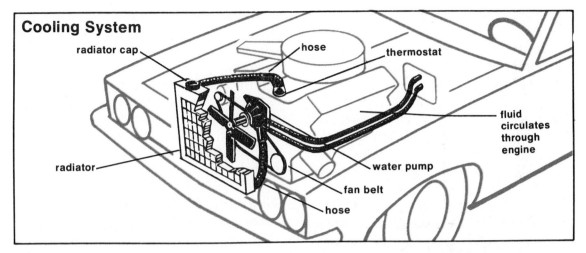

Cooling System

radiator cap

hose

thermostat

radiator

fluid circulates through engine

water pump

fan belt

hose

THE COOLING SYSTEM

How It Works   Although oil carries away some of the engine heat, additional cooling is needed. Some engines are air cooled, but most American car engines are liquid cooled.

In a liquid-cooled engine, the **radiator,** which holds the coolant, is connected to the engine by two large **hoses.** The **water pump** forces coolant throughout parts of the engine. As the coolant circulates in the radiator, a fan draws in air for recooling. When the temperature falls below best operating level, a **thermostat** shuts off the flow of coolant until it heats up again. Then the coolant flows again and cools the engine.

Keeping It Running   **Radiator** fluid level should generally be checked before starting the engine.

If the **temperature gauge** shows the coolant in the radiator is overheating, it may be necessary to add fluid. *Never remove the cap from a boiling radiator. Hot fluid or steam will spurt out and burn you. The radiator must cool before adding fluid. The fluid must be poured in slowly, with the engine running.* Never drive with a boiling radiator.

Overheating may be caused by:

- Radiator low on fluid, or fluid not being cooled by air from fan.
- Faulty water pump or loose fan belt.
- Radiator grille clogged with particles.
- Frozen fluid in radiator.

Preparing for Winter   Cold weather puts a strain on the cooling system. Before winter, have the **fan belt** and **water pump** checked, radiator flushed and cleaned, and look for leaks in the radiator, heater, water hoses, and hose connections. It will be less costly to replace worn-out parts before trouble develops.

Engine damage can occur if the fluid in the radiator and engine freezes. To prevent this, add **antifreeze.** Antifreeze should be checked regularly and coolant added as needed.

If the weather gets cold before antifreeze has been added to the radiator, drain the cooling system by opening the **drain plugs** under the radiator and at the side of the engine. Close the plugs before adding the antifreeze.

THE FUEL AND THE EXHAUST SYSTEMS

How It Runs   The fuel system is made up of a **fuel tank, fuel line, fuel pump, fuel filter,** and **carburetor.**

Gasoline is drawn from the tank through the fuel line by the pump to the carburetor, which sits on top of the engine just under the air cleaner and to send it to each **cylinder** for the liquid gasoline with air drawn through the air cleaner and to send it to each **cylinder** for combustion. The more fuel fed to the cylinders, the greater the power and the faster the car will go. The amount of fuel fed into the cylinders is controlled by how far down the accelerator is pressed.

The exhaust system includes the **exhaust pipe, muffler, catalytic converter** (on many newer cars), and **tailpipe.**

Exhaust gases pass through the muffler, which cuts down the noise of cylinder explosions, and out the tailpipe at the back of the car. To reduce air pollution from car exhaust, emission-control devices, such as the catalytic converter, are added to most new cars.

Keeping It Running   The **carburetor** may need to be cleaned and adjusted so it will work well. This is generally done at tune-up time.

The **emission-control device** attached to the engine requires servicing according to instructions in the owner's manual.

Gasoline   The type of gasoline best suited to your car's needs depends largely on the engine of the car. Generally, four- and six-cylinder engines and small V-8's can use regular gas. Larger engines usually run best on premium gas; some small engines require premium gas.

Most cars produced during the 1975 model year or later must use lead-free gas because of the catalytic converters required by law.

For the kind of gasoline you need for your car, follow the advice in your owner's manual.

Vapor Lock   Sometimes the fuel line becomes blocked by bubbles of gasoline vapor. This condition, called vapor lock, keeps the fuel from reaching the carburetor and causes the engine to stall. It happens most often in heavy traffic on a hot day, especially if the air conditioning is on. It also occurs at higher altitudes where reduced atmospheric pressure makes it easier for the gasoline to vaporize before it reaches the carburetor. Uncomfortable as it may sound, the best way to prevent vapor lock in such situations is to turn off the air conditioner and turn on the car's heater. This draws heat away from the engine. If you do have a vapor lock and your car stalls, park on the road shoulder, lift the hood, and wait for the engine to cool.

Fuel System

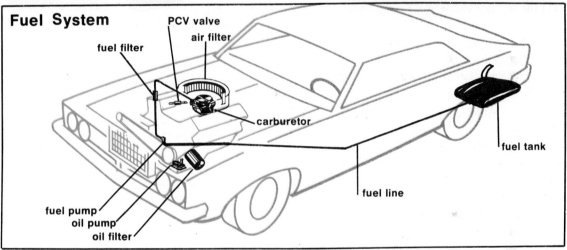

- PCV valve
- air filter
- fuel filter
- carburetor
- fuel tank
- fuel line
- fuel pump
- oil pump
- oil filter

Exhaust System

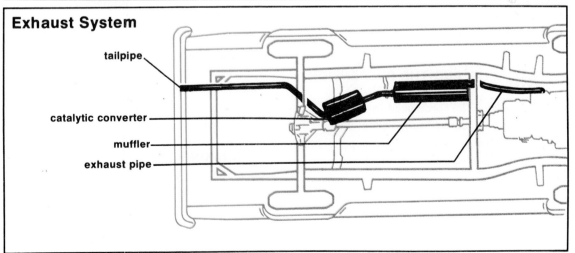

- tailpipe
- catalytic converter
- muffler
- exhaust pipe

THE LUBRICATION SYSTEM

How It Works   When two surfaces of moving parts rub against each other, they create friction and heat. If the friction between moving parts in a car could not be reduced, the engine would burn itself out. Oil is used to reduce friction. It plays an important part in a car's operation.

The oil in the **oil pan** at the bottom of the engine is forced under pressure by an **oil pump** through the filter to all moving parts of the engine. The oil reduces friction, carries away heat, and keeps the engine clean.

Keeping It Running   Cars need an **oil change.** When the dirty oil is drained and replaced with fresh oil, the oil filter is also changed.

Cold weather makes oil thicker. Thick oil will not circulate well, and the car won't start as easily. Use all-weather oil or a light-weight oil for cold weather. For summer, use a heavier oil.

If the oil-pressure warning light remains on when the engine is running, pull over to the side of the road, stop, and shut off the engine. Don't drive the car. Have the cause of low pressure corrected at once.

When a car is **lubricated,** grease is forced under pressure to lubricate the moving parts.

THE STEERING AND THE SUSPENSION SYSTEM

How It Works   The force used to turn the steering wheel is carried to the front wheels through the **steering column.** The suspension system, including **springs** and **shock absorbers,** are important for steering and car control as well as for riding comfort. The shock absorbers hold the wheels and tires down on the road so a normal bounce won't reduce steering and braking control.

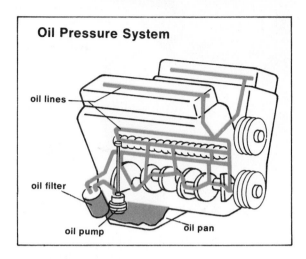

Oil Pressure System

oil lines

oil filter

oil pump   oil pan

Keeping It Running   *Any steering defect is serious and needs immediate attention.*
Have the steering system checked, if

- With power steering and the engine running, there is *any* "play"; with manual steering, there is more than two inches of "play" in the steering wheel.
- The steering wheel is hard to turn and tires are properly inflated.
- There is a "shimmy" or wobbling in the front wheels, or the car pulls to one side and the brakes are not wet. Check front wheels for alignment and balance.
- You feel a sudden bump as you turn the wheel, but you did not hit a bump.
- The car "wanders" from one side of the road to the other.

Shock absorbers should be checked at each 24,000 miles or earlier and replaced if they show signs of leaking.

THE BRAKING SYSTEM

How It Works   Pressure on the brake pedal forces hydraulic brake fluid in the **master cylinder** through **brake lines** to the **wheel cylinders.** One part of the dual master cylinder

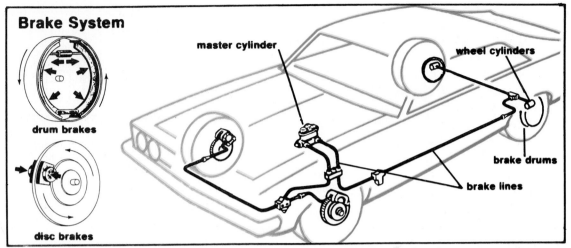

Brake System

drum brakes

disc brakes

master cylinder

wheel cylinders

brake drums

brake lines

connects with the front wheels, the other with the rear wheels. Stepping on the brake pedal activates the brakes on all four wheels.

At each wheel the pressure of the fluid pushes the brake shoes with their special **lining** against the inside of the turning **brake drum.** On cars with **disc brakes, pads** are forced against the turning **disc.** Friction between these slows the wheels down. The harder the brake pedal is pressed, the more quickly the car slows down because friction is increased.

If the fluid in one part of the master cylinder leaks out, or if there is a leak in a brake line, fluid will not reach one pair of wheels. The other two wheels still get fluid from the other part of the dual master cylinder, and the brakes on those wheels will still work, but braking efficiency will be reduced.

The **parking brake** is connected by a steel cable to the brakes on the rear wheels. It should be adjusted to hold the car on any hill.

Keeping It Running   Brakes, whether disc or drum, are self-adjusting. Have them adjusted as the owner's manual recommends.

If the brake pedal goes down too near the floor when you press on it hard, drive backwards and forwards several times, applying the brake firmly each time. If the problem is not corrected, have the brakes checked as soon as possible.

Keep the brake fluid in the master cylinder at the proper level. Check it every 2,000 miles or so. The brake warning light warns of trouble in the braking system. The warning light is not a substitute for having the fluid level in the master cylinder checked regularly.

Early warning signs of brake trouble:
- Low brake level—power brakes less than two inches from floor; standard brakes less than three inches when pressed hard.
- Uneven pull to right or left when applying the brakes when brakes are dry.
- Grabbing or sudden braking action at some point when applying the brakes.
- ''Spongy'' feel or ''squealing'' noise when brakes are applied.
- Need to pump brakes to slow the car.
- Master cylinder brake fluid level low.
- Signs of fluid leaking on inside of tire.

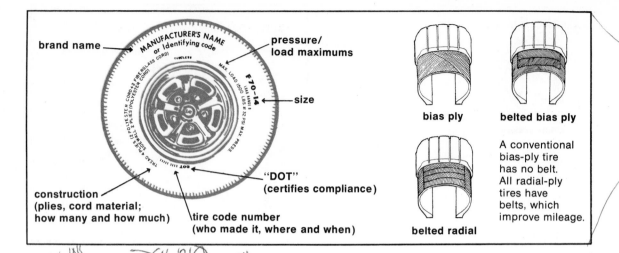

brand name — MANUFACTURER'S NAME or Identifying code

pressure/load maximums

size

"DOT" (certifies compliance)

construction (plies, cord material; how many and how much)

tire code number (who made it, where and when)

bias ply

belted bias ply

belted radial

A conventional bias-ply tire has no belt. All radial-ply tires have belts, which improve mileage.

TIRES

Types of Tires   In recent years, **radial tires** have improved car handling as well as tire strength and tread mileage. The less expensive, conventional **bias-ply tire** offers less tread mileage and is best suited for light driving around town. **Belted tires** add special cord belts to the bias-ply tire for improved strength and mileage.

A tire's construction, size, and other information are clearly marked on the sidewall of every tire. Some points to remember about buying tires are:

- Never select a replacement tire smaller than the original equipment tire.
- Stick to the same size and kind of construction for all four tires, if possible, for better car handling.
- If you buy a single replacement tire, make sure it is the same construction as the other tire on the same axle.
- If you buy two radial tires to pair with other tires, the radials must always be placed on the rear axle.

- Unless mixed with radials, new tires should go on the rear wheels for better car handling and safety.

Inflation and Tread   Keep proper air pressure in the tires. Too little air in even one tire can make the car difficult to control. *Low tire pressure is probably the major cause of tire wear and tire failure.*

The air pressure in tires rises in warm weather and falls in cold weather. When temperatures fluctuate, pressures should be checked often, but do not let air out of tires to reduce pressure when tires are hot.

Replace a tire when the **wear indicators** (smooth bars across the tread) are showing. Tires with worn tread will skid more easily on wet pavement and are more likely to blow out without warning.

Tires should be rotated and balanced every 6,000 miles. After rotation, tire inflation must be adjusted to the inflation recommended in the owner's manual.

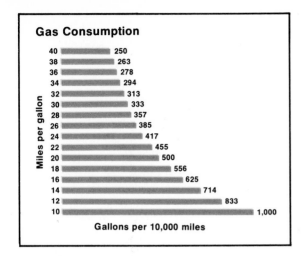

Gas Consumption

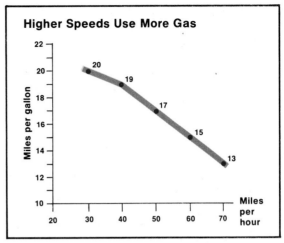

Higher Speeds Use More Gas

Economy Measures

If you follow the maintenance directions in your owner's manual and have service done at the scheduled time, your car will last longer and cost less to run.

CALCULATING MILES PER GALLON

The rising cost of gasoline has made people more concerned with good gas mileage. Smaller cars and smaller engines usually give better gas economy.

To calculate the miles your car runs on a gallon of gas, follow these procedures:

- Fill gas tank to the top. Record the odometer reading.
- Drive as you normally would until the tank is about half full.
- Fill the tank to the top again. Record the odometer reading.
- Divide the number of miles driven by the number of gallons required to fill the tank the second time.

Do this several times over several weeks to obtain an average miles-per-gallon for your car.

TIPS FOR GOOD GAS MILEAGE

- Drive at a steady, moderate speed.
- Avoid sudden stops.
- When making a long stop, turn off engine.
- Avoid jack-rabbit starts.
- Keep engine tuned and spark plugs gapped.

AVOID THESE WASTEFUL PRACTICES

- Racing the engine.
- Driving fast in cold weather before engine has warmed up.
- Squealing tires around turns.
- Spinning the wheels when stuck on ice, in snow, or in mud.
- Starting from a dead stop in SECOND gear.
- Killing the engine.
- Starting suddenly in cold, wet weather when brakes are wet or frozen.
- Not pressing down on clutch of a stick-shift car before starting the engine.
- Driving a stickshift car too fast and too long before shifting to a higher gear.

Vocabulary

antifreeze, 305	fuel line, 306	shock absorber, 308
brake fluid, 309	fuel pump, 306	spark plug, 300
brake shoe, 309	fuse, 302	starter motor, 302
carburetor, 306	master cylinder, 308	tailpipe, 306
catalytic converter, 306	muffler, 306	thermostat, 305
differential, 300	oil pan, 308	transmission, 300
disc brake, 309	oil pump, 308	tune-up, 300
driveshaft, 300	power train, 300	water pump, 305
drum brake, 309	preventive maintenance, 299	wheel cylinder, 308
	radiator, 305	

Summary

1. To find a good mechanic, ask friends, neighbors, and auto shop instructors. If in doubt, a new-car dealer is usually a good choice.
2. Preventive maintenance is the day-to-day and periodic attention to stop car trouble before it starts.
3. A driver can take preventive maintenance measures before and after starting the engine, while driving, at a gas stop, and when the car is lubricated and tuned.
4. Power train—Engine should be tuned once a year; transmission fluid checked monthly.
   Ignition and electrical systems—Keep water level up in the battery, terminals clean, cables tight, lights clean, fuses replaced when burned out.
   Cooling system—Keep coolant level up in the radiator. Don't drive with a boiling radiator. Check cooling system before winter. Keep antifreeze in radiator.
   Fuel and exhaust systems—Have carburetor cleaned and adjusted as needed. Use proper gas for engine.
   Lubricaton system—Have car lubricated and the oil and oil filter changed according to the schedule in the owner's manual.
   Steering and suspension systems—Replace shock absorbers every 24,000 miles or if they are leaking. Check steering system often and correct problems at once.
   Braking system—Have brakes adjusted or repaired when needed, or the master cylinder repaired if brake fluid leaks.
5. Bias ply, belted, and radial tires offer a choice in price, tread mileage, and strength. A replacement tire should match the other tire on the same axle. Inflation, balance, front wheel alignment, and rotation should receive careful attention.
6. Gas mileage is determined by size of car and engine and by driving practices. Gas usage can be calculated by dividing number of miles driven by the number of gallons required to fill the tank the second time.

Driving Situations

1. You are driving through the mountains when the engine sputters and dies. What could be wrong? What should you do?

2. Your headlights suddenly go out while driving on a road at night. After bringing the car to a safe stop, what should the driver do to correct the problem?

3. Your radiator suddenly boils over while you are driving. What should you do?

4. You need a tire to replace one that has just failed. What guidelines should you use in deciding what kind to buy?

Chapter Review Questions

Car Maintenance

1. What purpose do car clinics serve? (298)
2. List five preventive maintenance measures to keep the engine and transmission running efficiently. (300-301)
3. What are four preventive maintenance measures to keep the battery in good condition? (302)
4. Why is it harder to start an engine in cold weather than in warm weather? (302)
5. What are four possible causes for overheating of the cooling system? (305)
6. Why should you not remove the cap from a hot radiator? (305)
7. What should you do if the oil-pressure light comes on while you are driving? (308)
8. How can you tell if the car's shock absorbers need to be replaced? (308)
9. List five warning signs of brake trouble. (309)
10. When should tires be rotated and balanced? (310)
11. What are two important effects of too little air pressure in tires? (310)
12. How can you tell when a tire's tread is too worn for safe use? (310)

Economy Measures

13. Name ten driving and maintenance practices that will keep down the cost of driving and add longer life to a car. (311)
14. What are five driving practices for good gas mileage? (311)
15. What are the steps in calculating how many miles a car runs on a gallon of gas? (311)

Projects

1. Undertake a survey of car owners, auto shop teachers, and others to compile a list of competent auto mechanics in your town or region.
2. Watch a car being tested at a car clinic. Make a list of the various tests and explain the results of a sample test to the class.
3. Observe a car at a service station or garage for lubrication and oil change. Make a record of all preventive maintenance measures taken in the process.
4. Interview several mechanics regarding car systems or parts that break down most often, and their opinions as to how many could have been prevented by proper preventive maintenance.
5. Check the gas mileage for two or more cars of the same make, model, and engine size. Determine why the gas mileage for the cars are not the same.

Chapter 18 · Test

(Write the correct answers on a separate sheet of paper.)

True-False

1. Car clinics can save an owner money by discovering defective parts before they cause trouble. (298)
2. Transmission fluid level should be checked before starting the engine. (301)
3. When waiting on an upgrade for the light to change, you should speed up the engine to hold the car in place. (300-301)
4. If a car is operated for a period of time while the alternator light remains on, the battery may go dead. (302)
5. If car fuses continue to burn out, a larger size fuse should be used. (302)
6. When adding water to an overheated radiator, you should keep the engine running. (305)
7. The purpose of oil in an engine is to reduce friction and remove heat. (308)
8. If the oil-pressure warning light stays on while the car is running, it should receive attention the next time the car is in for a lubrication and oil change. (308)
9. If a brake line should leak, all braking control from the foot brake is lost. (309)
10. The parking brake is connected to just the rear wheel brakes. (309)
11. Radial tires should always be used in pairs on the rear wheels for best car handling. (310)
12. Low tire pressure is the major cause of tire wear and tire failure. (310)
13. A car that averages 30 miles per gallon of gas will use half as many gallons in 10,000 miles as one that averages 20 miles per gallon. (311)

Answer the Question

14. How is the transmission fluid level checked? (301)
15. Where is the hot coolant in the cooling system cooled? (305)
16. What are two important purposes for the use of oil in the lubrication system? (308)
17. Which are two of the places where brake fluid can escape from the braking system? (309)
18. How can a driver easily tell when the tread on a tire is reaching a dangerous level? (310)
19. What two problems can result from low tire pressure? (310)
20. How can a driver easily adjust the brakes on a car that has self-adjusting brakes? (309)

Chapter 19

Buying and Insuring a Car

Objectives

1. Explain the problems and responsibilities of car ownership for a high-school student.
2. Describe the process of deciding what kind of used car to buy and from whom to buy it.
3. Describe the steps to take when choosing the best used car.
4. List the major costs of owning and driving a car.
5. Explain the principle of automobile insurance.
6. Tell what is covered by each of the following kinds of insurance: liability, uninsured-motorist, collision, comprehensive, medical-payments, and towing.
7. Describe no-fault insurance.
8. List eight factors that affect the cost of automobile insurance.
9. Describe the procedures a driver should follow if involved in a collision.

Introduction

Owning and driving an automobile offer a freedom of movement and independence that is important to young adults. Owning a car also means that the owner must be able to pay the costs of buying, using, maintaining, and insuring it.

Before deciding what car to buy, decide whether owning a car now is really necessary. You can easily find good reasons for having your own car. However, it is more important to weigh those reasons against the problems a car may bring. For example, will car ownership make you work longer hours to pay for the car and the continued maintenance and operational costs? In many cases, students with cars have had less time for study, sports, and other desirable activities and thus have lower grades or drop out of school. A delay in purchasing a car until graduation may be a wise decision.

For most people, the cost of owning and operating a car will be their greatest single expense, other than buying a home. Knowing how to buy a car, what insurance coverages are desirable, and what procedures to follow in the event of a collision can help save much money and inconvenience.

Buying and Owning a Car

If you decide you have sufficient need and money to own your own car, what kind of a car should you buy? The right car depends on your answers to these questions:

- How well will the car meet your needs?
- Are you interested in a high performance engine or in economy and efficiency of operation?
- What is the maximum amount of money you can spend?

Reach some firm answers before you go to the car dealers.

FROM WHOM SHOULD YOU BUY?

A used car can be bought from a private owner, a used-car dealer, or a new-car dealer.

A car would probably cost least from a private owner. You have the advantage of talking to the owner, and both of you can share in the profit a dealer would have made. However, this person can offer no warranty, and sales are usually final.

Used-car dealers often have a good selection of cars. However, these dealers seldom have facilities for repairing cars and generally do not offer any guarantee on cars sold.

New-car dealers probably have the best selection of used cars from the many traded for new cars, and they usually have the highest prices. With facilities and qualified mechanics to recondition used cars, these dealers can extend guarantees on newer used cars.

HOW MUCH SHOULD YOU PAY?

The used-car *Blue Book* reports the average price paid to dealers throughout the country for various makes and models of used cars. This monthly report lists average prices, but

Check the engine thoroughly.

Check the outside and inside of the car.

dealers do not have to follow these prices. They may charge less for a used car in poor condition and more for the same model in good condition.

Regardless of the initial price of the car, be sure to set aside at least $200 to cover unexpected repairs during the first year of ownership, plus an additional amount to pay the costs of registration, licensing, and insurance.

CHOOSING THE BEST USED CAR

Allow plenty of time, even as long as a month, to find the best car. When you see a car you like, check further to see if it is in good condition. The following checks will help you judge a used car:

Outside and Inside Checks

- See if the doors sag. Is the paint on one panel different from the rest of the car?
- Open and close all doors from inside and outside. Do all doors lock?
- Look for rust along chrome edges, under headlights, and around fenders.
- Get behind the car. Does it lean to one side?
- Raise the trunk mat and look for rust or crash damage. Check jack and spare tire.
- Look for oil drips on the ground under car.
- Raise hood and check inner fenders and front frame for damage. Does the paint under the hood match the car?
- Sit behind the wheel. Does front seat sag? Does the back feel firm?
- Check brake, clutch, and gas pedals. Badly worn pedals may indicate high mileage.
- Look for worn upholstery. This shows much use and therefore high mileage.
- Move steering wheel. With power steering, there should be no play when engine is running. With manual steering, more than two inches shows excessive wear.
- Operate heater, defroster, radio, horn, lights, windshield wipers, and washers.
- Press brake pedal hard. It should be firm and not give way when pressure is maintained.

Check Under Hood

- Check radiator and fan for accident damage. Check for leaks.
- Check coolant level in radiator. Underside of radiator cap should be free of oil.
- See if battery is free of cracks and cables free of corrosion.
- With hood up and engine running, listen for any unusual noises. Check for water and oil leaks.

Driving Test

- If the dealer refuses to let you drive the car or requires a deposit, forget about the car and the dealer.
- Turn the switch to "on" position. Warning lights should come on.
- Start the engine. It should start promptly each time you turn the key. Warning lights should go out in a few seconds.
- At low speeds, test the brakes several times to be sure they stop the car well.
- Turn some corners. The car should steer easily.
- Acceleration should be smooth and steady from 0 to 40 mph.
- Brakes should not pull or grab. Try them at various speeds.
- Drive on a stretch of rough road at 25 mph. Check for vehicle stability. Listen for rattles.
- Check temperature gauge for overheating.

Mechanic Check   If the car you have been considering passes most of these tests, have a mechanic make a final check. Try to get an unbiased person who has nothing to do with the sale. A car clinic will check the car completely at moderate cost.

BEFORE YOU CLOSE THE DEAL

Pay cash for the car, if possible. If you must borrow some money, shop as carefully for your loan from different lending agencies, such as banks and credit unions, as you did for the car itself. Car dealers loan money at higher interest rates than lending agencies and can often afford to sell a car at a bargain price if they then loan the buyer the money.

Never close the deal on the condition that something will be fixed later unless you get it in writing.

COST OF OWNING AND DRIVING A CAR

After you buy the car, the costs of ownership and maintenance begin. Only by keeping a record of car expenses can you tell the actual costs.

Depreciation   No matter how little a car is driven, it is worth less each year. This decrease in the value of a car is called *depreciation.* Generally, the newer the car, the more it depreciates each year.

Other Costs   Besides depreciation, operating costs (gasoline, oil, tune-ups, repairs, and tires) and fixed costs (insurance and registration) are high. It could cost about $1,000 to drive a $1,000-used car 10,000 miles a year. This cost does not include parking fees or such hidden costs as making more trips than you would if you did not own a car.

Insuring a Car

The largest expense that may arise from owning and driving a car is paying for damages resulting from a collision. State financial responsibility laws require persons involved in collisions that result in death, injury, or property damage over a certain amount to show they can pay for damages to others. Owners and drivers can prove this ability by protecting themselves with auto insurance. It is also legal to deposit cash or post a bond rather than buying auto insurance, but insurance is cheaper.

WHAT IS AUTOMOBILE INSURANCE?

Car owners pay a specified amount, called a *premium,* to an insurance company. Owners are assured that the company will pay (up to specified limits) for any damage to persons or property for which the owners are responsible. The agreement or contract between an owner and an insurance company is called a *policy.*

KINDS OF BASIC COVERAGE

The most important insurance for car owners is liability coverage. This insurance protects car owners against claims for damage to other persons and property. It is usually separated into bodily-injury and property-damage liability coverage.

The other main types of auto insurance protect car owners from large expenses for themselves and their passengers. The chart on the next page gives the details of these various kinds of coverage.

Car Insurance

Kind of Insurance	Coverage	Claim Includes	Minimum Amount	Notes
Bodily-injury liability	Pays claim against owner if someone is killed or injured if owner is at fault.	Hospital and doctor bills Legal fees Court costs Loss of wages	States normally specify minimum: $10,000-$15,000 for one person; $20,000-$30,000 for several persons.	Compulsory in many states. Needed by all owners. Minimum required is too low.
Property-damage liability	Pays claim against owner if property of others is damaged and owner is at fault.	Other car House Telephone pole Traffic light	States normally specify a minimum: $5,000-$10,000.	Compulsory in many states. Needed by all owners.
Uninsured-motorist	Pays for injuries to you and your passengers in case of hit-and-run collision or uninsured motorist.	Hospital and doctor bills Legal fees Court costs Loss of wages	Usually same as bodily-injury limits.	Compulsory in many states. Needed by all owners.
Collision	Pays cost of repairing or replacing owner's car when owner is at fault or when owner cannot collect from person at fault.	Any car driven by owner or with owner's permission	Insures for depreciated value of car. Owner decides on $50 to $250 deductible.	Important for new or expensive car. Drop after 6-8 years of ownership.
Comprehensive	Pays cost of repairing or replacing owner's car.	Fire Storm Theft Earthquake Flood Riots Wind Vandals	Insures for depreciated value of car. $50-$100 deductible.	Important for new or expensive car. Drop after 6 years of ownership.
Medical-payments	Pays medical costs for you and your passengers injured in any collision regardless of fault.	Pays all immediate medical costs in addition to other medical insurance	Insures up to $500 to $5,000.	This does not require a legal procedure while bodily injury usually does.
Towing	Pays cost of towing or minor repair to disabled car.	Dead battery Out of gas Flat tire Accident	Usually pays amount validated by towing company.	Not needed if belong to automobile club.

NO-FAULT INSURANCE

The question, "Who was at fault?" is raised after nearly every collision. The insurance company representing the driver at fault must pay for injury and property damage to the other driver and passengers.

Recently, many states have adopted a new form of auto liability insurance that no longer raises the question of fault. Under no-fault insurance, the insurance company pays all costs to its own policyholders, up to specified limits, no matter who was to blame for the collision. Claims for damages beyond those limits can be made in court against the driver at fault.

The major advantage of no-fault insurance is the quick settlement of claims. When blame must be determined, it may take years before a claim is settled in court. No-fault insurance largely eliminates the need for legal suits between owners or drivers of cars involved in collisions. This kind of insurance cuts the cost of settling minor claims, as well as the cost of premiums.

Started in Massachusetts in 1971, no-fault insurance plans have spread quickly. By 1976, more than half of the population of the United States was covered by no-fault insurance in more than 20 states, while most other states had plans under consideration.

ESTABLISHING AUTOMOBILE INSURANCE RATES

Premium rates are determined mostly by the amount paid out in claims. Determining the fair costs of insurance is so difficult that each

This driver should have insurance to cover damage to property.

state regulates the rates that companies can charge.

How Rates Are Determined The actual amount a car owner pays for insurance protection is based on the following factors:

- Where you live. Collision rates are lower in rural communities than in metropolitan areas.
- Miles driven. The more miles driven, especially if the car is used in business, the more the car is exposed to collisions.
- Collision and violation record. Drivers with convictions for moving violations are more likely to be involved in collisions.
- Who does most of the driving (principal driver). Premiums are higher on cars whose principal driver is under 25 years old.
- Cost of the car. Premiums on expensive cars are higher because repairs and replacement costs are higher.
- Age. Insurance records show younger drivers have a greater proportion of collisions than older drivers.

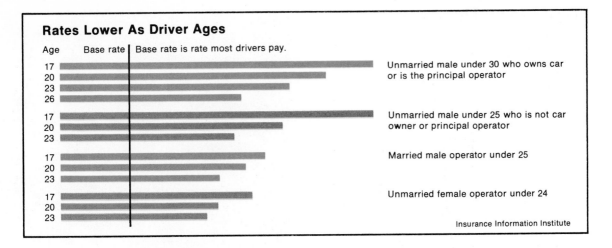

Rates Lower As Driver Ages

| Age | Base rate | Base rate is rate most drivers pay. |

Unmarried male under 30 who owns car or is the principal operator
(Ages: 17, 20, 23, 26)

Unmarried male under 25 who is not car owner or principal operator
(Ages: 17, 20, 23)

Married male operator under 25
(Ages: 17, 20, 23)

Unmarried female operator under 24
(Ages: 17, 20, 23)

Insurance Information Institute

- Marital status. Married drivers have proportionally fewer collisions than single drivers.
- Sex. Males under 25 usually pay more than females because they drive more, have more collisions, and have more severe collisions. Thus, repairs are costly.
- Number and cost of claims against the insurance company, especially on comprehensive and collision coverage.

Assigned-Risk Plan   An insurance company may cancel the policy of a driver who has a bad collision and/or violation record, or whose license has been suspended or revoked. Such drivers may then be unable to buy insurance from any other company at standard rates.

The assigned-risk plan provides bodily-injury and property-damage liability insurance to those drivers at a considerably higher cost.

Each company shares the assigned-risk business in a state and is assigned a percentage of these drivers.

Reduced Rates for Special Groups   Some insurance companies provide special reduced rates for car owners and drivers who meet one or more of the following conditions:

- Have no claims against the company or no citations for moving violations in the past year.
- Have more than one car in the family insured with the same company.
- Have compact or smaller size car.
- Have successfully completed a course in driver education (classroom and in-car).
- Have maintained a "B" grade average while in high school and college.
- Do not drink or smoke.

Some companies also offer better payments for injured drivers who were wearing seat belts and shoulder harnesses at the time of a crash.

Accident Procedures

While most collisions can be prevented, everyone must be prepared for the time when he or she might be involved in a crash.

FIRST STEPS

For your own protection, you should know the step-by-step procedures to follow.

1. **Stop Immediately**   It is illegal to leave the scene of an accident. Even a minor collision becomes a serious offense if a driver fails to stop. If possible, stop off the road.

   If you cause slight damage to a parked car, try to locate the owner. If this is impossible, leave your name, address, and phone number in a note to the owner. Put it under the windshield wiper or attach it to the car where it can easily be seen. Notify the police.

2. **Aid the Injured**   Send for a doctor and ambulance. Do not move an injured person unless there is extreme danger of fire or further injury. Carry a first-aid kit as part of your car's equipment.

3. **Prevent Further Damage**   Turn off the ignition of the wrecked car to reduce chances of fire. Warn oncoming traffic. Flares should be placed at least 100 feet behind and ahead of the wreck (500 feet in high-speed traffic). If no flares are available, station a person at the side of the road to wave a flashlight or a white cloth.

4. **Send for Police**   Police must be called if anyone is killed or injured. Some states require that the police be called in any collision. Even if no one is injured, the police should still be called.

5. **Exchange Information**   Write down the other driver's name, address, license plate, and insurance company. Ask to see

the driver's license. Make a note of the names and addresses of all passengers, of the position they were sitting in, and of the extent of their injuries.

ADDITIONAL STEPS

In addition to the first five essential steps, the following procedures are important:

- **Get Witnesses and Record Information** Obtain the names and addresses of any witnesses as soon as possible. Make a diagram of the situation and write down all the facts, such as time, date, exact location, and weather. Get the name of the hospital to which any injured person was taken and the badge number of the police officer.

- **Give Facts to the Police** When the police ask you for a statement, be as honest and accurate as possible. Don't become involved in an argument with the other driver about who was to blame. Remain at the scene of the crash until you are sure all information has been taken.

- **See a Doctor** If you were shaken up, even if you notice no special ill effects, see a doctor as soon as possible.

- **File Necessary Reports** All states require drivers involved in an accident to file a written accident report with the state if someone has been killed or injured, or if damage is over a certain amount. This report includes a statement of financial responsibility that shows a driver's ability to pay for the damages or injuries. Some states require these reports within 24 hours; others, within 5, 10, or 30 days. You should also notify your insurance company without delay.

Summary

1. A high-school student who owns a car usually must work longer hours to pay for the car and its upkeep, often resulting in lower grades and less participation in school activities.

2. Buyers should determine how the car will be used, whether high performance or economy and efficiency are more important, and how much they can spend. Used cars can be bought from private owners, used-car dealers, or new-car dealers.

3. Some on-the-lot and driving checks will help narrow the choice to one or two cars. These should be checked further by a car clinic or qualified mechanic prior to purchase.

4. Regardless of how much the car is used, depreciation, insurance, and registration are fixed costs for every owner. Operating costs include gas, oil, tires, repairs, and tune-ups.

5. Many policyholders pay annual premiums to an insurance company. In the event of a claim, the insurance company pays the policyholder for damages up to policy limits.

6. Liability insurance pays for injury or property damage to others. Uninsured-motorist and medical-payments pay for injury to the policyholder and his or her passengers. Collision, comprehensive, and towing cover repairs to the policyholder's car.

7. No-fault insurance pays for injury to policyholders, their passengers, and their cars regardless of who was at fault in the collision.

8. The cost of auto insurance is affected by sex, age, marital status, car equipment and engine size, cost of car, miles driven, where owner lives, accident and violation record of driver, principal driver, and claims against company.

9. Drivers involved in a collision must stop, aid the injured, prevent further damage to the cars, call police, and exchange information. They should also get witnesses and collect information, give facts to police, see a doctor, and file necessary reports.

Driving Situations

1. You are a high-school junior working part-time to save for college. What are the arguments for and against buying your own car?

2. Newspaper ads display the same model car at about the same price from a private owner, a used-car dealer, and a new-car dealer. How would you decide which of the three to buy?

3. You have just bought a used car and are trying to decide what insurance coverage best meets your needs. List the insurance coverages you should consider, in order of priority.

4. You find your car covered with paint. What kind of insurance will cover this damage?

Chapter Review Questions

Buying and Owning a Car

1. What problems do many students face when they own a car before high-school graduation? (317)
2. In deciding the kind of car to buy, what three important questions should a person answer? (318)
3. What are the advantages and disadvantages of buying a used car from a private owner? From a used-car dealer? From a new-car dealer? (318)
4. List eight checks that should be made inside and outside a used car before buying it. (319)
5. What two major costs of car ownership do not depend on how much a car has been driven? (320)

Insuring a Car

6. Explain the principle of automobile insurance. (320)
7. What is meant by liability insurance? What two important types of collision expenses does it cover? (320)
8. Whom does comprehensive insurance cover? What kinds of damage are covered by comprehensive insurance? (321)
9. Explain the deductible feature of comprehensive and collision insurance. (321)
10. Whom does collision insurance cover? Under what conditions is this coverage desirable? (321)
11. Explain the principle of no-fault insurance. What are its advantages? (322)
12. List three conditions under which many insurance companies grant special reduced rates for automobile insurance. (323)

Accident Procedures

13. List five major steps a driver must take when involved in a collision. (324)
14. In case a driver hits a parked car, what procedures are required? (324)
15. What four additional steps should a driver take when involved in a collision? (324-325)

Projects

1. Interview several car mechanics for tips on buying a used car. Report your findings to the class.
2. Find out from a representative of the department of motor vehicles what the financial responsibility law in your state requires of drivers and owners who are involved in a collision. What reports must be completed?
3. Interview an automobile insurance agent regarding insurance rates for young drivers. Report to the class what students can expect to pay for different kinds of insurance.
4. Invite an auto insurance agent to explain to the class why a person's life-style affects his or her insurance rates. Also have the agent explain the effects of no-fault insurance in your state or its possible effects if your state does not have no-fault insurance.

Chapter 19 · Test

(Write the correct answers on a separate sheet of paper.)

True-False

1. The main reason some drivers pay more for auto insurance than other drivers is their collision involvement record. (323)
2. When a used-car dealer offers a car at a good price, it will probably cost less to borrow the money for the car from the dealer. (320)
3. Comprehensive insurance covers replacement of a stolen car. (321)
4. Car ownership by high-school students can lead to lower school grades. (317)
5. The primary purpose of automobile insurance is to protect car owners and drivers against large financial losses. (320)
6. Under no-fault insurance, the insurance company pays its own policyholders for damages in a collision, regardless of who was at fault. (322)
7. The *Blue Book* tells future buyers exactly how much they will pay for a used car. (318)
8. Repairs to your car resulting from a collision caused by another driver are covered by your property-damage liability insurance. (321)
9. Many states require drivers to have collision insurance. (321)
10. When involved in a collision, you should first determine who was at fault. (324)
11. A used car purchased from a private owner generally costs less than the same type of car at a new- or used-car dealer. (318)
12. Towing coverage generally is not necessary if a driver belongs to a motor club. (321)
13. Insurance rates are generally the same for all car owners in a state. (322-323)
14. Liability insurance pays for injuries to someone else when you are at fault. (321)
15. Replacement of the windshield damaged when someone threw a stone is covered by collision insurance. (321)

Answer the Question

16. What is a written agreement between a car owner and an insurance company called? (320)
17. What must a driver file with the state if he or she is in a collision with injuries, death, or damage over a certain amount? (325)
18. What does worn upholstery on a used car tell a prospective buyer? (319)
19. What are the two most important kinds of insurance for a car owner? (320)
20. What two major fixed costs of car ownership do not depend on how much a car has been driven? (320)

Chapter 20

Driving for Pleasure

Objectives

1. List at least three planning steps a driver can take to make local driving easier.
2. List the important vehicle checks that should be done before leaving on a long trip.
3. Describe the emergency equipment to take on a long trip.
4. List special equipment to take if the trip is planned for winter driving.
5. Describe preparations you should make for a long trip.
6. Explain how to use a road map.
7. List four questions to consider when selecting a route for a trip.
8. Describe three navigating techniques that can help make a trip plan work.
9. Describe the proper way to load a car, truck, or trailer.
10. List at least five cautions a driver should take when towing a trailer.

Introduction

Every year, more and more people are driving campers and recreational vehicles. Many others are using trucks and trailers to move heavy loads. Because of their unusual handling characteristics, size, or power, advanced planning and special skills are needed to operate these vehicles.

Driving on local or long distance trips can often be made easier just by simple advance preparations. For example, if you must drive during peak traffic hours, listening to a local radio station that gives weather and traffic reports may save you time and help avoid possible trouble.

Plans for a long trip should be made well in advance. The car should be checked and serviced. Special emergency equipment should be packed, and the safety of home and belongings ensured.

When preparing to drive a truck, a van, or a car towing a trailer, a driver needs to know how to load these vehicles properly. The manner in which the weight is distributed makes a big difference in how these vehicles respond to a driver's controls. The combination of careful preparation and special skills can improve one's chances for a successful trip and safe return.

Planning for Local Driving

Planning ahead can prevent many serious difficulties even on routine, local trips.

SELECTING DEPARTURE TIME

Selecting the right time for travel is important. In most big cities, driving in the morning or afternoon rush hour can double the time it takes to get from one place to another. If you have a choice, try to avoid rush-hour traffic.

USING ADVANCE INFORMATION

Listening to a local radio station for weather and traffic reports before leaving home can help you avoid bad weather or traffic jams. It is a good idea to keep listening to local stations while driving.

CHOOSING A SAFE ROUTE

If you do not know the area you will be driving in, advance warning of weather and road conditions will help you even more. To become familiar with the area, check a local map before leaving.

PREPARING THE VEHICLE

Running out of windshield washer fluid, driving on a low-pressure tire, or having a turn-signal light fail do not sound like big problems. But if a minor problem occurs in a complex driving situation, serious trouble can develop. Anytime you use a car, make a routine pre-driving check of the car's tires, lights, and controls. If you find anything wrong, have the problem corrected promptly.

CHECKING FOR STREETS AND ADDRESSES

You should know ahead of time the destination address and what streets to take. Passengers can also help find street signs and address numbers. If you miss a street, do not try to make a last-second turn or stop. Go around the block and try again.

Planning a Long Trip

Taking a long trip by car can become one of the most expensive ways to travel if you do not plan ahead.

VEHICLE PREPARATION

Before a long trip, you should have the car checked and serviced. Check the owner's manual for what has to be done and when. Determine the next mileage figure recommended for a major service check. If a major service check is needed within one to two thousand miles, you should have it done before your trip. You will have more confidence in a car that has been completely checked and serviced.

Sometimes emergencies occur on the road. In addition to the jack, lug wrench, and spare tire carried in the trunk, you should take the following emergency equipment:
- Fire extinguisher.
- Flashlight.
- Friction tape for repairs.
- Spare parts (fan belt, can of motor oil, fuses, windshield washer fluid) and tools.
- First-aid kit.

If you are planning to drive in winter, the following equipment should be included:
- Chains or snow tires.
- Tow line or safety chain.
- Battery jumper cables.
- Window scraper.
- Blanket.
- Food and warm clothing for cold weather.

PERSONAL PREPARATION

Before leaving on a long trip, a driver should check other things besides the car:
- Plan to pay for major expenses with traveler's checks or with credit cards.
- Pack clothing for all expected weather conditions. Don't forget sunglasses.
- Secure your house or apartment. Notify neighbors of your plans, stop home deliveries, and arrange for lights to be turned on at night.
- Schedule your trip so all travelers can be well rested before starting.
- Carry a spare set of keys.

LOADING VEHICLES

When loading a car, keep weight low, centered, and secure. Place heavy items in the trunk. Do not have loose objects in the passenger compartment that can injure someone in a sudden stop or quick maneuver.

If a car-top carrier is needed, do not overload it. The more weight there is in a car-top carrier, the more top heavy the car.

An overloaded car will be more difficult to control, especially in an emergency situation or in a strong wind. Steering, acceleration, and stopping must be done more slowly. The aim of the headlights may also be changed by the load.

READING MAPS

In planning a trip, you must have a map of the cities or states to be visited. These maps are usually available at gas stations, travel clubs, or from chambers of commerce. It may be more convenient to buy a road atlas containing all the maps in one booklet.

To read a map correctly, you must look at the *legend.* The legend is usually located in one corner of the map and explains the markings and symbols used. In addition to the regular mileage markings, the legend provides a scale which can be used to estimate mileage.

It is helpful to know the basic numbering system used for the national system of Interstate routes. North-south routes usually have odd numbers, while east-west routes are even numbered. Interstate expressways that bypass cities carry a three-digit number beginning with an even number. If the road leads into the city, a three-digit number is used, except the first digit is odd.

Most maps have a listing of cities in addition to the legend. This listing shows all the major towns and cities on the map in alphabetical order. After the name of the city or town, there will be a letter and a number that refer to the letters and numbers around the edge of the map. If a city has R-9 beside it, as Detroit does, a person must find R and 9 on the outside edges of the map. By putting one finger on the R in the margin and the other on 9 and following these lines until your fingers meet, you will find the approximate spot where the city of Detroit is located.

Some maps provide all sorts of additional information. They may help you locate fish and game areas, airports, golf courses, and points of historical or geographical interest.

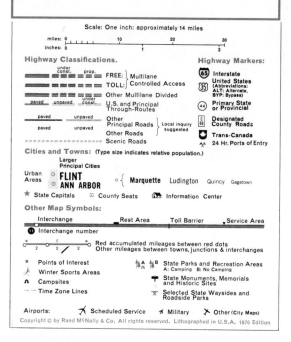

East-and-west routes are even numbered. North-and-south routes are odd numbered.

Three-figured routes, with the first figure odd, are routes that lead into a city.

Three-figured routes, in which the first figure is even, are bypasses around cities.

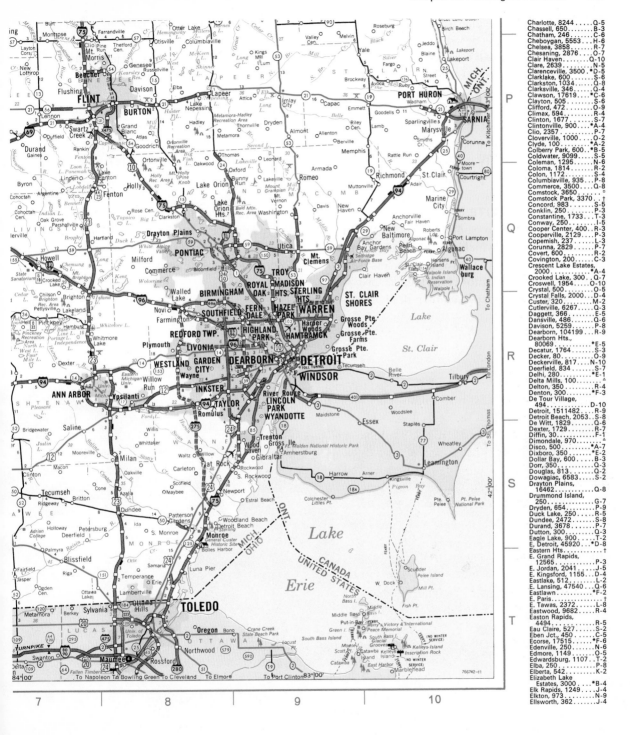

Time and mileage charts on some maps tell a driver how far it is between two points and about how long it will take to drive that distance. Times given are for ideal conditions, and should be increased for bad weather, road construction, or heavy traffic conditions.

Some maps do not give enough detailed information. For example, to locate a small suburb of a large city you might need to use the metropolitan map for that city.

PLAN YOUR ROUTE

Decide whether you want to travel on the Interstate highways which are faster and more direct, or on other roads for a more leisurely and scenic route. Motor clubs usually provide its members with maps and help in planning a trip.

Consider the following questions when selecting the routes to be used:

- How many miles can be traveled a day? Plan to drive no more than eight hours, covering 300 to 400 miles.
- What type of roads can you take? Are any under construction? Will there be Interstate expressways, two-lane highways, toll roads, and bridges and tunnels?
- Will you encounter heavy traffic?
- What will the weather be?
- Will there be facilities for eating, resting, and lodging? For summer and holiday trips, it is wise to reserve space in advance at hotels, motels, or camp sites.

After the route has been mapped out, make a brief outline of the routes to take and the stops to make. This outline can be used to look for key route numbers and stops ahead of time.

NAVIGATING

Trip planning will pay off on the road if drivers and passengers keep these things in mind:

- Plan each day's drive the night before. Don't try to push too far in one day.
- Rotate drivers every one to two hours whenever possible.
- Use the prepared trip plan outline to keep track of routes along the way.
- Make gas, food, and rest stop decisions ahead of time.
- When lost, stop and ask questions at once. Don't just drive on blindly.

- If you hear bad traffic or weather reports on the radio, change plans to avoid trouble.

If you need to consult your map while you are driving, pull over to the side of the road and stop. If all you need is a quick glance, take advantage of a stop at a traffic light. *Never try to look at a map when your car is moving.*

When following a numbered route through cities and towns, look for the standard route markings posted before every turn. Then watch for confirming route signs after the turn. A road map cannot show the route through small towns, so you will have to watch for road signs that are posted. Another place where signs must be carefully watched is on detours.

When backing or maneuvering in tight places, a driver must be alert and careful.

Trucks, Trailers, and Recreational Vehicles

Occasionally, most drivers will drive a truck or recreational vehicle, or pull a trailer.

TRUCKS AND RECREATIONAL VEHICLES

In most states, individuals who hold a driver's license for a car are allowed to drive pickup trucks, vans, and even some fairly large trucks. Anyone who drives one of these vehicles should remember that they handle differently than a car.

Trucks and recreational vehicles get fewer miles per gallon of gasoline, which means more frequent gas stops.

When loading these vehicles, the basic rule of keeping the weight low, centered, and secure applies. If you are going to carry a large load, it should be loaded correctly and checked en route. Speed must also be watched closely. Keep in mind the truck or camper will not accelerate, brake, or steer as easily as a car.

Hitting overhead obstructions is one of the most common accidents with rental trucks or large campers. This happens so often that many truck rental insurance policies do not cover this type of damage. So drivers of these vehicles must be alert to identify low overhead obstructions, such as gas station or motel overhangs, to avoid running into the obstruction. Many times clearance heights are posted on bridges and overhanging obstructions. Have someone outside the vehicle guide you when backing or maneuvering in tight spaces.

TRAILERS

Before pulling a trailer, check the equipment on the tow car. Cars that are fitted for towing big trailers have heavy duty power, cooling, electrical, and suspension systems. To make sure the car is equipped to pull the trailer, check the owner's manual.

If a trailer is to be rented, the car must be fitted with the right trailer hitch assembly, and have hookups for lights, mirrors, and safety chains. Since large trailers require a second braking system, most rental trailers are limited to under 1000 pounds.

When hooking up a trailer, check the lights, tires, and safety chains. All lights should operate on the car and the trailer.

In turning a corner with a trailer, all turns must be slow and wide.

When loading the trailer, place heavy items over the axle. Weight should be evenly distributed on left and right. About 10 to 15 percent of the total weight should be on the tongue of the trailer.

Before actually driving with a trailer, practice slow maneuvers with an empty trailer. Part of the practice should include backing. To *start* a trailer backing, turn the steering wheel *right* to back left and *left* to back right. Then creep back slowly and make small steering corrections.

When pulling a loaded trailer, remember the ''two times'' rule. It will take about *two times as long* to pass, stop, accelerate, or turn. In addition, a car-trailer combination is likely to react about twice as much to normal road hazards like dips, rough pavement, or wind.

Rules for pulling a trailer
- Turning should be done slower and wider.
- Travel on four-lane roads whenever possible.
- Do not drive faster than posted speed limits for trailers.
- Start slowing as soon as you notice trouble ahead.
- Allow about twice as much time when passing.
- Use mirrors and ask a passenger to check traffic whenever possible.
- Avoid traveling in heavy cross winds.
- Shift to a low gear ahead of time when going up or down hills.
- If the trailer starts to sway or ''fishtail,'' steer for the center of the lane and slow gradually. If the trailer has a separate set of brakes, use them *first* while accelerating slightly. When the trailer stops swaying, use the car brakes carefully.

legend, 334

map scale, 334

navigating, 337

recreational vehicle, 338

road atlas, 334

safety chain, 338

trailer hitch, 338

trip plan, 332

Summary

1. To make short trips easier, select a departure time and route by using advance information. Before leaving, routine pre-driving car checks should be made.

2. Before going on a long trip, have the car carefully checked and serviced. The owner's manual serves as a basic guide for items that may need attention.

3. Emergency equipment to take on a long trip should include a fire extinguisher, flashlight, spare parts, simple tools, first-aid kit, and tire-changing equipment.

4. Special equipment should be taken for driving in winter, such as chains, if snow tires are not used, a safety chain, battery jumper cables, window scraper, and a blanket. In severe weather, food and clothing should also be included.

5. In preparing for a long trip, arrange for traveler's checks and credit cards, pack all-weather clothing, secure the home or apartment, and establish a schedule which will enable the driver and all passengers to start the trip well rested.

6. To read a map, you must know how to use the map's legend. Most maps also have special charts and listings to tell a driver where to locate towns and special points of interest. The mileage between points and the time needed to drive that distance is also generally provided.

7. Before selecting a route to travel, a driver should consider the miles to be driven and the type of road, traffic, weather, and facilities at anticipated stops.

8. To make a trip plan work on long trips, each day's drive must be planned the night before. Rotate drivers every hour or two, use route outlines, and make decisions to stop ahead of time.

9. A car, truck, or trailer should be loaded so that the weight is low, centered, and secure. Heavy vehicles do not accelerate, brake, or steer as easily as a car.

10. When towing a trailer, a driver should make turns slow and wide, use four-lane roads whenever possible, count on taking twice as long to pass, start slowing as soon as trouble is spotted, and shift to a lower gear ahead of time to go up or down hills.

Driving Situations

1. How would you go about finding out how bad the weather is or will be before you travel?

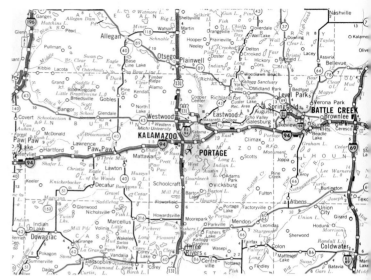

2. What main routes would you take to go from Allegan to Three Rivers, Michigan? How far is it, and how long will the drive take? What other routes are available?

3. The trailer ahead is "fishtailing." What should the driver do to control the "fishtailing" action?

4. The driver of this rental truck is stopping for gasoline. What problem might develop? How can it be avoided?

Chapter Review Questions

Planning for Local Driving

1. When selecting a departure time for local travel in a large city, what important factor should you consider? (332)
2. What is the best way to get advance information before driving locally? (332)
3. If a driver is lost in a city and the state map does not have enough information, what should the driver do? (332)
4. To avoid car trouble, what should the driver do before every trip? (332)
5. How can a passenger help a driver in city driving? (332)

Planning a Long Trip

6. Before leaving on a long trip, what should the driver do to a car? (333)
7. What is the main thing to remember when loading a car? (333)
8. What does the legend on a map tell? (334)
9. When selecting a driving route, what four questions should you consider? (336)
10. What can you do to make a trip plan work better while driving? (337)

Trucks, Trailers, and Recreational Vehicles

11. What is one of the most frequent minor accidents experienced by drivers who rent large trucks? (338)
12. What special equipment should a car have before being used to pull a large trailer? (338)
13. When loading a trailer, what caution should you take? (339)
14. What specific driving techniques should a driver keep in mind while towing a trailer? (339)
15. What correct actions should a driver take if a trailer starts to "fishtail?" (339)

Projects

1. Get a set of maps and plan a trip to a point 900 miles away. Plan a scenic route one way to your destination and a quick route for your return trip.
2. Get a large city map and find the quickest way to two points across town. Are there other routes that can be taken during rush-hours?
3. Use the trip plan developed in Project 1 and estimate the amount of money needed to take the trip. Then contact a travel agent to find out how much the same trip would cost by air or bus.
4. Visit a gas station that rents trailers. Find out how to use a trailer hitch, safety chains, and lighting hookups.
5. As a class project, prepare a pre-trip checklist that can be used to get ready for a trip to a point 1500 miles away.

Chapter 20 · Test

(Write the correct answers on a separate sheet of paper.)

True-False

1. Regular pre-driving car checks should be made before each local driving trip. (332)
2. Interstate routes that run north and south have odd numbers. (334)
3. The most important thing about loading a truck or trailer is to get everything in that you plan to take. (339)
4. The letter and number alongside a city or town listed on a map refer to its size and importance. (335)
5. When loading a trailer, most of the weight should be placed as far to the front as possible. (338)
6. It is best to drive into large cities during the morning hours and leave during the late afternoon hours. (332)
7. The aim of a car's headlights may be changed as a result of a heavy load. (333)
8. When loading a car, heavy objects should be placed in the car-top carrier where they will be out of the way. (333)
9. All truck rental insurance policies will cover damage from any kind of collision or upset. (338)
10. When starting to back a car and trailer, the steering wheel should be turned in the opposite direction from which the trailer is expected to move. (339)

Answer the Question

11. What is the most important check a driver should make when preparing a car for a long trip? (333)
12. When planning a long trip, what is the maximum number of miles you should plan to drive in a day? (336)
13. What special rule should be kept in mind when pulling a trailer? (339)
14. If a car is overloaded, what can happen in a strong wind? (333)
15. In what two ways can a driver overcome problems of vision to the rear when pulling a trailer? (339)

Careers in the Highway Transportation System

Introduction

Transportation in the highway transportation system means the safe and efficient movement of people and goods from one place to another. This movement process is the very lifeblood of the daily activities and needs of people in our society. Imagine what would happen if every vehicle in the nation did not move for three or four days. There would be no service trucks, delivery trucks, taxis, buses, ambulances, fire trucks, garbage trucks, milk and grocery trucks, and mail trucks to bring the products and provide the services people need. Even if trains and airlines still operated, there would be little opportunity to use them because much of their freight and most of their passengers arrive by some sort of motor vehicle.

Over 7 million people are employed in various types of careers that use the HTS or help to keep it working properly. These careers cover a wide range of abilities and call for different kinds and amounts of preparation and education. In many of these careers, a person can succeed with a basic high-school or vocational education. Others require college or university education and special talents.

Jobs in the automotive and other highway transportation industries are so widespread and varied that people can choose what section of the country, or even what foreign country, they wish to work in.

Careers in Driving

Career and job opportunities for men and women are many and varied in the HTS.

DELIVERY ROUTE DRIVING

Many first jobs held by young people involve driving a small truck or van. The chief requirement for success in these jobs is the ability to drive safely and efficiently. Collisions interfere with business. Not only is the delivery delayed and goods damaged or destroyed, the vehicle cannot be used until it is repaired.

Many people earn a good salary driving delivery trucks. This kind of driving job can also be an excellent starting point for other careers.

TRUCK DRIVING

After graduating from high school, many young people get a job with a trucking company as a loading dock worker or city pickup truck helper. These same workers can advance to being a driver, and finally to becoming a longhaul driver traveling from coast-to-coast. These jobs usually require a driver to be on the road for days. Some jobs enable a driver to return home regularly at the end of the day.

The big semi-trailer trucks that are driven coast-to-coast are handled by drivers who have proven themselves to be safe, experienced drivers.

TRANSPORTING PEOPLE

Many career opportunities are offered in this area. Drivers who transport people have the additional obligation of protecting them from harm. These drivers must also be able to deal successfully with people.

Careers in Manufacturing, Sales, and Maintenance

The automobile manufacturing industry employs many people with a variety of talents and abilities.

MANUFACTURING

In the planning stage, market researchers determine what styles, types, and qualities of products people will probably buy. Automotive stylists, who are artists with a basic understanding of engineering, work on the total styling features of a car. Design engineers make a great number of sketches. Sculptors then make a full-size clay model from the sketches. Designs are developed several years in advance of the current model, which involves artistic planning ahead of time. Talents of people who deal with metals, plastics, paints, colors, adhesives, light, sound, textiles, and fabrics are coordinated to make better products.

Cars that are produced from this combined team effort then go through a "proving" process to test the cars for endurance, reliability, safety, and performance.

Once a car's qualities have been tested, production begins. Three basic areas of the making of parts are foundry, stamping, and machining. In a foundry, metal is melted and poured into molds to give it shape. In stamping, sheet metal and other materials are forced into shape by pressure. Machining trims away unwanted material.

Workers on the assembly line then put the car parts together and a car is made.

The women above are working on a clay model of a future car design.

AUTOMOBILE SALES AND MAINTENANCE

A new-car dealership offers a variety of careers, such as sales, mechanic, and body repair. A sales person must be able to meet and talk with people and must have a complete knowledge of the product to be sold, such as new cars, used cars, or trucks. Sales people may advance to sales manager or to general manager. Some may even own their own dealerships some day.

The service department offers good opportunities for specialization and advancement. With high-school auto mechanics or work-training programs in mechanics, a person can start in a service department on the lubrication rack, or as car washer, or in light mechanical repair. Aptitude and in-service schools enable a person to advance to heavy repair mechanic and truck mechanic or to repair of specialized areas, such as transmission, brakes, or tune-up.

SERVICE STATIONS

Service station operation is a small business opportunity in every community. The basic business of servicing cars can be expanded to washing, light repair jobs, and various kinds of specialist services.

OIL PRODUCTION

The oil fields furnish the energy that powers the automobile. The process of recovering oil from deep in the earth's surface, sometimes offshore in the ocean, requires the services of many people. Geologists determine what parts of the earth may yield oil. Engineers work at the drilling site or in a refinery.

Many opportunities may be found in the oil industry associated with refineries, pipelines, oil tankers, and gasoline delivery trucks.

Careers in Traffic Safety

HIGHWAY ENGINEER

Engineers are employed by state highway departments to design and oversee the building of roads and bridges. They deal with problems of curves, slopes, drainage, building materials and many other problems that are concerned with the planning, construction, repair, and maintenance of highways.

Highway engineering requires advanced education at a college or university. A person interested in this area needs ability in mathematics and science.

Many highway construction and maintenance jobs require travel far from home for extended periods.

TRAFFIC ENGINEER

Traffic engineers plan the movement of traffic. In cities where the street system is already built, they determine how the streets can be used to move traffic safely and efficiently. They study traffic flow and collision records and check for areas where traffic jams occur regularly. This information is used to eliminate those trouble spots. Traffic engineers may then make some streets one-way, change signal-light sequences, or add special pavement markings to help traffic flow.

Traffic engineering is concerned with making present roadways more efficient and safer for everyone. They help plan future roads with people safety as well as people movement in mind.

Traffic engineering also requires a college or university education. Traffic and highway engineers need many of the same abilities. The work of one goes hand-in-hand with the other.

DRIVER LICENSING

The purpose of a state driver licensing agency is to establish a standard of good driving performance and screen out incompetent drivers. If drivers become bad driving risks, it is the job of this agency to remove them from the road.

Driver license examiners are civil service employees in many states. Each state determines what training its examiners shall receive. A driver licensing agency also employs data processing people, traffic specialists, and administrative personnel.

TRAFFIC ENFORCEMENT

Police officers in most cities have many duties, the largest of which may be traffic supervision and traffic law enforcement. The best "enforcement" is self-imposed; a driver learns the traffic laws and obeys them. Part of the job of a police department is to help inform the driving public about traffic laws.

Many cities have training courses for police officers. A person qualifies by satisfactorily completing a training program. Courses in police science and traffic regulation are offered by some colleges and universities. Most police departments have continuing on-the-job training.

TRAFFIC COURTS

Traffic courts are another link in the HTS chain. The judges decide on the guilt or innocence of drivers who receive traffic tickets. The court notifies the driver licensing agency if drivers are found guilty, and the licenses of drivers convicted of too many violations are suspended or revoked.

Most traffic court judges were formerly lawyers. A law degree and passing a state examination are usually required to be a judge.

Careers That Depend on Driving

Most people drive to work. Or they ride a bus or travel by car to a train which takes them to work. Most jobs, therefore, depend on somebody driving a vehicle.

Many careers depend on the use of a special-purpose vehicle which contains the tools of their trade or other equipment. The career is not the driving, but driving is necessary to the business. An example is a tree-removal service. The truck itself is used to provide a service. Failure to drive the truck successfully to the work location would delay starting the removal service.

Many one-person businesses do not need a specially-equipped vehicle. A self-employed TV repairman could use a van or car and carry several cases of tools and parts.

Sales representatives, the people who present their company's products to prospective buyers, are especially dependent on cars. These sales people must serve their customers who live in different states. They must drive to see their customers in order to demonstrate the products successfully.

Certain large companies have need for special-purpose vehicles to carry on their business. A telephone company or an electric power company has installation and repair vehicles. Trained career people work with these vehicles as a base for installation of lines and equipment. Such companies carry out continuous safety programs, not only in industrial safety but also in defensive driving skills.

Driving plays a major part for people engaged in real-estate sales, TV repair, and telephone installation and repair.

Most governmental agencies have civil service jobs that depend on driving. The postal system, for example, has a great number of positions that require driving some type of vehicle. All of the agencies that have a product, such as the Government Printing Office, need dependable truck drivers. The National Park Service depend on good driving to carry out their functions. The military services use vehicles of many kinds for routine, noncombat business. State and local governments also have many driving jobs. They generally demand a dependable, no-collision style of driving.

RECYCLING

Recovering and reusing metals from junked automobiles is not a new industry but is becoming more and more important as natural resources are being used up. At some junk yards, parts are available for older cars. The most important function, however, is reclaiming the metals for reuse.

THE HIGHWAY TRANSPORTATION SYSTEM: TOTAL INVOLVEMENT

There are many other related careers in the HTS including mining, traffic safety education, car insurance, tire companies, replacement parts companies, diagnostic shops, car repaint businesses, and nurseries, which deal in shrubs and sod for highway landscaping.

There are also numerous unsolved problems that will lead to more and new careers in the next generation: problems about pollution, energy, and mass transit in highly populated areas.

High schools have helpful information in their libraries. From vocational counselors, you can obtain additional information about any career area. Personnel departments of

large companies also have information about careers available in their company.

The HTS offers many different career opportunities. A great many other jobs require the use of a motor vehicle to get to work or to perform a service. They all have one thing in common for success—safe and efficient driving.

True-False

1. A driver can usually compensate for a physical condition, whether temporary or permanent, that reduces driving ability. (255)
2. A driver with good daytime vision may have poor night vision. (258)
3. As speed increases, a driver's vision generally becomes sharper and wider. (259)
4. Emotional control while driving cannot be expected among young drivers. (274)
5. The best indicator of good driving is the lack of passenger reaction at the end of the ride. (277)
6. The driving ability of young drivers is usually impaired at lower blood-alcohol levels than older drivers. (286)
7. Elimination of alcohol from the body can be speeded up by strenuous exercise. (287)
8. The side effects of medicines and drugs are multiplied when taken before or after an alcoholic drink. (290)
9. A car's engine should be tuned every time the car is lubricated. (300)
10. Once the engine is running, the battery generates electricity to run the car. (302)
11. In hot weather, tire pressure should be reduced since pressure may become too high for safety. (310)
12. The major costs of owning and operating a car are depreciation, operating costs, and fixed costs. (320)
13. The most important insurance for car owners is liability coverage. (320)
14. Before starting on a long trip, the car should have a major service check. (333)
15. The letter and number after the name of a city or town listed on a map refers to its population and size. (334)

Answer the Question

16. What steps can a driver take to lower the dangers from carbon monoxide? (261, 262)
17. What possible effects might strong emotions, such as anger, have on a driver's vision? (271)
18. At what rate does the average person "burn" alcohol? (286)
19. What two types of insurance can an owner drop as the car gets older? (321)
20. What three control problems can be expected when driving an overloaded car? (333)

Final Test

True-False

1. Since many drivers have been taught to drive in schools, the human element of the HTS has become less important than in earlier years as a major cause of accidents. (4)
2. Drivers are expected to know and obey speed limits set for different types of roads even where signs are not present. (23)
3. Force of impact is affected by distance between impact and stop, weight, and road condition. (64)
4. Most traffic hazards can be minimized by proper car positioning. (82)
5. Choice of a gap in traffic when turning at a controlled intersection depends on the speed of approaching vehicles. (108)
6. When other drivers keep cutting in front of your car and reducing your following distance, maintain a shorter following distance. (129)
7. Reduced speed when approaching complex traffic situations provides more time for IPDE. (158)
8. If another driver attempts to pass your car on a two-lane, two-way highway in an unsafe manner, you should position your car to prevent the pass. (187)
9. As falling snow covers the outer edges of the road, drivers tend to drive closer to the center of the road. (223)
10. Most emergencies in a motor vehicle occur as a result of driver error. (235)
11. Strong emotions over a period of time may cause mental and physical fatigue. (270)
12. Driver impairment is not likely to occur if the beverage drunk is beer. (287)
13. When buying a used car, borrow as much money as possible for the price of the car. (320)
14. On a long trip, drivers should rotate every one to two hours. (337)
15. It is illegal to cross a broken yellow center line at any time. (28)
16. Turning on the turn signal gives a driver the right to enter a lane of traffic. (45)
17. Learning to make good judgments is an essential driving skill. (75)
18. Usually, the safest type of turnabout is backing into an alley or driveway on the right and pulling out into the street. (96)
19. A delayed green traffic signal at an intersection is intended to protect left-turning vehicles from oncoming traffic. (110)
20. The driver of a car should allow extra following distance when driving behind a motorcyclist. (148)
21. By increasing speed from 50 to 60 mph, a driver can save eight or ten minutes on a 10-mile trip. (183)
22. A map legend provides a scale for estimating mileage between different places. (334)
23. When merging on an expressway, accelerate to the speed of approaching traffic. (200)
24. When a tire blows out at highway speeds, it is important to stop the car as quickly as possible to prevent further damage to the tire. (238)

25. Temporary or partial loss of hearing may be more of a handicap for a driver than permanent deafness. (261)
26. Passengers should avoid talking to the driver on long trips in order not to cause any distraction. (276)
27. Low brake pedal level is an early indication of possible brake trouble. (309)
28. Success in backing depends on posture, seeing, steering, and speed control. (95)
29. When backing in a stickshift car, speed is controlled with the brake. (95)
30. When you are driving in late afternoon with the sun behind you, glare is no problem. (222)

Answer the Question
31. What do the letters HTS represent? (4)
32. What traffic law makes it illegal to drive at an unsafe speed? (23)
33. Which device changes the headlights from low to high beam and back? (40)
34. When rounding a curve, when do you reduce speed? (63)
35. Which Smith System rule applies to keeping a space cushion? (75)
36. When parking uphill with a curb, in what direction should wheels be turned? (100)
37. What term means allowing cross-street traffic to pass through the intersection? (114)
38. What unsafe action are tailgaters taking in traffic? (124)
39. Why should motorcyclists ride with headlights on at all times? (141)
40. Under what conditions must a pedestrian yield the right-of-way to motorists? (170)
41. Why do drivers fail to see some road signs on side roads that enter through highways? (180)
42. What are three parts of expressway entrances? (199)
43. What term means driving at speeds that make stopping distance longer than the distance lighted by headlights? (221)
44. If your brakes fail, what is the first step you should take? (236)
45. For which kind of visual disability can a driver easily compensate? (259)
46. What are some emotions that can interfere with driving? (270–271)
47. What part of the body is first affected by alcohol? (284)
48. What two serious problems can result from worn tire tread? (310)
49. If you run over a bicycle left near the curb, what insurance coverage protects against the loss? (321)
50. When loading a car for a trip, what basic rule should be followed? (333, 338)

Metric Measures

Speed

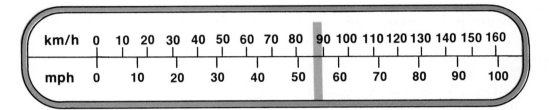

1000 metres per hour (m/h) = 1 kilometre per hour (km/h)

Distance

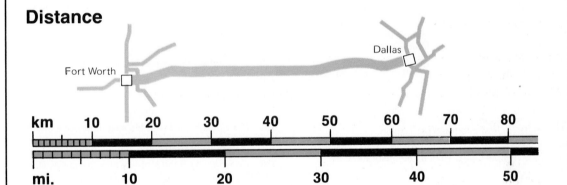

10 millimetres (mm) = 1 centimetre (cm)
100 centimetres = 1 metre (m)
1000 metres = 1 kilometre

Volume

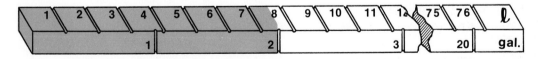

1 cubic centimetre (cm³) = 1 millilitre (ml)
1000 millilitres = 1 litre (l)
1000 cm³ = 1 litre (l)

Acknowledgments

Cover by M. Leon Lopez

Source for statistics
Most of the statistics used throughout the book are from *Accidents Facts,* 1975 Edition, published by the National Safety Council. Copyright © 1975, National Safety Council.

Charts
11 Statistics from *Accidents Facts,* 1975 Edition, published by the National Safety Council. Copyright © 1975, National Safety Council.

166 Statistics from *Accidents Facts,* 1975 Edition, published by the National Safety Council. Copyright © 1975, National Safety Council.

284 *Source:* Baker, S., from a Johns Hopkins study funded by the United States Department of Transportation.

286 From chart entitled "Blood Alcohol Concentrations" in *The Drunk Driver May Kill You,* published by Allstate Insurance Company. Reprinted by permission.

289 "Drinking-Driving Crash Chart" is reprinted by permission of the Highway Users' Federation for Safety and Mobility.

298 From "Pontiac Owner's Manual for 1976." Reprinted courtesy of Pontiac Motor Division, General Motors Corporation.

310 From "Construction & Tire Information" from *Driver Magazine* (May 1975). Reprinted courtesy of the Air Force's *Driver* Magazine.

311 From the chart "Gas Consumption vs. Gas Mileage" from *Journal of Traffic Safety Education,* October 1975. Reprinted with permission.

323 From "A Family Guide to Property and Liability Insurance." Copyright © 1976 by the Insurance Information Institute, and reprinted with their permission.

Pictures and Diagrams
21 Courtesy U.S. Department of Transportation, Federal Highway Administration

25 Courtesy Ohio Department of Transportation

36–37 Courtesy General Motors, Chevrolet Motor Division

38 Courtesy American Motors Corporation

43 Courtesy American Motors Corporation

54–55 Courtesy *Road and Track* Magazine

64–65 Insurance Institute for Highway Safety
90–91 dduve

101 dduve

103 Courtesy San Francisco Visitors' Bureau

142 Courtesy American Honda Motor Co., Inc.

144 Courtesy American Honda Motor Co., Inc.

155 Shostal Associates

163 Wide World

176–177 Bob Hammond/Stock, Boston

208 Maje Waldo/Stock, Boston

224 Aetna Life & Casualty

240 U. P. I.

245 Wide World

282–283 Shostal Associates

301 General Motors Corporation, Oldsmobile Division, Lansing, Michigan

302 Courtesy Firestone Tire and Rubber Company

305 Courtesy Firestone Tire and Rubber Company

307 Courtesy Firestone Tire and Rubber Company

309 (r) Courtesy Firestone Tire and Rubber Company
(l) Courtesy General Motors Corporation

310 (r) Courtesy Goodyear Tire and Rubber Company

322 Wide World

324–325 Shostal Associates

330–331 Shostal Associates

334 (t) Copyright by Rand McNally and Company, R. L. 76-S-13
(b) Courtesy Bethlehem Steel Corporation

335 Copyright by Rand McNally and Company, R. L. 76-S-13

336 Oregon State Highway Division

337 Iowa State Highway Commission

341 Copyright by Rand McNally and Company, R. L. 76-S-13

347 (b) Courtesy Greyhound Lines, Inc.

348 (t) Courtesy General Motors Corporation
(b) Owen Franken/Stock, Boston

349 (b) Bill Gillette/Stock, Boston

Answers to Driving Situations

Page 13

1. Identify: Driver is opening the door on the street side.
Predict: Door may open all the way. Driver may get out of the car and walk into your path.
Decide: Slow; prepare to stop if necessary; tap horn; swing out if the way ahead is clear.

2. Identify: Cement truck forced the oncoming car to swing into your lane.
Predict: There is not enough room between the oncoming car and cars parked at the curb for you to continue in your lane.
Decide: Slow down; stop if necessary. Allow the oncoming car to complete the pass around the truck before you continue.

3. Identify: Child on bicycle partly hidden by parked car is approaching the street from a driveway.
Predict: If neither you nor bicyclist change speed or position, you will hit the child and hurt or kill her.
Decide: Slow down; stop if necessary; tap horn

4. Identify: School bus is stopped, and red lights will be flashing. Passengers just got off bus.
Predict: Passengers may dash across street in front of your car.
Decide: Stop behind the bus (state laws require you to stop when red lights are flashing). Wait until red lights stop flashing before moving on.

Page 31

1. You should drive in the left lane. Lane signals are located over this street so the number of lanes going in a certain direction can be changed during different hours of the day.

2. Center line should be broken yellow rather than broken white. White means traffic going in the same direction. Check lane-line color before turning into a street.

3. STOP sign is hidden. The sign should be mounted in a more obvious way. A person could easily assume that no stop is required, and a crash might result.

4. The orange construction signs indicate that the lane is closed. You should slow down and move to the right when there is a gap in traffic.

Page 51

1. The problem and the action to take for the panel gauges are as follows:
a. Fuel tank is almost empty. Stop at first service station to fill up.
b. Battery is discharging. Stop at first service station to check the electrical system.
c. The oil is not circulating properly in the engine. Pull over at the first safe place, turn off the engine, and send for a tow truck.
d. Coolant in radiator is overheated. Pull over at first safe place, turn off the engine, and wait for it to cool before proceding to nearest service station.

2. The driver has made these errors: seat is too far forward; driver is not sitting up straight behind the wheel; driver is not wearing safety belts; driver is using only one hand on steering wheel; mirror is crooked; driver is smoking; and loose objects are piled on dash. Devices and indicators are important to help drivers keep their cars running safely and efficiently, communicate with other road users, protect cars' occupants, and help prevent theft.

3. The selector lever should be in DRIVE on expressway and LOW on downgrade.

4. The gearshift should be in THIRD or FOURTH on expressway and SECOND on downgrade.

Page 67

1. Take foot off accelerator until tires stop spinning; then apply pressure on accelerator very slowly. The physical force is friction.

2. It will take you four times longer to stop. You should stop if there is enough room or swerve into the other lane if there is no oncoming traffic.

3. The curve should be four times larger. Slow down to the speed given on the sign before entering the curve.

4. Ease up on the brakes so the wheels do not lock and steer toward the shoulder.

Page 85

1. Children are playing near the street. Children will get careless when they are playing. It is up to the driver to be alert to the actions of children and watch out for them. By "aiming high," you can keep an eye on them because what they do may affect you.

2. One boy has suddenly decided to run across the street. You see this and begin to prepare for it.

3. You should tap the horn, reduce speed, and swerve away from children if necessary.

4. Stop. The child's actions allow you no other choice.

Page 103

1. It is important for a driver to check behind the car before backing to see if the area is clear for safe backing.

2. Driver must check traffic over left shoulder (as well as traffic ahead), give a left signal, and pull into traffic lane. If there is a collision, the driver leaving a parallel parking space is at fault because the parked car pulled into the traffic lane.

3. Driver should choose to do a two-point turn by driving into the driveway on the left. The driver will then be able to drive forward into the street instead of backing into the street.

4. Downhill car's wheels are turned *right* toward the curb. Uphill car's wheels turned *left* to rest against the curb. This position will allow the car to hit curb first if it starts to roll and thus prevent it from rolling down a hill.

Page 119

1. The driver on the left is required to yield the right-of-way, but you have no guarantee from the other driver. Brake until you are sure the other driver will yield. Otherwise, make a full stop at the intersection.

2. You should stop and wait for the other car to pass before completing the turn. If you try to turn too soon, you might sideswipe the parked truck.

3. You should stop short of the tracks, not on them. If you pull onto the tracks, a train might come before you can clear the tracks.

4. You should check the traffic light, inside lane, outside oncoming lane, and turn path. The special problems are the driver's inability to see the signals of all oncoming cars in the inside lane, the difficulty of seeing the oncoming truck because of cars in the inside lane, and the possibility that the pedestrians might step into the turn path.

Page 135

1. The danger is that the oncoming car might take more than half of the space on the bridge. You should yield. Never depend on the other driver to yield. Both drivers should slow down.

2. The yellow car has no open space to the side and is being tailgated by C. In an emergency, the only option the yellow car has is to brake hard. This could result in a rear-end collision. You should drop back to increase your following distance and position your car so that there is open space on at least one side.

3. The tailgating driver is taking away the choice of your using the brakes as hard as you might need to use them. You should increase your following distance ahead so you both can stop with moderate braking.

4. With A tailgating the driver ahead, there is increased danger of A rear-ending B. You should increase your following distance so that you could stop safely with only moderate braking even if A crashed into B.

Page 151

1. The cyclist is riding in the driver's blind spot. The car driver should check over the right shoulder before making a right turn.

2. The cyclist is following these correct procedures: signaling for a turn, leaning into the turn, and wearing protective gear. The driver's defensive strategy should be to allow the cyclist an extra space cushion. The driver should predict that the cyclist might fall.

3. The cyclist is riding in the wrong side of the lane and following the truck too closely. In adverse conditions, the truck will kick up water, thus reducing the cyclist's vision. Wet road reduces traction and makes control difficult. To

correct the error, the cyclist should move over to the right lane where there is more space and sight distance.

4. Cyclist should yield. Driver should predict that the cyclist will not yield. Cyclist should predict that driver might turn left into cyclist's path. Driver must be prepared to stop if cyclist does not yield.

Page 173
1. Wheels are turned, and someone is sitting in the driver's seat.

2. There may be a pedestrian attempting to cross the street in front of the cars in the other lane. You should slow down in case the pedestrian steps in front of your car.

3. You should predict the car might swing out into your path just as you are passing.

4. The bike rider is in the center of the street. The driver should slow and wait for a good opportunity to go around the rider.

Page 193
1. The special problem is decreased traction on the side road due to the gravel surface; too much speed could cause the car to skid into the ditch. A traffic hazard could be vehicles following that might strike the rear of your car as you are about to turn right. Another hazard might be that a car coming from the gravel road is traveling too fast and is unable to stop at the intersection, thus sliding into you.

2. Slow down so that you can stop within the distance you can see. Keep checking the farthest point you can see, as you would at hill crests. Do this especially on a *left* curve, in case a driver is coming around a blind curve in your lane.

3. Reduce speed; let the oncoming truck pass first on the bridge; then proceed.

4. If the car being passed continues to speed up, you should brake and drop back.

Page 215
1. The driver of the last car should be checking for a gap in expressway traffic. The driver of the middle car should be concerned about holding a space cushion to the front and rear. The driver of the van should already have identified a gap in expressway traffic.

2. The driver should predict that the merging car may force traffic in the right lane to move into the center lane. To avoid trouble, the driver of the yellow car should thus move to the far left lane in front of or behind the car already in the far left lane.

3. The driver should have identified flashing brake lights on vehicles ahead, predicted traffic ahead is going to slow down and that there may be conflicts, decided to reduce speed while warning others to the rear, and executed a pumping-brake action to slow and warn others to the rear by flashing brake lights.

4. To avoid trouble, the driver of the yellow car will have to cooperate with those who want to merge. If possible, the merging drivers should go first. If the driver of the yellow car cannot exit, that driver should drive on to the next exit.

Page 231
1. Water on the windshield restricts a driver's view. Traction is poor; the car may hydroplane.

2. The headlights do not light the car's path on a curve. The driver should slow down enough to be able to see and stop within the lighted area. An alert driver will brake *before* reaching a curve.

3. Drivers must make sure that all windows are clear of snow before attempting to drive in bad weather. Snow on the windshield and other windows seriously restricts a driver's view of the road.

4. A driver must drive slowly enough to be able to stop within the distance lighted by the range of the headlights in order to stop short of the rock slide. A reduction of speed is necessary to reduce stopping distance. If the driver steps on the brakes too hard, the car might go into a braking skid. *Overdriving headlights* means driving at a speed at which you cannot stop within the distance lighted by your headlights.

Page 249

1.   Slow down as much as possible; move toward the right shoulder; blow horn and flash headlights.

2.   Hold the steering wheel firmly; position the car so it straddles the edge of the road; steer sharply left toward the pavement; countersteer sharply to the right when the front tires hit the pavement.

3.   Let up on the accelerator; do not brake. Steer hard to the right to keep car on the Exit ramp. When car has slowed, steer and brake gently to a stop in a safe area so that the tire can be changed.

4.   Hold the steering wheel firmly; quickly turn the steering wheel so that the car will swerve to the left around the bicyclist; then quickly countersteer in the opposite direction to return to the right lane.

Page 265

1.   With the limited use of his right arm, the driver would be unable to steer and shift in a normal manner. Pain from his injury might distract him from the driving task. A safer alternative would be for him to have someone drive him or find another way home.

2.   Slow down. Drive toward the right edge of the road. Glance to the right or beyond the approaching car to check your position on the road.

3.   A driver can compensate for his hearing defect by using his eyes more.

4.   Medicines or drugs can slow down a driver's identify processes and the driver would not be able to stop in time to avoid a collision. A driver who takes medicines or drugs should not drive because they have a tendency to make a person drowsy.

Page 279

1.   The people are feeling fear and anxiety. The driver evidently failed to identify and predict an unexpected hazard, and so did the passenger.

2.   Ignore the challenge. You should be mature enough to ignore such foolhardy challenges. By accepting the challenge, you would be taking unnecessary risks and possibly endangering lives and property.

3.   The passengers are distracting the driver by handing him food and drink and by pointing for him to look at something. The passengers should be helping him pay attention to his driving and assist in looking for dangers.

4.   The driver might be feeling impatience, frustration, irritation, or anger. The driver should be patient, stay in line, regain following space, and proceed normally. The left elbow should be withdrawn.

Page 293

1.   Accept responsibility for driving. If friend refuses to let you drive, find other means of transportation. Otherwise, follow the rules to reduce passenger risk on p. 287.

2.   Student must give his or her own personal answer here.

3.   Reduced inhibitions and poor reasoning and judgment might lead driver to take risks. Poor depth perception, vision in dim light, glare recovery, slowed reaction time, and poor coordination might make it more difficult to perform the passing maneuver.

4.   The people should use the following criteria: how much each one had eaten and drunk; how long since each had the last drink; how much each weighed; and, how experienced each was in drinking and driving.

Page 313

1.   You are either out of gas, or you have vapor lock. If the first, try to get gas. If the second, raise the hood, and wait for the engine to cool and the gas vapor to condense so the fuel pump can work.

2. When headlights go out suddenly, it usually means a fuse needs replacing or the circuit breaker needs to be reset. You can correct this problem in a few minutes unless there is additional trouble that requires the attention of a mechanic.

3. Stop immediately in the first safe place. Wait until the radiator cools before attempting to remove the cap. If overheating was caused by insufficient coolant, add coolant slowly while engine is running. Tighten fan belt if it has slipped off. Otherwise, have car towed to a garage for repair.

4. Replace with tire of the same size and construction on all four wheels, if possible, or at least the same size and construction as the other tire on that axle.

Page 327

1. Owning a car makes it convenient to get to many places, but the cost of the car will probably force you to work longer hours and possibly to neglect school work and activities.

2. Check the three cars thoroughly. If all cars are about the same condition and price, it would probably be wise to buy from the new-car dealer who can offer some guarantee for the car and for repairs, if necessary.

3. The most important kinds of insurance in order of priority are bodily-injury liability (if you kill or injure anyone); property-damage liability (if you damage property); and uninsured-motorist (if someone who is uninsured injures you or your passengers). Other kinds include collision, comprehensive, medical-payments, and towing.

4. Vandalism is covered under comprehensive insurance.

Page 341

1. Listen to local radio stations for weather and traffic reports before undertaking any kind of travel in threatening weather.

2. Main route to take from Allegan to Three Rivers, Michigan, would be Route 89 to Interstate 131. Since there are about 50 miles between the towns, it would take an hour of driving at the posted speed limit under ideal conditions. An alternate route would be Route 40 to Route 60.

3. The driver should let up the accelerator to slow gradually and steer for the center of the lane. Once the trailer is under control, the driver should stop and check to see if the trailer hitch and safety chains are in good condition.

4. The body of the truck might hit the overhang on the gas station. To avoid trouble, the driver should stop and have someone check for clearance as the truck is moved slowly toward the gas pump.

Glossary

Abutment: the structural support at either end of bridges or culverts.

Acceleration lane: an extra lane that permits drivers entering a high-speed highway to pick up speed and merge with other traffic.

Accelerator: the pedal that controls the flow of gasoline to the engine to regulate speed.

Alternator: a device similar in function to a generator that produces electrical current while an automobile engine is running.

Alternator light: a warning light on the instrument panel indicating the alternator is not working.

Amphetamine: a non-narcotic drug or pep pill used to stimulate the central nervous system.

Angle parking: parking a car diagonally to the curb.

Antifreeze: coolant with a low freezing point used in an automobile radiator to prevent freezing.

Antihistamine: a medicine commonly used to treat the symptoms of colds and allergies, which often has a sedative effect.

Assigned-risk plan: insurance provided for drivers who cannot buy insurance at regular rates because of their accident or violation record.

Automatic choke: valve opened and closed automatically by a thermostat to control the air flow through the carburetor.

Banked curve: curve sloped down on the inside and up on the outside to overcome car's tendency to tilt or slide toward the outside of the curve.

Barbiturate: a drug that depresses the central nervous system and is found in sleeping pills.

Basic speed law: drive at a speed that is safe for traffic, pavement, visibility, and vehicle conditions.

Bike flag: a pennant on a pole attached to a bicycle to alert others of the bicyclist's presence.

Bike reflector: device on a bicycle that reflects light so bicyclist can be seen at night.

Blood-alcohol level: the percentage of alcohol found in the bloodstream as measured by chemical tests of blood, breath, or urine.

Bodily-injury liability insurance: a type of insurance that covers the medical and hospital expenses, wage losses, and other costs of those injured in a collision caused by the insured.

Brake fluid: the liquid used in the brake system.

Brake shoe: a part of the brake that is forced against the brake drum on a wheel to produce friction, thus stopping a car.

Brake system warning light: warns driver of locked parking brake or of a brake-system failure.

Braking distance: the distance traveled from time brakes are applied to time car is stopped.

Carbon monoxide: a colorless, odorless, poisonous gas found in the exhaust gases of motor vehicles.

Carburetor: part of the engine that mixes air and gasoline in the proper proportion and sends it to the combustion chambers as a fine mist.

Catalytic converter: a pollution control device that uses a chemical reaction to convert harmful engine exhaust emissions to harmless gases.

Central vision: the three-degree area of clear vision used when the eyes focus on something.

Clutch: device in a stickshift car operated by a foot pedal that connects or disconnects the engine from the transmission.

Collision: contact between two or more objects, generally resulting in damage and/or injury or death, as when two cars crash into each other.

Collision insurance: insurance coverage that pays for damage to the vehicle of the insured.

Color vision: ability to tell one color from another.

Common speed: speed at which most vehicles move.

Communicating: telling other road users by turn signals, hand signals, car position, and other means where you are going and what you plan to do.

Compensate: to substitute or make up for some shortcoming, generally one which cannot be corrected.

Comprehensive insurance: a type of automobile insurance that covers most losses other than collision, such as fire, theft, storm, and vandalism.

Compromising: positioning a vehicle to allow sufficient space to avoid the most critical of several hazards.

Controlled intersection: an intersection where traffic is regulated by traffic-control signs or signals.

Controlled railroad crossing: a railroad crossing controlled by flashing lights and/or crossing gate.

Coping: recognizing a problem or task and dealing with it successfully.

Cornering: the controlled movement of a vehicle around a corner.

Countersteer: to steer in the opposite direction in order to keep a car going straight.

Covering the brake: putting the foot just above the brake pedal to be ready to apply pressure to the pedal.

Crossbuck: large, white X-shaped highway warning sign located beside a railroad crossing.

Crush area: the part of a car that receives early impact in a collision and collapses to reduce the force of impact on vehicle occupants.

Deceleration lane: an extra lane that permits drivers leaving a high-speed highway to slow down without obstructing traffic before entering the exit ramp.

Deciding: the third step of the IPDE process in which the driver selects the best course of action based on what the driver sees and predicts will happen.

Defroster: device that blows hot air from front heater to keep windshield free of fog, ice, and snow.

Delayed green light: traffic light that remains red while opposite traffic lanes clear; then it turns green.

Depreciation: the decrease in the value of a car as a result of its increasing age.

Depth perception: the ability to judge distances between you and other objects.

Differential: an arrangement of gears in the rear axle that allows one wheel to revolve faster than the opposite wheel during a turn.

Dimmer switch: a switch, generally operated with the left foot, for changing the headlights from high to low beam and back.

Disc brake: a type of brake that applies friction by pressing brake pads against a steel disc attached to the wheel.

Downshifting: shifting to a lower gear.

Driveshaft: shaft turned by the transmission that transmits power to the differential.

Driving task: applying knowledge and IPDE process to operate a car successfully in the HTS.

Drum brake: a type of brake that applies friction between brake shoes and a steel drum or hollow cylinder attached to the inner side of the wheel.

Emergency flare: a device which burns with a bright, red light to warn approaching traffic of a hazard in the road.

Emergency flasher: a device that flashes front car lights and taillights to warn others of an emergency situation.

Emotion: a strong feeling of any kind. Joy, grief, fear, hate, love, anger, and excitement are emotions.

Energy of motion: the energy an object has because it is moving.

Entrance ramp: a ramp leading into an expressway or tollway.

Evasive action: action taken by a driver to avoid a collision.

Executing: the fourth step of the IPDE process in which a driver takes the action decided upon.

Face shield: a clear, plastic device attached to a motorcycle helmet which protects the face and eyes from particles of dust, dirt, and insects.

Fading brakes: loss of braking power that occurs when brakes are overused and become very hot.

Field of vision: the area to the right and left that a person can see with the eyes focused straight ahead.

Financial responsibility law: a law that requires persons to prove their ability to pay damage claims resulting from a collision.

Fishtailing: side to side motion of the rear of a vehicle as a result of skidding.

Fixation: momentary stop in movement of the eyes, which permits eyes to focus on an object.

Flashing signals: red or yellow traffic light that flashes on and off to indicate stop (red) or caution (yellow).

Following distance: space between a car and the vehicle moving just ahead of it.

Foot brake: a brake operated by foot pressure on a pedal. It operates the brakes on all four wheels at the same time.

Force of impact: the striking force of colliding objects which varies according to their speed, weight, and distance between impact and stop.

Formation: a group of vehicles moving in the same direction.

Friction: resistance to motion between surfaces that touch. The rougher the surfaces, the greater the friction.

Friction point: the point where the engine begins to turn the transmission as you release the clutch in a standard transmission car.

Fringe vision: See Peripheral vision.

Front brake lever: the hand control which operates the front wheel brake of a motorcycle.

Fuel gauge: a gauge in the instrument panel that shows the amount of gasoline in the tank.

Fuel line: small pipe through which gasoline is pumped from fuel tank into carburetor.

Fuel pump: a device for pumping the gasoline from the fuel tank into the carburetor.

Fuse: a safety device in a car's electrical system which prevents damage to the system.

Gap: the distance a driver has between approaching cars in which to cross an intersection or to join traffic.

Glare recovery: the return of seeing ability after having been temporarily blinded by a strong light.

Glare resistance: the ability to see in spite of glare at night.

Hallucinogen: a drug that tends to distort one's perceptions of time, distance, and the shapes and colors of objects.

Hand-over-hand: a method of turning the steering wheel, in which one hand always grips the wheel firmly, so the wheel turns quickly and smoothly.

Head restraint: padded support to minimize whiplash injury to front-seat occupants in a rear-end crash.

High-beam indicator: a light on the instrument panel that glows only when the headlights are on high beam.

Highway hypnosis: a dulled or drowsy, trance-like condition caused by concentration on the road ahead and monotony of long hours of driving.

Highway transportation system (HTS): a complex system made up of people, machines, and roads.

Hydroplaning: a condition in which the tires of a moving vehicle ride on the surface of water, causing loss of steering and braking control.

Identifying: first step of the IPDE process in which drivers become aware of objects that may affect their continued movement.

Ignition switch: a switch on the steering column, operated by a key, which starts or stops the engine.

Impairment: physical, mental and/or emotional conditions that reduce an individual's ability to drive safely.

Implied consent law: state law providing that when a driver is granted a license, that driver agrees to take a chemical test for intoxication whenever asked by proper authority or to give up the license.

Information signs: a rectangular-shaped sign, on expressways, green with white letters or on smaller roads, white with black letters, that indicates directions, distances to places, and other information of interest to road users.

Inhibition: a person's sense or feeling of restraint to behave in a certain way as a result of prior experience or conditioning.

IPDE process: steps of the driving task that include identifying, predicting, deciding, and executing.

Jaywalking: walking across the street at places other than intersections or pedestrian crosswalks.

Joining: fitting into a gap in the flow of traffic.

Lane change: lateral movement from one lane to another on a multilane road.

Lane signals: signals, usually overhead, that designate a lane can or cannot be used at that time.

Legend: boxed area on a map containing explanations of the codes and markings on that map.

Low beam: headlight position so they do not blind oncoming drivers.

Manual shift lever: device for shifting gears in a stickshift vehicle attached to the right side of the steering column or on the floor.

Map scale: a line several inches long appearing in the legend of a road map indicating a measurement in miles for distances on that map.

Master cylinder: the device in the brake system that forces brake fluid to the wheel cylinders when you step on the brake pedal.

Medical-payments insurance: coverage for medical and funeral expenses for occupants in insured car who are injured or killed in a collision, regardless of fault.

Merge area: a stretch of roadway at the end of an acceleration lane on a multilane highway where cars join the flow of traffic.

Mid-block U-turn: a maneuver to turn the car around in a single movement so that the car proceeds in the opposite direction.

Minimizing: reducing the risk in a developing traffic situation by adjusting the car's position and/or speed in relation to a single hazard.

Minimum speed law: lowest legal speed a car may travel on certain roads under good conditions to prevent wide differences in speed among vehicles.

Muffler: a device attached to the exhaust system to deaden the sound of the engine.

Multiple cause: more than one cause contributing to a collision.

Narcotic: a drug that, in moderate doses, deadens the senses, relieves pain, and produces sleep. Narcotics are addictive.

Navigating: process of driving from one place to another using available signs and other aids to complete the trip safely and efficiently.

Night visual acuity: the ability to see clearly with very little light.

No-fault insurance: an insurance plan that pays expenses for insured collision victims regardless of who was held responsible for the collision.

Odometer: device showing total number of miles a car has traveled.

Oil pan: container for oil under the engine from which oil is pumped under pressure to various parts of the engine.

Oil-pressure warning light: a light on the dashboard that glows red if the engine oil pressure is low.

Oil pump: a pump that pumps oil from the oil pan to parts of the engine needing lubrication.

Overdriving the headlights: driving at a speed from which you cannot stop within the distance lighted by your headlights.

Overtaking: approaching and passing a slower-moving vehicle.

Parallel parking: parking the car parallel to the curb.

Parking brake: primarily used to hold a parked car in place; also used to slow vehicle when floor brake fails.

Passenger crash: the second crash in a collision when unrestrained occupants hit vehicle interior.

Passenger hand grips: attachments on motorcycles for passengers to hold onto for safety.

Pavement markings: yellow and white solid and broken lines on most hard-surfaced roads that regulate, warn, and guide traffic.

Pedestrian-actuated signals: traffic signals activated by a pedestrian pushing a button.

Pedestrian signals: traffic signal for the use of pedestrians—usually reading WALK and WAIT, or WALK and DON'T WALK.

Perception distance: distance covered while driver is taking time to see and identify an object ahead.

Perception time: time it takes a person to become aware of an object or situation ahead.

Peripheral vision: ability to see at either side while looking straight ahead.

Perpendicular parking: parking at a right angle to the curb.

Policy: a contract between a vehicle owner and an insurance company specifying the amount and type of insurance coverage.

Potential hazard: the possibility that a situation can develop that may become dangerous.

Power train: the parts of the car that transmit power from the engine to the rear wheels.

Predicting: the second step of the IPDE process in which the driver foresees what is apt to happen before it happens in a particular traffic situation.

Premium: amount of money paid at regular intervals for insurance.

Preventive maintenance: care given to a vehicle to keep mechanical problems from developing.

Progressive-signal system: the timing of traffic signals at consecutive intersections so that cars can travel at a given speed.

Property-damage liability: insurance that covers damage to the property of others in a collision caused by the policyholder.

Protected left turn: turn at a corner where left-turning vehicles are allowed to complete the turn without the hazard of oncoming traffic.

Protective clothing and equipment: special equipment, such as helmet, face shield or goggles, and heavy clothing, which a motorcyclist should wear to prevent or reduce injury in the event of a spill or a collision.

Pumping: applying and releasing pressure on the brake pedal repeatedly.

Radiator: part of the cooling system of a car in which the coolant that circulates around the engine is cooled by a current of air.

Railroad crossing flashers: a warning signal of flashing red lights placed at railroad crossings.

Reaction distance: distance the car travels during a driver's reaction time.

Reaction time: the time it takes a driver to respond to driving hazards once they have been perceived.

Rearview mirrors: mirrors to give driver broader rear view for passing, turning, and lane changing.

Recreational vehicle: vehicles used for recreational purposes and not used as commercial vehicles.

Regulatory signs: signs that inform highway users of traffic laws or regulations and indicate requirements to perform in a certain manner.

Revocation: cancellation of a legal permit to drive.

Riding the brakes: driving with a foot on the brake pedal so that the brake lights remain on and the brakes are partially applied.

Riding the clutch: driving with clutch partially depressed.

Right-of-way: the privilege of immediate use of the roadway.

Risk-taking: taking chances when consequences can be dangerous.

Road atlas: a collection of road maps usually bound into a single book.

Rocking: a means of loosening a car's wheels from snow, mud, and sand by alternately putting the car in LOW gear and moving ahead, then shifting to REVERSE and moving back.

Rumble strips: sections of rough pavement usually before road construction, toll booth, or other traffic condition to alert drivers to slow or stop.

Safety chain: a chain linking a vehicle and the trailer being towed. It serves as a safety device in the event that the trailer hitch breaks loose.

Safety helmet: a protective head covering worn by motorcyclists to prevent head injury in case of a spill or collision.

Scanning: glancing quickly and continuously.

School zone: a portion of a street or highway near school grounds subject to special speed limits set by state law or local ordinance.

Searching: a more intense process of scanning to gather as much information as possible about the traffic scene.

Seat adjustment lever: device to adjust front seat.

Sedative: a drug that depresses the central nervous system and causes drowsiness.

Selector lever: device in an automatic transmission car used to select forward or reverse gears.

Separating: the process of adjusting speed of a vehicle to handle a hazard one at a time when two or more hazards threaten a driver.

Shift indicator: device on a car that shows the different driving gears and the one being used.

Shock absorber: device that absorbs the bouncing action of the wheels.

Shoulder harness: arrangement of straps used together with a seat belt to keep the upper part of the body in place in the event of a collision.

Sight distance: how far you can see ahead.

Skids (braking, cornering, power): to slip or slide straight ahead or sideways because the tires have lost their grip on the road and the car is out of control.

Snow tire: a type of winterized tire with special tread for rear wheels.

Space cushion: area of space surrounding a car, consisting of adequate following distance between it and the cars ahead and behind, plus swerve paths to left and right.

Spark plug: device in the cylinder head which produces a spark to ignite the fuel-air mixture.

Speedometer: instrument that indicates the speed being traveled.

Speed smear: the distortion of the driver's side view as a result of speed.

Stale green light: a traffic signal ahead that is green at the time it is first noticed.

Starter motor: the electric motor that starts the engine when the starter switch is turned on.

Stimulant: a drug that speeds up the central nervous system.

Stopping distance: the total distance in feet it takes to stop a car. It includes perception distance, reaction distance, and braking distance.

Stopping time: the length of time it takes to stop a vehicle. It includes perception time, reaction time, and braking time.

Straddle: positioning a vehicle so that the right wheels are on one side of a lane line and the left wheels on the other side.

Strategy: plan which drivers use to cope with common and unusual traffic situations.

Stress: an emotional condition that adversely affects the performance of a driver.

Sun glare: created by sunlight reflecting from shiny surfaces, this glare can cause temporary blindness.

Sun visor: a padded device just above the windshield that can be pulled down to keep glare out of the eyes of people in the front seat.

Suspension: temporary withdrawal of a driver's license, generally as a result of one or more convictions for moving violations.

Tailgating: following a vehicle too closely.

Tailpipe: a pipe at the end of the exhaust system of a vehicle through which exhaust gases escape.

Temperature indicator light: a warning light on a vehicle's instrument panel, which glows red when the coolant in the cooling system becomes too hot.

Thermostat: an automatic device for regulating temperature of the coolant in the cooling system.

Three-point turnabout: a maneuver to turn the car around in the middle of the block.

Three-speed transmission: a standard transmission with three forward gears.

Through-lane: a lane of traffic, generally the middle lane of a road with three lanes in each direction, on which vehicles can continue to travel without interruption.

Tire chains: devices placed over the tire tread to increase friction when driving on roads covered with snow and ice.

Tireprint: the imprint of a tire left on a wet road pavement.

Tire wipes: same as tireprints.

Towing insurance: insurance coverage that pays for towing the policyholder's disabled vehicle to a garage for repairs.

Traction: the friction between a body and the surface on which it moves.

Traffic-actuated signal: a signal in which the amount of green light time given to each intersecting street is controlled by traffic as it moves over detectors in the street.

Traffic-control device: any sign, signal, or pavement marking used to control the movement of traffic.

Trailer hitch: a device for hooking a trailer to a vehicle for towing.

Trail riding: use of a motorcycle for off-road riding.

Tranquilizer: a drug used to relieve tension and anxiety, to treat high blood pressure, and to calm the nerves by depressing the central nervous system.

Transmission: the mechanism that transmits power from the engine to the rear axle.

Tread: the grooved surface of a tire.

Trip plan: organized preparation for a trip, which involves such activities as checking the vehicle, reading a map, selecting routes, and arranging for rest stops.

Tune-up: the process of checking, repairing, and adjusting the various parts of the ignition and fuel systems to obtain maximum engine performance.

Tunnel vision: a very narrow field of vision.

Turn signals: signal device showing other drivers which way a driver intends to turn.

2-second interval: following interval between moving cars that should be maintained under normal traffic and road conditions.

Uncontrolled intersection: an intersection at which there are no traffic-control devices, signs, or pavement markings.

Uncontrolled railroad crossing: a railroad crossing at which there are no signals or crossing gates.

Uninsured-motorist insurance: protection from bodily injury losses due to hit-and-run or uninsured motorists.

Unprotected left turn: an intersection where a traffic signal does not hold back oncoming traffic that may interfere with the movement of a left-turning vehicle.

Vehicle code: the organization of state laws regulating the owning and operating of motor vehicles on public roads.

Velocitation: condition of reduced ability to judge speed as a result of driving for long periods at a high speed.

Visual acuity: the ability to see an object sharply and distinctly.

Warning signs: yellow and orange signs that inform drivers of dangerous conditions ahead.

Water pump: pump that circulates coolant through the radiator and the engine block.

Wheel cylinder: the unit of the hydraulic braking system that activates the brake shoe on the individual wheel in response to the fluid pressure from the master cylinder.

Wolf pack: a group or formation of vehicles traveling on a multilane road.

Yield: the process of allowing another vehicle to proceed first.

Index